Ludwig Lavatar

Of Ghosts and Spirits

Ludwig Lavatar

Of Ghosts and Spirits

ISBN/EAN: 9783744670876

Printed in Europe, USA, Canada, Australia, Japan

Cover: Foto ©Thomas Meinert / pixelio.de

More available books at **www.hansebooks.com**

Ghoſtes and Spirites, VValking by Night,

And of ſtraunge Noyſes, Crackes, and ſundrie forewarnings, which commonly happen before the death of men: Great ſlaughters, and alterations of Kingdomes.

One Booke,

VVritten by *Lewes Lauaterus* of *Tigurine.*

And tranſlated into Engliſh by *R. H.*

Imprinted at London by Thomas Creede.
1 5 9 6.

To the Reader.

BEing desirous (gentle Reader) to exercise my selfe with some translation, at vacant times, and seeing, that since the Gospell hath beene preached, this one question, touching the appearing of spirits and soules departed, hath not bin much handled amongst vs, and therfore many, otherwise well affected in religion vtterly ignorant heerein, I thought it not amisse to take in hand some good and learned Treatise concerning this matter. Wherein as many haue both learnedly, painfully, and religiously trauelled: so amongst others, none in my iudgement hath more handsomly & eloquently, with more iudgment & better method discoursed the same, the *Lewes Lauaterus*, Minister of Tigurine. Others haue hādled it indeed wel, but yet *Nihil ad nostrū hunc*, being either too short, or too long, or too

dark-,

darke, or too doubtful, or otherwise so cōfused, that they leaue the Reader more in suspence in the end, then they found him in the beginning. As for Maister *Lauaterus* his discretion heerein, I will no otherwise commend it, then to desire the Reader to view, and iudge himself. For thus much at the first sight he shall see: A cleare methode, with a familiar and easie stile, the matter throughly handled *Pro* and *Con*, on both sides, so that nothing seemeth to be wanting, nor any thing redounding. And if it be true that Horace saith, *Omne tulit punctum, qui miscuit vtile dulci*, that is, He winneth the prize, that ioyneth pleasure with profit: I thinke this Authour may also in this respect be pronounced *Victor*, and adiudged to the best game. For he so intreateth this serious and terrible matter of Spirits, that he now and thē inserting some strange story of Monks, Priestes, Friers, and such like counterfeits, doth both very liuely display their falshood, and also not a litle recreate his Reader: and yet in the end he so aptly concludeth to the purpose, that his histories seeme not idle tales, or impertinent vagaries, but very truthes, naturally falling vnder the compasse of this matter. And how profi-

table

table this his woorke is, those may best iudge, which are most ignorant in this question, some thinking euery small motion & noyse to be Spirites, and some so fondly perswaded that there are no Spirits, who being better enformed herein by this Authour, I suppose will confesse his work to haue done them some profit: if knowledge be profitable, and ignorance discommodious. And againe, those which being hitherto borne in hande that mens soules returne againe on earth, crauing helpe of the liuing, and haue spent much of their substaunce on idle Monkes and Friers, to relieue them, will confesse the like. For when they shall see they haue bene falsely taught, and that they were not the soules of men which appeared, but either falshood of Monks, or illusions of diuels, franticke imaginations, or some other friuolous & vaine perswasions, they will thinke it profitable to haue knowne the truth, as well to auoid error hereafter, as to saue their mony from such greedy caterpillers. Some also which be otherwise well trained vp in Religion, and yet not knowing what to thinke of these matters, will not iudge their labour euill imployed, nor the worke vnprofitable, wherby they may be brought out of doubt, and know certainly what to beleeue. There be many also euen now a dayes, which are hanted & troubled with ſpirites, and know not howe to vſe themſelues, who when they ſhall learne how a Chriſtian man ought to gouern himſelfe, being vexed with euil ſpirits, wil think it a very profitable point of doctrine, that ſhal teach them to direct themſelues. Profitable therefore it is, and ſhalbe, no doubt, vnto many, and diſprofitable vnto none, except perchance vnto popiſh Monks and Priests, who are like hereby to loſe a great part of their gaines, which ſometimes they gathered togither in great abundaunce, by their deceifull doctrine of the appearing of dead mens ſoules. But this their wicked and diuelliſh doctrine, togither with all the patches and appendices therto belonging, he ſo notably teareth and cutteth in peeces, that I am well aſſured they ſhal neuer be able to cobble and clout them vp again. And this doth he with ſuch a moderation of breuitie and tediouſneſſe, that I may rightly ſay; He hath ſaid well, and not too much, and written truly, and not too litle.

Now as touching my tranſlation, although I

haue

haue not made him ſpeake with like grace in Engliſh, as hee dooth in Latine: yet haue I not chaunged his meaning, nor altered his matter, endeuouring my ſelfe rather to make thee vnderſtand what thou readeſt, then to ſmoothe and polliſh it with fine & picked words, which I graunt others might haue done more exquiſitely, and perchaunce I my ſelfe alſo ſomewhat better, if I would haue made thereof a ſtudy and labour, and not a recreation and exerciſe. But howſoeuer I haue done herein, verily good reader, I truſt thou wilt take in good part, which is all that I eſteeme: if any man ſhall miſlike thereof, let him amend it. I truſt it be ſufficient to teſtifie my good will to do thee good, and to let thee vnderſtand the Authours meaning.

Farewell.

To the right excellent and most wise and vertuous Lord *Iohn Steigerus* Consull *of the noble Common wealth of* Berna, *his good Lord and Patrone*, Lewes Lauaterus of Tigurine, *wisheth health.*

MAny and diuers things are reasoned vpon, both of the learned and vnlearned, as wel of other matter, as also of Spirites, which are seene and heard, and make men afraid in the night season, and in the day time, by sea and by lande, in the fields, woods, and houses: And likewise concerning such straunge things which for the most part happen before the death of certain men, especially great Princes, and before notable innouations of Kingdomes and Empires. Many which neuer sawe or heard any of these things, suppose all that is reported of them, to be meere trifles and old wiues tales: for so much as simple men, and such as are fearefull and superstitious, perswade themselues they haue seen this or that, when indeed the matter is farre otherwise. Againe, there are some, which assoone as they heare of any thing, especially if it happen in the night, they by and by thinke some spirite dooth walke, and are maruellously troubled in minde, because they cannot discerne naturall things from spirites. And some (chiefly those whiche hunt after gaines, by the soules of dead men) affirme that the most part of such things which are heard or seene, are the soules of dead men, which craue helpe of them that are liuing, to be deliuered out of the torments of most cruell paine in Purgatorie. Many not only of the common sort, but also men of excellent knowledge, do maruell whether there be any spirits or no, and what maner of things they are. Yea and some of my familiar friends haue many times requested me, to shew them my opinion concerning these matters. Wherfore me seemeth it shall be worth my laboure, if I declare briefly and plainly out of the word of God, what we ought to iudge concerning these things. For the Ministers of Gods Church can take nothing more profitable in hande, than to instruct the people of God purely and plainly, in such necessary matters as come in question out of the word of God, which is a lanterne (as the Psalmist saith) vnto our feete, and a light vnto our pathes: and to deliuer them from all errour and superstition, and bring them out of all wauering and doubt. And verily their studie & diligence is to be highly commended, who for these fewe yeares ago, haue set forth certaine bookes drawne out of the scriptures, written in the Germaine tongue against sundrie errours: and theirs likewise who in these our dayes by writing of bookes do teache, instruct, and confirme the rude and vnlearned people. For amongst many other excellent benefits, which God our heauenly Father hath bestowed vppon mankinde, this

also

also is a great and most liberall gift, that in this latter, and as it were old age of the world, he hath brought to light by the Art of Imprinting, aswel many other good Authours, as also the holie scriptures of the old and new Testament, written in diuers languages: whereby he doth not onlie teach vs amply and fully what to beleeue, and what to doo, but also mightily subuerteth and quite ouerthroweth diuers and sundrie errours, which by little and little haue crept into the Church. Truly all such are verie vngrateful towards God, which do not willingly acknowledge this so notable a benefit.

As touching this my treatise concerning Spirits, and straunge wonders, I haue deuided it into three partes for the more cleare vnderstanding therof. In the first parte I shewe, that there are visions and spirits, and that they appeare vnto men sometimes, and that many & maruellous things happen besides the ordinarie course of nature. In the second I discusse what maner of things they are, that, is not the soules of dead men, as some men haue thought, but either good or euill angels, or else some secret and hid operations of God. In the third I declare why God doth somtime suffer Spirits to appear, and diuers forewarnings to happen: and also how mē ought to behaue themselues when they happen to meete with such things. In these points or partes, the chiefest thing wheron men vse to reason touching this matter, are conteined. Now I meanto handle this matter, being very obscure and intricate, with many questions, (I trust) so plainly, & clerely out of the holy scriptures, whereon we may surely stay our selues, out of the

The diuision or partes of this booke.

anciēt fathers, allowed historiographers, and other good writers, that those which are studious and louers of Gods truth, may well vnderstand what may be denied & thought of those apparitions, & other straunge & maruellous matters. And I also trust that euen our aduersaries also, (in case they wil lay their affections aside, but a litle while) wil say that I haue truly alleaged all their arguments, and confuted thē without any railing or bitternesse. For my purposed ende is according to the doctrine of Saint *Paule*, to edifie and not to destroy.

As touching diuinations, blessings, iuglings, coniurings, and diuers kinds of sorcerie, and generally of all other diuellish practises, certaine learned men of our time haue written bookes, as *Gasper Pencerus*, *Ioannes Viera*, *Ludouicus Mellichius*, and perchaunce some others also, whose worke I haue not yet seene. It is not long ago since *Ioannes Riuius* a man learned and eloquent, published a booke in the latin toong, entreating of spirites and superstition. In the which booke albeit very briefly, yet doth hee as he is wont in all things, very finely & eloquently intreat of this matter, and of other foolishe superstions. And albeit that I do write more largely of this, yet was it not my minde to gather togither al those thinges which I could haue spoken and alleaged touching the same matter: but only such as seeme the chiefest and most especiall points, partly because I would not be tedious to the reader, & partly also least my books shuld grow vnto an ouer great quantity. I haue great hope that *Ioachimus Camerarius*, that excellent man, who readeth the auncient writers both greeks and latins,

with

with exquisite iudgemēt, and hath great experience in all things, will shortly write learnedly & at large of this matter, and also of others like vnto it. For so muche hee seemeth to promise in his preface to *Plutarches* Booke, *De defectu oraculorum, & figura, & consecrata Delphis* (wherin he handleth the nature and operatiōs of diuels) and also in other of his writings. I for my parte had once written this my treatise in the vulger tong, and now bicause I trust it shal be also profitable to other men, I haue translated it into latin, adding certaine things thereto.

This my booke which I haue with great labour and study gathered out of other mēs writings I present & offer vnto you (most noble consul) according to the ancient fashion & custome: not for that I suppose you haue any neede of my teaching, touching these things which are herein hādled. (For I am not ignoraunt, vnder what teachers you haue atteined vnto true learning, and how you haue and do continually read ouer sundry good authors with perfect knowledge in many tongues.) But partly that I might purchase credit and authoritie vnto this my booke with those men, vnto whome your goodnes, godlinesse and constancie (which you haue alwaies hitherto euermore shewed, and yet do shewe, in setting forth true religiō, & mainteining good lawes) is throughly knowne: and partly that I might shew my selfe in some respecte thankfull vnto you. For your honour hath bestowed many benefits on me, whom you onlie knowe by sight, and vppon other Ministers of the Church, wherby ye haue so bound me vnto you, that I shall neuer be able to make any recompence. The dedication.

Wherefore I most earnestly beseech you, not to refuse this signe and token of my good wil, be it neuer so simple: but rather to vouchsafe, whē ye haue leisure from the laboure and toile of the common wealth, to reade ouer this my booke: for I haue good hope it will not seeme vnpleasaunt vnto you & others in the reading, as wel for the plaine order I vse therin, as also for the sundrie and manifold histories in it recited.

Almightie God, who hath so blessed you with his heauenly gifts, that for them, (albeit very yong) you haue aspired vnto the highest degree in your noble citie and dominiō of *Berna*, vouchsafe to preserue you in health; and increase and multiply his good gifts in you. My Lords & brethren the ministers of *Tigurin*, and also your old companion master *George Grebelius*, that excellent man in lerning, vertu, and nobilitie, hartily salute your Lordship. From *Tigurin* in the month of Ianuary, the year of Christs Natiuitie. 1570.

The

A Table of the Chapters of the three principall parts, touchings Spirits walking by Night.

Of the first part.

COncerning certaine words which are often vsed in this Treatise of Spirites, and diuers other diuinations of things to come. Chapter.1. Folio.1.

Melancholike persons and madde men, imagining things which in very deed are not. Chaper.2. Fol.9.

Fearefull men, imagine that they see and heare straunge things. Chap.3. Fol.14.

Men which are dull of seeing and hearing, imagine many things which in very deed are not so. Chap.4. Fol.16.

Many are so feared by other men, that they suppose they haue heard or seene spirits. Chap.5. Fol.21.

Priests and Monkes fained themselues to be spirits: also how *Mundus* vnder this colour defiled *Paulina*, and *Tyrannus* abused many noble and honest matrons. Cha.6. Fol.23.

Timotheus Aelurus, counterfeiting himselfe to be an Angell, obteined a Bishopprické: foure Monkes of the order of Preachers, made many vaine apparitions at *Berna*. Chapter.7. Fol.28.

Of a counterfaite and deceiuing spirite at *Orleaunce* in *France*. Chap.8. Fol.37.

Of a certaine parish priest at *Clauenna*, which fained himselfe to be our Lady, and of an other that counterfeited himselfe to be a Soule, as also of a certaine disguised Iesuit Frier. Chapter.9. Fol.41.

That it is no maruell if vaine sightes haue bene in olde time,

time, neither yet that it is to be maruelled at, if there be any at this day. Chap.10. Fol.45.

That many naturall things are taken to be ghostes. Chapter.11. Fol.49.

A proofe out of the Gentiles histories, that ghostes do oftentimes appeare. Chap.12. Fol.53.

A proofe out of the histories of the auncient Church, and of the writings of holy Fathers, that there are walking spirits. Chap.13. Fol.62.

That in the bookes, set foorth by Monkes, are many ridiculous and vaine apparitions. Chap.14. Fol.65.

A proofe by other sufficient writers, that spirits do sometime appeare. Chap.15. Fol.68.

Daily experience teacheth vs, that spirites do appeare to men. Chap.16. Fol.71.

That there happen straunge wonders and prognostications, and that sodain noyses and cracks and such like, are heard before the death of men, before battail, and before some notable alterations and chaunges Chap.17. Fol.77.

It is proued by testimonies of holy scripture, that spirites are sometime seen and heard, and that other strange matters do often chaunce. Chap.18. Fol.85.

To whom, when, where, and after what sort, spirits do appeare, and what they do worke. Chap.19. Fol.88.

The Chapters of the second part.

The opinion or beleef of the Gentils, Iewes, and Turks, concerning the estate of soules seperated from their bodies. Chapter.1. Fol.92.

The Papists doctrine touching the soules of dead men, and the appearing of them. chap.2. Fol.102.

What hath followed this doctrine of the Papists, concerning

Testimonies of the auncient Fathers, that deade mens soules parted from their bodies, doo not wander here vppon earth. Chap.5. Fol.116.

A confutation of those mens arguments or reasons, which affirme, that dead mens soules do appeare. And first, that is answered which certaine do alleage, to wit, that God is omnipotent, and therefore that hee can worke contrary to the ordinary course of nature. Chap.6. Fol.123.

That the true Samuel did not appeare to the Witch in Endor. Chap.7. Fol.127.

A confutation of their arguments, which woulde haue Samuell himselfe to appeare. Chap.8. Fol.1'3.

Whether the Diuell haue power to appeare vnder the shape of a faithfull man? Chap 9. Fol.140.

Moses and *Elias* appeared in the Mount vnto Christ our Lorde: many haue beene raised from the dead both in bodie and soule, and therefore soules after they are departed, may returne on earth againe. Chap.10. Fol.145.

Whether the holy Apostles thought they sawe a mans soule, when Christ sodeinly appeared vnto them after his Resurrection. Chap.11. Fol.148.

Concerning the holy Fathers, Councels, Bishoppes, and common people, which say that soules doo visibly appeare. Chap.12. Fol.151.

Whether soules doo returne againe out of Purgatorie, and the place which they call *Limbus puerorum*. Chapter.13. Fol.155.

What those things are which men see and heare: and first that good Angels do sometimes appeare. Chap.14. Fol.159.

That sometimes, yea and for the most part, euill angels

 doo

Of wondrous monsters, and such like. Chap.16. Fol.164.

That it is no hard thing for the diuell to appeare in diuers shapes, and to bring to passe straunge things. Chap.17. Fol.167.

Diuels do sometimes bid men do those things which are good, and auoyde things that are euill: sometimes they tell truth, and for what cause. Chap.18. Fol.171.

The Chapters of the third part.

God by the appearing of Spirits doth exercise the faithfull, and punish the vnbeleeuers. Chap.1. Fol.175.

What the cause is that in these our dayes, so fewe spirites are seene or heard. Chap.2. Fol.183.

Why God doth suffer straunge noyses, or extraordinary rumblings to be heard before some notable alterations, or otherwise. Chap.3. Fol.186.

After what sort they should behaue themselues, which see good or euill spirits, or meete with other straunge aduentures: and first how both Iewes and Gentiles behaued themselues in the like cases. Chap.4. Fol.187.

How Christian men ought to behaue themselues when they see spirits, and first, that they ought to haue a good courage, and to be stedfast in faith. Chap.5. Fol.190.

It behoueth them which are vexed with spirites, to pray especially, and to giue themselues to fasting, sobrietie, watching, and vpright and godly liuing. Chap 6. Fol.193.

That spirits which vse to appeare, ought to be iustly suspected: and that we may not talke with them, nor enquire any thing of them. Chap.7. Fol.199.

Testimonies out of the holy Scripture, and one example whereby it is prooued, that such kinde of apparitions are not

to

to be credited, and that we ought to be verie circumspect in them. Chap 8. fol.201.

After what sort the faithfull in the primatiue church, vsed themselues, when they met with spirits. chap.9. fol.204.

That sundry kindes of superstition haue crept in, wherby men haue attempted to driue away spirits. chap.10. fol.206.

That spirites are not to bee driuen away by cursing and banning. chap.11. fol.214.

After what sort we ought to behaue our selues, when we heare straunge cracks, or when other forewarnings happen. Chapter.12. fol.216.

FINIS.

An answer [illegible] in the primitiue Church, [illegible] to them since [illegible] with spirits. chap.9. fol.[illegible]
That [illegible] superstition haue crept in, whereby men haue [illegible] spirits [illegible] fol.[illegible]
[illegible]
After what sort we ought to behaue our selues, when we heare strange noises [illegible] or when other forewarnings happen. Chap.[illegible] fol.[illegible]

FINIS.

The first parte of this Booke, concerning Spirits walking by night. Wherin is declared, that Spirits and sights *do appeare, and that sundry strange and monstrous things doo happen.*

CHAP. I.

Concerning certaine wordes whiche are often vsed in this Treatise of Spirits, and diuers other diuinations of things to come.

TO the intent, that those men which occupie themselues in reading of this my Booke, and especially in perusing of other auncient writers, may the better vnderstand euery thing, I will at the first enteraunce briefly expounde those things which shall seeme to concern the proprietie of wordes and termes vsed in this my Treatise of Spirits.

Spectrum, amongst the Latines doth signifie a shape or forme of some thing presenting it selfe vnto our sight. Spectrum.

Scaliger affirmeth, that *Spectrum* is a thing which offereth it selfe to be seene, either truly, or by vaine imagination. The Diuines take it to be a substance without a bodie, which being heard or seene, maketh men afraide.

Visum, signifieth an imagination or a certaine shewe, Visum.

which men being in sleepe, yea and waking also, seeme in their iudgement to behold: as we read of Brutus, who saw his owne angell. Cicero in his first booke Acadæm, quest. writeth, that *Visum*, amongst the Grecians is called φαντασία, a fantasie, or vaine imagination.

Visio. Also the Latines call those things *Visiones*, which the Grecians name φαντασίας.

Terriculamenta. *Terriculamenta*, are vain visions or sights, which make men afraide. The Latines also call it *Terriculum*, because it breedeth feare.

Phantasma. *Mat.24. Marke 6.* That which S. Matth. 24. and Marke 6. call φαντασμα, Erasmus doth translate it *Spectrum*: but the old interpreter vseth the Greeke word.

Phasma. φασμα in like manner doth signifie an elfe, a sighte or vaine apparition. Suidas maketh a difference betweene *Phantasma* and *Phantasia*, saying, that *Phantasma* is an imagination, an appearance or sight of a thing which is not, as are those sightes which men in their sleepe do thinke they see: but that *Phantasia*, is the seeing of that onely which is in very deede.

Pneuma. *Luk.24.* πνεῦμα is taken in Luke 24. chapter, for a spirite or vaine imagination. Howbeit most commonly some other word is ioyned vnto it, if it bee put for an euill spirite: as πνεύματα πλάνα, πονηρα. The Gentiles (as S. Augustine and other Fathers do testifie) supposed that the soules of men became *Dæmones*, that is, good or euil angels: which if they had done well, then were they called *Lares*, that is priuate gods: but if they haue done euill, then were they named *Lemures*, or *Larue*, bugs and Elues. But if it were doubted whether they had liued well or ill, then were they called *Manes*. Apuleius and other old writers affirme, that *Geny* and *Lares* were all one.

Lares. It was supposed (as Festus witnesseth) that *Lares*, were the soules of men, or else infernall gods. *Lares* were called

præstites. *Præstites*, because they made all things safe with their eies: that

that is, they saued and preserued all things.

And Authors affirme, they were called *Hostilij*, for that they were supposed to driue away enemies. Neither were they thought to beare rule only in priuate houses, & in crosse meeting waies, but also to defend Cities. They were likewise worshipped priuately in houses, and openly in the high wayes. As touching those that were called *Lares*, you may read more in Anthonius Constantius, of Fauentia his Commentaries, and in Ouid.lib.5.Fastorum. Hostilij.

Genius (say the Grammarians) is the naturall god of euery place, of euery thing, or of euery man when we are borne, as it is written, we haue two *Genij*, whereof the one encourageth vs to doo well, the other to doo euill. *Genius* (saith Censorinus) is a god in whose gouernance euery man doth liue, so soone as he is borne: either because hee taketh care for our begetting, or that he is engendred with vs, or else that he taketh charge and defence of vs when we are begotten. Sure it is, he is called *Genius*, *à gignendo*, that is, of begetting. Genius.

Penates likewise are domesticall gods. Macrobius affirmeth, that they are gods by whom we onely breathe, by whom we enioy this body, and by whom we possesse the reason of our mindes. Nonius saith, *Lemures* are spirites walking by night, and terrors rising of pictures of mē & beasts. Other say, that *Lemures* are euil and hurtfull shapes which appeare in the night, yea and that they be the soules of those that make men black and blew, called after that name. Penates.

Some men call the ghosts of all dead things by ẏ name of *Lemures*. Thus saith Apuleius, Of those *Lemures*, he that hath care of his posteritie, and inhabiteth the house with a peaceable and quiet kinde of rule, was called *Lar familiaris*, god of the house. And because among the people of olde time, as they counted *Lares* good, so they supposed *Lemures* to be naught, therefore to driue them away, they did sacrifice vnto them. Vmbræ.

Lemures. Some other affirme, that *Lemures* are soules which tarry about the bodies. Porphyrius calleth them the wandring soules of men departed before their time, as it were *Remures*, taking their name of Remus, whose soule folowed his brother Romulus: who to the intent he might pacifie them, instituted feastes called *Lemuria*.

Laruæ. Seruius writeth, that *Vmbræ* were called Laruæ: and they called dead mens soules by the name of V*mbræ*. Of L*aruæ* men are called L*aruati*, that is to say, frantike men, and such as are vexed with spirits. Who also as (Nonius witnesseth) are called *Ceriti*.

Ceriti.

Manes. Seruius saith, that mennes soules are called *Manes*, at suche time as departing from their bodies, they are not yet passed into other bodies. And he iudgeth that they are so called by the figure ἀντίφρασις, (whiche is when one speaketh by contraries) of the olde adiectiue *Manus*, that is good, because they were nothing lesse than good. For the auncient people supposed, that *Manes* were infernall gods, and therefore did they number them amongst their euil gods, and pacified them with sacrifice, least they should hurt them. Some affirme that *Manes* are indeed infernall gods, but yet good: whereof commeth *Mane*, which signifieth good, and *Dii Manes*, as if you would say, good and prosperous gods, and thereof also is said *Immanes*, for, not good.

Some other suppose, that soules separated from the bodies, were called after this name: Wherby we see the auncient monuments of tumbes haue bene dedicated to *Diis Manibus*, to the infernall gods: In the which opinion Apuleius was, as we said a little before.

There are some that iudge *Manes*, to be the very same, that the old people called *Genii*, and that there were two of these *Manes* assigned vnto mens bodies, euen immediately after their begetting, which forsake them not whē they are dead, but continue in the graues after the bodies are consumed. For the which cause, those men who defaced Monu-

ments,

ments, were thought to doo wrong vnto the gods called *Manes*. The sothsayers called as well the celestiall as the infernall gods by the name of *Manes*, and that because they beléeued (as Festus doth write) that all things did *manare*, that is, were deriued from them. Other thinke they were so called *à manando*, of flowing, because the places betwéen the circle of the Moone and the earth, from whence they come, are full of soules.

Maniæ are deformed creatures, as Festus saith: and also vgly shapes, wherwith nurses make children afraid. Maniæ.

μορμω is a woman with a face almost of a monstrous fashion: hereof it is taken for a hag: as also μορμολύκειον, doth signifie a terrible sight, a spirit, or an elfe. Nicephorus saith in his Ecclesiasticall history, that a woman vsing to walke by night, is called by the name of Gilo. Mormo.

Lamiæ were supposed of the auncient people to be women hauing eies to put out or in at their pleasure, or rather certaine shapes of diuels, which taking on them the shewe of beautifull women, deuoured children and yong men, allured vnto them with swéete inticements. Lamiæ.

Philostratus in his booke Appollonio, writeth a maruellous history or fable of one Menippus, beloued of an hegge. The same authour writeth, that *Lamiæ* are called of some men *Laruæ*, spirits walking by night: and *Lemurei*, night spirits of horrible shapes: and of many *Empusa*, ghoasts of variable fashion: and that nurses so named them to make their children afraide.

Chrysostomus Dion writeth, that in the inmost part of *Affrike* are certain wild beasts, hauing the countenance of a woman, which in like manner are called *Lamiæ*: and he saith that they haue their paps and al the rest of their breast so faire as any Painters wit can deuise, which being vncouered, they deceitfully allure men vnto them, and when they haue taken them, doo forthwith deuoure them.

In the fourth chapter of the Lamentations of Hieremie, Lament. of Hier. chap. 4.

 it

it is saide: *Lamiæ nudauerunt mammas suas, &c.* Apuleius writeth, that *Lamiæ* are things that make Children afraide.

Striges. *Lamiæ* are also called *Striges*. *Striges* (as they say) are vnluckie birdes, which sucke out the blood of infantes lying in their cradles. And hereof some men will haue Witches take their name, who also are called *Volaticæ*, as Festus writeth.

Gorgones. The name of *Gorgon*, was inuented to make children afraid: for they say these *Gorgons* are rauening spirites, such as men faine *Lamiæ* to be.

Incubi. Succubi. *Ephialtæ*, and *Hyphialtæ*, that is, *Incubi & Succubi*, (which we call Maares) are night spirits or rathers Diuels, which leape vpon men in their sleepe. The Phisitians do affirme, that these are nothing else but a disease.

Empusa. *Empusa*, is an apparition of the Diuel, or a spirit which sheweth it selfe vnto such as are in misery, chaunging his shape into diuers formes, and for the most part appeareth at noone time. Read more hereof in Suidas.

Dicelon. *Dicelon*, is so called, because it is sent to make men afraid: those kinds of terrors the Grecians call *Hecatæa*, as
Hecatæa. Apollonius writeth, because Hecate or Proserpina is the cause of them, who therefore is called βειμώ ἀπὸ τοῦ βειμᾶν, that is of terrifying, and that by reason that terrours by night were thought to be stirred vp by her.

Acco. Alphito. Plutarchus writeth, that *Acco* and *Alphito*, were monstrous women, by naming of whome, mothers kept their children in awe, and made them feare to do euil.

Cardanus calleth these Diuels which keepe vnder the earth, and many times kill men as they are vndermining,
Telchinnes. by the name of *Telchinnes*. Men vsing witchcraft, and such as are possessed with a Spirit, and out of their wits, are called amongst the Grecians, πλάχῖνες.

Pan. Faunus. Of these sort are those monsters, halfe like men, and halfe like beastes, whiche men say are founde in woode,

and

and oftentimes haue appeared unto men. It is saide, that *Panes* and *Fauni*, are all one, hauing their nether parts like unto Goates féete.

And menne saye, that *Satyri*, are almost lyke unto men: And those whiche are of full age are called *Sileni*. Satyri. Sileni.

Onocentaurus, is a beast of a straunge fashion, which is reported to be like a man in the upper part, and downward like an asse. Onocentaurus.

Onosceli, as it is written in Plutarche, are Diuels, hauing legges like unto asses. Onosceli.

The olde people imagined, that *Hippocentauri*, were creatures, who before were like to men, but the hinder parts had the similitude of horses. Hyppocentaurus.

And they do faine, that *Sphinx* is *Animal* ἀνθρωπόμορφον, a beast of the similitude of a man. Sphinx.

Scilla, and *Harpyæ*, are rauening Diuels, with faces like unto maydens. Scilla. Harpyæ.

As touching men liuing in the Sea, as *Tritones*, *Nereides* and *Syrenes*, who as the auncient people affirmed, had faces like unto men. Reade Gesnerus in *Historia Aquatilium*, where he intreateth of them. For he prooueth out of many Authors, that there are founde Monsters in the Sea, hauing shapes and countenaunces somewhat like unto men. Triton. Nereides. Syrenes.

Some of these Monsters which are indéede, bee of the kinde of Apes, and some are onely fabulous, or false: yet notwithstanding, it may be, that the Diuell doth deceiue men under the formes of them.

Thus much concerning tearmes, which we must use in this our Treatise of Spirits or Visions.

Hereunto haue I adioyned straunge happes, and foretokens, which for the most part chaunce before great matters. And therefore I knit them unto these, because they haue great resemblance unto them.

For vaine imaginations also appeare unto our sights: armed men as it were are seene on earth, or in the aire: and other such like shapes, voyces, noyses, crackes, and such like. But as touching the very words, *Portentum* is that which foresheweth some thing to come, as when straunge bodies appeare in the aire, or blazing starres, or thunder in faire weather, or whirlewindes do chaunce. Festus saith, that albeit *Portentum* be a naturall thing, yet it happeneth sildome, and doth betoken some thing to come to passe after a certaine season.

Portentum.

Ostentum.

Ostentum, is some straunge thing, which sheweth some thing to come to effect speedily. They giue the like examples of them both.

Prodigium.

Prodigium, is a thing which albeit it often chaunce by course of nature, yet notwithstanding it doth alwaies betoken some euill thing, being called *Prodigium*, as it were of *porro agendum*, to be done afterward.

Monstrum.

Monstrum, is that which hapneth against nature, as when any thing is brought forth hauing members belonging to an other kinde: the which is also called *Promonstrum*, as who should say, *Porro aliquid monstrans, siue monens*, that is, shewing or warning some thing to happen afterward. Notwithstanding these termes are many times confounded togither, and taken in one signification, and that because they respect one ende, that is, to tell before or giue warning of things to come. The vaine visions wheron we here intreat, appertaine nothing to naturall philosophers, neither yet these things which we haue ioyned with them. For if a sodaine cracke, or sound, or groning, or rumbling, as though the house would fall, or if any other thing chance which standeth by naturall reason, it doth not properly belong unto this matter which we haue in hand. But letting these things passe, we will by Gods helpe and aide come nearer to the matter it selfe.

Melan-

CHAP. II.

Melancholike persons, and mad men, imagine many things which in verie deed are not.

There haue bin very many in al ages, which haue vtterly denied that there bee any spirits or straunge sightes. The Philosophers of Epicurus sect, did iest & laugh at all those things which were reported of them, and counted them as fained and counterfeyt, by the which only children and fooles, and plaine simple men were made afraide. When Cassius, who was an Epicurian, vnderstood by Brutus, that he had seene a certaine vision, he (as Plutarch doth testifie) indeuoured to attribute the matter vnto naturall causes. We read in the 23. chapter of the Actes of the Apostles, that the Sadduces did not beleeue there should be any Resurrection of the dead, and that they denied there were any spirites or angels: Yea and at this day, many good & godly men beleeue those things to be but tales, which are talked of too and fro concerning those imagined visions: partly because in all their life, they neuer sawe any such, and partly or rather especially, because in time past men haue bin so often deceiued with apparitions, visions and false miracles done by Monkes and Priestes, that now they take things yͤ are true, to be as vtterly false. Whatsoeuer the cause is, it may be proued, by witnesse of many writers, and by daily experience also, that spirites and strange sightes do sometime appeare, and that in very deed many strange and maruellous things do happen.

Some men deny there are Spirits.

Act. 33.

True it is, that many men do falsly perswade themselues that they see or heare ghoasts: for that which they imagine they see or heare, proceedeth either of melancholie, madnesse, weakenesse of the senses, feare, or of some other perturbation: or else when they see or heare beasts, vapors, or some other naturall thing, then they vainly suppose, they haue ſéene ſightes I wotte not what, as hereafter I will ſhewe particularly by many and notable examples.

There is no doubt, but that almoſt al thoſe things which the common people iudge to be wonderfull ſightes, are nothing leſſe than ſo. But in the meane ſeaſon it cannot be denied, but that ſtraunge ſightes, and many other ſuch lyke things, are ſometimes heard and alſo ſéene.

Sundry imaginations of melancholike perſons.

And firſt it cannot be denied, but that ſome men which either by diſpoſitions of nature, or for that they haue ſuſteined great miſerie, are now become heauie and full of melancholy, imagine many times with themſelues being alone, miraculous and ſtraunge things. Sometimes they affirme in great ſoothe, that they verily heare and ſée this or that thing, whiche notwithſtanding neither they, nor yet any other man did euer ſée or heare. Which thing we ſometimes ſée by experience to be true in thoſe men, which be troubled with great headache, or ſubiect to other diſeaſes of the bodie, or cannot take reſt in the night, or are diſtraughted of their wittes. Theſe which dwell with ſuche kinde of men, when they here them tell ſuch abſurd tales, ſuch ſtraunge things, and ſuch maruelleus viſions, albeit they pittie their vnfortunate eſtate, yet can they not many times containe themſelues from laughing. Ariſtotle in his booke *de rebus mirandis*, writeth of a certaine man diſtraught of his wittes, who going into the Theatre of *Abydos* a Cittie of *Aſia*, when no man was therein, and there ſitting alone, by clapping of his handes, ſignified that he liked as well euery thing there, as if ſome Comedie or Tragedie had bin notably ſet forth on a ſtage.

Theatrum a place to behold plaies and paſtimes in.

The verie lyke Hiſtorie hath Horace, in his ſecond booke of Epiſtles, of a certain man, who comming into the Theatre at *Argos*, behaued himſelfe euen as the other man did: And when his kinſfolke through the helpe of good Phiſitians, had reſtored him to his right wittes againe, he was very angry with them, ſaying, that he neuer liued

more

more pleasantly than while he was beside himselfe. Atheneus lib. 12. writeth of one Tresilaus, whose braines were so distempered, that he verily supposed all the ships which arriued at Port Piræus, to be his owne: he would number them, he commaunded the Mariners to launch from shore, and when they returned after their voyage home againe, he as much reioyced as if he had bene owner of all wherewith they were laden. The same man affirmed, that in all the time of his madnesse he liued a verie pleasant life, untill the Phisitian had cured him of his disease. I my selfe haue seene a man, Iohannes Leonardus Sertorius by name, whom very honest and graue men, which knew him well, would testifie to be a godly man, which was throughly perswaded with himselfe, that hee could proue our Religion which we now professe, to be true and Catholike, euen by a miracle from heauen as sometime Helias did. He desired the Magistrates of certain Countries to call togither their Papists, and Protestants: for he was readie (he sayd) to shewe this miracle, and in case he did it not openly before them all, he refused not to sustain any kynd of punishment. The lyke reason is also of other men whiche are besides themselues: for they take on them marueillous things, either because they haue mused long time on some matter conceiued in their minds, as cunning Artificers oftentimes do: or because they haue bin long wearied with sicknesse, or else because they loue extremely. You shall finde some that imagine themself as it were armed with horns of an Oxe: other appeare to themselues to be earthen vessels, and therfore they wil shun euery thing for feare they be broken. Of such an one writeth Galene, *De locis affectis lib. 3. cap. 6.* and also *lib. 4. cap. 1.* Other suppose themselues dead, other thinke themselues great Princes, other to be learned men, other to be Prophets & Apostles, & therfore they wil foretel things to come. The same he writeth of them that are taken with frenzie, and namely, of one Theophilus a Phisitian,

Ioannes. Sertorius.

Ste. Ludouic. Cælius li. 17. ca. 2. antiquicat.

Galen de loci affectis.

Libro de Simtomatum diff. chap. 3.

who in other things was wise, and coulde dispute wel and perfectly knowe euery man: yet notwithstanding, hee thought there were certain minstrels did haunt that corner of his house where he vsed to lye, and that they tuned their pypes and played on them euery daye: And hée verily thoughte, that he sawe them, some sitting, and some standing, and in such sorte continually pyping without intermission, that they ceased at no time, neither in the day, nor in the night. And therfore he neuer ceased to crie, and to commaunde his seruants to driue them out of his doores. When he was throughly recouered of his sicknesse, then he tolde all other things which euery one of them had sayd or done: and also he called to mind the imaginations which he conceiued of the tediousnesse of the minstrels.

Paulus Aegineta. Licanthropia.

Paules Aegineta writeth in his thirde bo̅oke and xv. chap. that those that are taken with *Licanthropia* (which is a kynde of madnesse) leape out of their houses in the night, in all things imitating the nature of wolues, and that vntill it waxe day, they kéep about the graues of dead men. Moreouer, somtimes the diuel (enemie to mankinde) so deceiueth men, that they séeme vnto them selues to bée beastes.

Augustine vpon Genesis. Hidrophobia.

Wherof Augustin writeth In Genesin ad litteram lib.7. cap.11. they which are bitten with madde Dogges are afraide of water. This disease they call *Hidrophobiam*: out of which Aegineta lib.5.ca.3 reporteth, that they which are troubled with this disease, looking on the water, and béeing broughte vnto it, flée from them soone: other vtterly refuse all kind of moisture: and that there are some which barke like Dogges, and bite them that come vnto them.

Rufus.

Rufus shewing the cause of their feare, saith that they suppose they sée in the water the shadowe of the Dog which bitte them.

Ephilates the maare.

Ephialtes, which the Phisitions call the Maare, is a disease of the stomacke, concerning which, reade Paulus Aegineta li.3 cap.16. Many which are taken with this disease, imagine

to creepe vp by little and little on the bed, as it were to deceiue them, and anon to runne downe. They see me also to
themselues to heare him. This disease is called by an other
name πιγαλίων, and πιγάμων.

Madde men which haue vtterly lost the vse of reason, Mad men.
or are vexed by Gods permission, with a Diuell, whome
the Gospell calleth δαιμονιζομένους, doo maruellous thinges,
talke of many visions and diuers other matters. Their
sight deceiueth them, in so much as they mistake one man
for another: which thing we see by experience, in Bedleme
houses where madde and frantike men are kept. We read
that Aiax tooke the matter so greeuously, when Achilles
armour was adiudged vnto Vlisses, that becomming mad
through griefe, and drawing out his swoorde, he set vpon
herds of swine, supposing that he fought with the whole
army of the Grecians. Afterwards hanging vp two of the
greatest of them on postes, with rayling words he whipped them, thinking one of them to be Agamemnon, the o-
ther Vlisses, of whom with the first he was angry as an e-
uil iudge, with the other bicause he was by him vanquished
in iudgement. But afterwards when he came againe to
himselfe, for very shame he slew himselfe. It hath many
times chaunced in battaile, that the souldiers falling into
great fury, their captaines haue bene forced to take away
their armour, because by rage they tooke their own felowes
for enemies, and began to set on them violently.

Tertullianus saith thus: Those which are mad see one Tertullian.
man in an other, as Orestes sawe his mother in his sister,
Aiax beheld Vlisses in an heard of swine, Athamas and A-
gaue wilde beastes in their owne children, &c.

 Fearefull

CHAP. III.

Fearefull men, imagine that they see and heare straunge things.

That whiche we haue hitherto spoken concerning melancholicke men, and men out of their wits, may also be vnderstood of timorous and fearefull men. For if any man be timorous by nature, or subiect to feare through great daungers, or by some other wayes, he also imagineth straunge things which indéed are not so, especially if he haue in him any store of melancholy. Women, which for the most part are naturally

2.*Pet*.3. giuen to feare more than men, (for which cause S. Peter in his first Epistle speaking of the dutie of married folks, calleth them the weaker vessell,) do more often suppose they sée or heare this or that thing, than men do. And so do yong women, because commonly they are afraide. If when men sit at the table, mention be made of spirites and elues, many times women and children are so afraide that they dare scarce go out of doores alone, least they should méete with some euill thing: and if they chaunce to heare any kinde of noise, by and by they thinke there are some spirites behinde them, such vaine perswasions they haue. A cowardly souldiour iudgeth his enemies to be more in number than they are: the noyse of a leafe being moued so affrighteth him (which thing God in his lawe threatneth his people of *Israel*, except they do their duties) that he betaketh himself to his héeles: if he but heare a woodspeck with his bill beating on a trée, he straight thinketh the enemy readie to leape on his shoulders: yea if he heare but a mouse moue, by and by his heart is in his hose. These and such like things neuer trouble a stout and couragious souldier.

And

And yet sometimes in the chase, lustie souldiers flying away from their companie, are so troubled in minde, that they thinke their friends enemies, and cannot tell in the world where they are, and whither they go: all the which commeth by feare.

Plutarche in his booke *De sera numinis vindicta*, reporteth a maruellous and notable historie, of one called Bessus: who after he had murthered his father, hid himselfe a long season. But on a time as he went to supper, espying a swallowes neast, with his speare he thrust it downe: and when those which supped togither with him, misliked and abhorred his cruelty (for we like not those men that trouble little birdes and other beastes, because we iudge them austere and cruell) he answered: haue they not (saieth hée) falsly accused me, a great while crying out on me, that I haue slaine and murthered my father. Those which were present, being striken with great admiration, reported these his wordes to the king, who immediately caused him to bee tormented, and examining the matter diligently, at the last found him guiltie, and punished him as a manquiller of his owne father. Hereof ye may gather what feare can doo: the swallowes coulde not speake, and yet he perswaded himselfe that they vpbrayed him with murthering his father. Euen so many through feare, imagine that they heare and sée many thinges whiche in déede are méere trifles. Plutarche.

Procopius in the beginning of the warres of *Italie*, declareth, that as Theodoricus satte at meate, after he had put to death Boethius and Symmachus his sonne in lawe, a fishes head being brought before him, he sawe in it the countenance of Symmachus looking horribly, which byting the nether lip with lowring eyes séemed to threaten him, wherewith the King being sore abashed, fell into a gréeuous sicknesse, whereof he afterwards died. Yea feare if it be Theodoricus imagining that he seeth Symmachus.

vnncavnmeasurable maketh vs to abhorre those thinges, which otherwise should be comfortable vnto vs. The apostles of our Lord Iesus Christ may be examples hereof. Who in the night season being in greate daunger in the Sea, when they sawe Christe walking on the water approching towardes them wer marueilously appalled. For they supposed they sawe a Spirit, and cried out for feare. But the Lorde came to deliuer them out of that present daunger wherein they were. After his resurrection they were marueilously affraide, and as S. Luke saith, they verily supposed they sawe a Spirit, when in déede he appeared vnto them in his owne body. Therfore the lord comforteth & hartneth them saying: Behold my hands & my féet, for I am euē he: hāndle me and sée: for a spirit hath not flesh and bones as ye sée I haue. They through great ioy could not beléeue it, but marueiled at it. Héere thou séest, by feare it came to passe, that the Disciples supposed ẏ Lord him self to haue bin a ghost. And therfore no man ought to maruell if we hindered by feare, mistake one man for an other, and perswade our selues that we haue séene spirits, whereas no such were. They which are of stout and hautie courage, frée from all feare, seldome times sée any spirits. It is reported of the Scithians, a warlike natiō dwelling in mountains (from whom it is thought the Turkes take their originall) that they neuer sée any vaine sightes of spirits. Authors write that Lions are not feared with any bugs: for they are full of stomacke and deuoide of feare.

Match. 14.

Luke. 24.

Stout and coragious men seldom see any Spirits.

CHAP. IIII.

Men which are dull of seeing and hearing, imagine many things which in verie deed are not so.

They whiche are weake of sight, are manye times in suche sorte deceyued, that they beholde one man in steade of an other. Poare-blinded men whome the Gréekes call Μύωπες whiche can not sée

sée any thing, except it be verie neare their eyes (as for the most part students are, which night and day turne over their bookes) are so much deceiued in their sight, that they are many times ashamed to vtter what they haue thought they haue séene. And it standeth by naturall reason, that an oare séemeth to be broken in the water: and a tower foure cornered, a farre off sheweth to be rounde. Those which drinke wine immoderately, in such sort that their eyes begin to ware dimme, and stare out of their heads, like hares which haue bin caried hanging on a staffe a mile or twaine, sée things farre otherwise than sober men doo. They suppose they sée two candles on the table, when there is but one: desiring to reach the potte, they put their hand amisse. In Euripides Tragedie named Bacchis, Pentheus affirmeth, that he seeth two Sunnes and two citties of *Thebes*: For his braines were maruellously distempered. It is a common saying, that if wine haue the victorie, all things séeme to haue turned vpside downe: trées to walke, mountaines to be moued, and riuers to run against the head, &c. Salomon exhorteth all men from drunkennesse, in his prouerbs, cap. 23. shewing what discommodities ensue therof, and amongst other thinges he saith thus: Thy eyes shall sée straunge (to wit) visitions and maruellous apparitions. For as timorous men imagine miraculous things, euen so doo drunken men, who of purpose corrupt and spoile their sight. And albeit God shew many wonders in the aire, and in the earth, to the ende he may stir men vp from idlenesse and bring them to true repentaunce, yet notwithstanding, we must thinke that dronken men which sit vp vntill midnight, do often say, that haue séene this or that vision, they haue beheld this or that wonder, when as indéed they are vtterly deceiued. For in case they had returned home in due season, and not ouercharged themselues with so much wine, no such thing had appeared vnto them. For indéede their eyesight had not bene blinded. Doth it not often come

Dronken men see straunge things.

Euripides.

Pro. 23.

to paſſe, that when men are once throughly warmed with wine, they miſtake one for another, of whom they thought they were abuſed in word or déede, and violently flie on them with weapon? The place before alleaged out of Salomon, may alſo be vnderſtood to this purpoſe: Thy eyes ſhall ſée ſtraunge (to wit,) women, to luſt after them. For experience teacheth vs that men being drunke, aſſaie to rauiſh matrones and maidens, which being ſober they would neuer once thinke vppon. Wine immoderately taken, is the nurſe of raſhe boldneſſe and filthie luſt.

Some ſee themſelues.

Ariſtotle writeth, that ſome men through the féebleneſſe of their ſight, beholding in the aire neare vnto them (as it were in a glaſſe) a certaine image of themſelues, ſuppoſe they ſée their owne angels or ſoules: and ſo as the Prouerbe is, they feare their owne ſhadow. Although men in obſcure and darke places can ſée nothing, yet do they not (I pray you) imagine they ſée diuers kindes of ſhapes and colours. And we many times ſuppoſe thoſe things which we ſée, to be farre otherwiſe than indéed they are.

It is well knowne, a mans ſight may be ſo deceiued, that he verily thinkes that one deuoureth a ſword, ſpitteth out money, coales, and ſuch like: that one eateth bread, and ſpitteth forth meale: one drinketh wine, which after runneth out of his forehead: that one cutteth off his fellowes head, which afterwardes he ſetteth on againe: and that a Cocke ſéemeth to drawe after him a huge beame of timber, &c. Moreouer it may be brought to paſſe by naturall things, as by perfumes and ſuch like, that a man would ſweare in earneſt, that all men ſitting at the table with him, haue no heads at all, or elſe that they are like the heads of aſſes: & that ſomtimes a vine ſpreadeth it ſelf as it were ouer al the houſe, whē indéed it is a mere deceit, or a plaine iugling caſt. Of which matter there be bookes commonly ſet abroad. The like reaſon is in hearing, & in the other ſenſes. Thoſe men whoſe hearing is ſomewhat decaied, many

Hearing deceiueth.

times.

times séeme in their owne imagination, to heare the noyse of boysterous winde, or violent tempest, the sparkling of fire, the roaring of waters sodeinly increased, singing and sounding of instruments, and also the iangling of belles, when as indéed these things are not so, but only chaunce by default of hearing: for others which are conuersant with them, hauing the right vse of hearing, do not heare any such thing at all. Somtimes in very déed such things are heard, as the crackling of wainscot walles, and such like, which are naturall signes of some tempest shortly after ensuing.

There are also certaine hollowe places, through the which the winde whisting, giueth a pleasant sound, as if were through a pipe, much like vnto singing, so that men wonder verie much thereat. We reade in writers of Philosophie, that the very same also chaunceth in bankes of riuers, which bende a little in compasse. Hearing is also deceiued when we thinke we heare thunder, and it is indéed but the rumbling of some Carte. There be many which thinke they handle something, and yet are deceiued: If men sicke of the ague, drinke wine of the best and swéetest sorte, yet they thinke it is more bitter than Gall: if they eate pottage neuer so good, yet they iudge it vnsauorie: which thing commeth not of any faulte in the Cooke, but of the mouth and stomacke which is distempered with sicknesse. For vnto them which haue abundance of choller, all things séeme bitter. And euen so it commeth to passe, that a man supposeth he seeth, heareth, féeleth, or is felt of some spirit, when indéed it is not so, and yet no man can perswade him the contrary.

The sense of feeling is deceiued.

If feare and weaknesse of the sight and of other senses méete togither, then men fall into strange and maruellous imaginations, beléeuing things vtterly false, to be verie true: Neither will they be brought from their owne opinions by any meanes or reason.

VVeakenesse of the sight and feare.

We reade that not only perticular and priuate men, but also whole armies of souldiers generally haue bene so deceiued, that they haue verily thought their enemies hard at their heeles, when as no man followed. And hereof haue proceeded many horrible flightes in battaile.

Cominæus. Cominæus, a knight and diligent writer of histories, in the ende of his first booke of the Acts of Lewes the II. King of *Fraunce*, writeth, that when Charles Duke of *Burgundie*, with other Princes, had remoued their armie to *Paris*, they vnderstood by their espials, that the next day the king had determined to set on them with all his power of men. Wherefore the next day Charles sent out certaine horsemen to view his enemies: who comming forth, by reason that the element was somewhat darke, supposed they sawe a huge number of pikes and speares, but when they had passed a little further and that the aire was a little clearer, they vnderstood the same place wherein they iudged the king to be with all his armie, to be planted and ouergrowne with many high thistles, which a far off shewed as it had bene long speares. For the night beguileth mens eyes. And therefore none ought to maruell, if trauellers towardes night or at midnight, mistake stones, trees, stubbes, or such like, to be sprites or elues. We reade in the last booke of the kings the 3. chap. that after the death

King.4. of king Achab, the Moabites reuolted from Ioram his sonne, wherefore he desired Iosaphat to aide him, and with all his power he determined to make warre on the Moabites, to reduce them to obedience, and subiection. Which thing when the Moabites heard, they prepared to defend themselues, so many as were able to beare armour. But when they had set forward verie earely in the morning against their enemies, supposing in the rising of the Sunne, the waters which God had miraculously brought out to be redde, they said amongst themselues: Surely the two Kings haue encountred togither, and eache haue de-

stroyed

stroyed other, whereuppon they running on heapes without order, to spoile the Israelites Tents, were by them vanquished and slaine: here you sée all the Armie mistooke water in stead of bloud.

CHAP. V.

Many are so feared by other men, that they suppose they haue heard or seene Spirits.

Furthermore, it commeth to passe many times that not only pleasant and mery conceited men, but also spitefull and malitious men, chaunging their apparell, make others extreamely affraide. It is a common custome in many places, that at a certaine time of the yeare, one with a nette or vizarde on his face maketh Children affraide, to the ende that euer after they should laboure and bee obedient to their Parentes, afterward they tel them that those which they saw, were Bugs, Witches and Hagges, which thing they verily beléeue, and are commonly, miserably affraide. Howbeit, it is not expedient alwayes so to terrefie Children. For sometimes through great feare they fall into dangerous diseases, and in the night crie out, when they are fast a sléepe. Salomon teacheth vs to chasten children with the rod, and so to make them stand in awe: he doth not say, we must beare them in hand they shall be deuoured of Bugges, Hags of the night, and such like monsters. Salomons Pro.

Many times, pleasant & mery yong men, disguise themselues like vnto Diuels, or else shroud themselues in white shéetes to make other men affraide: with whome if simple men chaunce to méete, they make no doubt of the matter, but verily thinke they haue séene spirites, and straunge sightes. And yet it is not alwayes the safest way, so to deceiue men with iests and toyes; for many examples might be brought to shewe how euill some men haue sped hereby. It is an vsuall and common thing that yong men merily disposed, when they trauell by the way, comming to their Inne at night, tie ropes to the bed side, or to the couerlet or garments, or else hide themselues vnder the bedde, and so counterfeiting themselues to be Spirites, deceiue and mocke their fellowes. It chaunced once at *Tigurin* where we dwel, that certaine pleasant yong men disguising themselues, daunced about the Churchyard, one of them playing on a béere with two bones, as it were on a drumme. Which thing when certaine men had espied, they noysed it about the citie, how they had séene dead men daunce, and that there was great danger, least there should shortly ensue some plague or pestilence.

Daunsing Spirits.

Moreouer, it is well knowne to all men, that harlots, and whoremongers, haue practised their wickednesse a long season vnder this cloake and pretence, perswading their family, that walking Spirites haunt the house, least they should bee taken with the déede doing, and that they might enioy their desired loue. Many times such bugges haue bin caught by the magistrates, and put to open shame. Théeues likewise vnder this colour haue many times robbed their neighboures in the night time, who supposing they heard the noyse of walking Spirits, neuer went about to driue the théeues away. Touching this point, that an euil Spirit, by means of naturall things which haue strange vertues, can do maruellous things, by deceiuing mens senses, I will at this present speake nothing.

Priests

CHAP. VI.

Priestes and Moncks fained themselues to be Spirites: also how *Mundus* vnder this colour defiled *Paulina*, and *Tyrannus* abused many noble and honest matrones.

TO these thinges may bee added, that there haue bin in all ages certaine Priests, which practising strange deuises, and giuing themselues to Necromancie, haue bewitched foolish men that highly esteemed them, to the ende they might thereby encrease their riches, and follow their lustfull pleasures. Touching which matter, to the ende godly disposed men may be the more heedfull, I will rehearse a fewe histories.

Iosephus a writer of histories, in his 18. booke and 4. chap. of Antiquities, remembreth a notorious deed which hapned at Rome, in the time of Tyberius Cesar vnder the pretence of sacrificing to the goddesse Isis. I will record the historie as it is translated by Galenius, a very learned man.

Iosephus de antiquitatib.

There dwelled at Rome a woman named Paulina, no lesse renoumed for honestie of life, than for the nobilitie of parentage: She was also very rich and exceeding beautiful, as one that was now in the floure of her age, and especially adorned with the great vertue of chastitie, and married she was to one Saturnius, a man worthie of such a wife. It chaunced that Decius Mundus, a famous yong knight, became very much enamored with her: and because she was a woman of greater wealth than that she might be won with rewardes and money, so much the more was this louers madnesse inflamed, in so much that he stuck not to proffer her for one night. 200000. groates. The Atticke groat and the Romain peny are by common valuation all one. Budeus accounteth one of them worth S. Crusados: so this summe according to his reckoning, amounteth to 26000. Florens.

Paulina and Mundus.

And

And yet not being able by these means to moue her constant mind, bicause he could not endure the rage of his loue, he determined, by abstinence and hunger to make an ende both of life and loue togither. This determination was not vnknowne to Ide, Mundus Fathers bondseruant, a maide cunning in many artes, but such as were not to be liked. She maruellously greeued with the yong mans wilfulnesse in absteining frō meat, talking with him, by sweete and flattring words began to encourage him, assuring him that she would bring to passe, that he should at his pleasure embrace Paulina. After that he had gladly condiscended to her entreatie, she telleth him she must needes haue fiftie thousand groates to ouerthrow the Gentlewomans chastitie. So putting the yong man in good hope, and receiuing as much mony as she required, because she wel knew Paulina could not be wonne with mony, she deuiseth a new way to deceiue her. Understanding therefore that she was maruellously addicted to the worshipping of Isis, she inuenteth these meanes: She talketh with some of Isis Priests, and hauing receiued sure promise of them to keepe all things secrete, and (which is most effectuall) hauing shewed their reward, promising presently 25000. groates, and when they had done the deed, other 25000. she openeth vnto them the yong mans loue, beseeching them to helpe by al means possible, that shee might enioy the same. They touched at the heart with desire of the mony, gently promised their helpe. Wherefore the eldest of them speedily goeth to Paulina, and being admitted to her speech, after hee had obtained to talke with her in secrete, he declareth that he is come vnto her being sent by the great God Anubis (this Anubis hauing a head lyke to a Dogge, was worshipped togither in one Temple with Isis) who is maruellously in loue with her beautie, and doth commaund her to repaire vnto him. She ioyfully receiued the message, and forthwith vaunteth among her familiar acquaintaunce, that the God

Anubis,

Anubis hath vouchsafed to loue her: And shée telleth her husband, that shée must suppe and lye with him. Which thing was so much the more easily graunted vnto her, for that her husband had had good experience and knowledge of her chastitie. Whereupon shée goeth to the Temple, and after supper when time of rest drew neare, being shut in by the priest, shée méeteth with Mundus, who had priuily hidden himselfe there, the darkenesse bringing them togither, without any suspition. And so all that night shée satisfied the yong mans desire, supposing she had done pleasure vnto the God. Afterwards he departing from hir, Paulina early in the morning, before the priestes (who were priuie to this deceit) were stirring, returned home to her husband, to whome she recounteth her méeting with Anubis, and also with great words setteth out the same amongst her gossips and friends. They could not beléeue her, considering the nature of the thing, and yet could they not chuse but maruell, waying the great chastitie of the woman. Thrée dayes after the déede done, Mundus méeting by chaunce with his beloued, saide vnto her: O well done Paulina, thou hast saued me 200000. groats wherewith thou mightest haue encreased thy riches, and yet notwithstanding thou hast fulfilled my desire, for I way it not that thou hast despised Mundus, sith vnder the title of Anubis, I haue enioyed my desired lust, which words said, he departed. But the woman then first perceiuing this villany, began to teare her garments, and opening the whole matter vnto her husband, beséecheth him that he suffer not such a notorious mockery to go vnpunished. Her husband then declareth the whole matter to the Emperoure Tiberius: who after he had learned all things by diligent examination, trusseth vp these iugling priests on the gallowes, togither with Ide, the author of all this mischiefe, by whose meanes chiefly the chastitie of this noble Gentlewoman was defiled: and ouerthrowing their temple, he commaunded the Image of Isis to be sunke in the riuer of *Tibris*. But it pleased him to chasten Mundus with banishment, a more gentle kind of punishmēt, ascribing his fault to ŷ weaknes of his immoderat loue. By this history it may easily be gathered how sathan in times past bewitcht the Gentils, and how their priests persuaded them ŷ their Gods appearing in visible forme spake this or ŷ vnto them, which notwithstāding were very false. Vnder the pretence of worshipping their gods, they gaue thēselues to wicked deuises. For how often may we wel thinke they cōmitted abhominable mischief (although indeed ŷ matter it selfe neuer came to light.) If they brought it to passe, ŷ Mundus by their meanes enioyed his desired loue, surely there is no doubt, but ŷ they thēselues vnder the colour of holinesse defloured other mēs daughters & wiues: for otherwise this deuise could neuer haue bin so ready in mind. This matron would neuer haue bin so wel cōtent, vnles ŷ very same had bin practised with other dames before. Neither yet wold her husbād haue suffered her to lodge in the Church all night. What need was there for ŷ gods to haue beds prepared for thē in ŷ Church, whē it was most aparant they neuer lodged in thē. Princes also may learne by ŷ example of Tiberius, although he were a wicked tyrant, how such varlets are to be restrained. To this purpose maketh ŷ historie which Ruffinus a Priest of *Aquilia* reporteth in Li.11.ca.25. of his ecclesiasticall history.

Ruffinus.

Tyrannus a wicked priest.

There was a priest in *Alexandria* in *Egipt*, vowed to Saturn, whose name was Tyrānus. This mā as it had bin frō the mouth of god, used to say vnto al such noble & principall men, whose Ladies he liked & lusted after, that Saturne had cōmanded, ŷ such a ones wife shuld lie al night in the temple. Then he which heard ŷ message, reioycing much ŷ the god vouchsafed to call for his wife, decking her vp brauely, & giuing her great gifts (forsooth lest she shuld be refused bicause she came emptie) sent her forth vnto ŷ temple, where the woman being shut vp in the presence of al men, Tirannus whē he had fast locked the doores, surrendring the keyes departed his wayes. Afterwards in great silence passing through priuie caues vnder the ground, he issued forth out of the open holes into the image of Saturne: which image was made hollow in the backe, and cunningly fastned to the wall. And as the candles burned within the Church, he spake sodeinly vnto the woman (giuing great eare, and praying deuoutly) through ẏ image made of hollow brasse, in such sort that the vnhappie woman, trembled betwéene feare and ioy, because she thought her selfe worthie of the spéech of so great a god. Now after the baudie god had talked his pleasure to bring her in great feare, or to prouoke her to lust and wantonnesse, sodeinly all the lightes were put out with the spreading abroad of shéets, by a certain cunning deuise. And then descending out of the image, he committed adultery with the woman much abashed and afraid, vsing most profane and wicked gloses vnto her. When he had thus dealt a long season, almost with all the wiues of these silly Gentlemen, it chaunced in the end, that a certain chast Gentlewoman began to abhorre and loath the déede, and marking the matter more héedfully, knew it to be Tyrannus voice: and thereupon returning home againe, declared the slie conueiance of this horrible déed vnto her husband. He being set on fire with rage for the iniurie done vnto his wife, or rather vnto his selfe, apprehēded Tyrannus, & brought him to ẏ place of torments, where being conuicted he cōfessed al ẏ matter, & thē other deceits being likewise detected, al shame & dishonor was spred throughout the houses of ẏ Pagans: the mothers were found adulterers, fathers incestuous persons, and their children illegitimate and bastardes. Which thing so sone as it was brought to light and noysed abroad, togither both Church and image, and wickednesse, and all was vtterly subuerted and destroied. We reade that Numa Pompilius bare the people of *Rome* in hande that hée hadde familiar company with

Egeria a Goddeſſe of the waters, to the ende he might purchaſe credit and authoritie to his lawes.

CHAP. VII.

Timotheus Aelurus, counterfeiting himſelf to be an Angell, obteined a biſhopricke: foure Monkes of the order of Preachers, made many vaine apparitions at *Berna*.

IT might be ſomewhat borne withall, if theſe things had only chaunced among the Gentiles, which were without the word of God, if we did not euidently ſee the like happen oftentimes amongeſt Chriſtians, and in caſe it were not to be feared leaſt many ſuch things ſhould happen euen at this day alſo. For it is well knowne to all men, that there haue bene many Magiciens, Soſſerers, and Coniurers, and thoſe eſpecially Monkes and Prieſts, who would eaſily counterfeit viſions, and miracles, and familiar talking with ſoules.

Lippis & tonſoribus notum

Theodorus.

Theodorus Lector, collectaneorum ex hiſtoria eccleſiaſtica lib. 1. writeth of Timotheus Aelurus, that he, before Proterius biſhop of Alexandria was put to death, gaping for the biſhopricke, in the night cladde in blacke apparell walked about the celles of the Monkes, and calling eache man by his name, they anſwering, ſayd vnto them, that he a ſpirit, one of Gods ſeruants came to warne them, that euery one reuolting from Proterius, ſhould ioyne himſelfe vnto Timotheus. And by his craft and deceit obteining the biſhopricke, hee made great vproares in the Church of God. Here I cannot refraine my ſelfe as touching this preſent matter, but that I rehearſe a famous hiſtorie, of foure Monkes of the order of Preachers (who were brent at Berna in Heluetia, in the yeare of our Lord 1509. the laſt day of May) by what ſubtilties they deceiued a poore ſimple

Foure Monks of Berna.

simple Frier whom they had lately reteined into their monasterie: concerning which thing, many bookes were written at the same time when these things were done, which are yet extant both in the Latin and in the Germain toong. There was great contention betwéen the Monkes of ye order of Preachers, and the Friers Minorites, or Franciscans, touching the conceptiō of ye virgin Mary. The Friers preachers affirmed, that she euen as other men also was conceiued in originall sin, that the Franciscans denied and stoutly denied. At the last the matter came to that issue, that the preachers determined to auouch and proue their opinion by false and fayned miracles: taking aduisement in a certaine Synode (which they call a chapter) holden at *Vimpenium* a cittie of *Germanie*, where the most conuenient and fittest place for this matter might be founde: and at the last they chose out *Berna* in *Heluetia*, because the people there were plaine and simple, and giuen to the warres. Foure therefore of the chiefest in the Abbay of the order of preachers beganne the pageant at *Berna*: and because the Supprior one of the foure, was well séene in coniuring, he bounde the Diuell to ioyne in councell with them by what meanes they might best bring their purpose to passe. Hée appearing vnto them in the likenesse of a Negro or blacke Morian, promised them all that he could doo, vnder this condition, that they should yéeld and giue themselues vnto him, which thing they willingly did, deliuering vnto him a writing written with their owne hand and bloud. And it chaunced at the same time very fitly, that one Iohn Iezerus, a plaine fellowe, a Taylour by occupation, was chosen into their order, who séemed to be verie fit for their purpose. They tryed him by throwing stones into his chamber in the night time, making a great noyse, and faining themselues to be Spirits. The matters séemed vnto them, euen from the beginning, that it would take good successe. On a certaine day being Friday, the Supprior shrouding himselfe in a shéete, togither with other Spirites, whom he had coniured vp for this purpose, brake into the Friers cell with great force and noyse, faining with many teares, that he desired his ayd and help. Now had they priuily conueied Holy water and the Reliques of Saints into his Cell before. The poore Frier halfe dead with feare, denied that he could by any meanes helpe him, recommending himselfe to Christ our Sauiour, and to his holy mother. The Spirite aunswered, that it was in his and his brethrens power to deliuer him out of this miserie, if he would suffer himselfe for the space of viij. dayes, euery day to be whipped vntill the blood followed, and moreouer, cause eight Masses to be sung for his sake in S. Iohns Chappell, himselfe while they were sung, lying in the floore with his armes spread abroad. After hée tolde him that the next Friday before midnight, he would come again with greater noyse, willing him in any wise not to be afrayd, for the Diuels could nothing hurt him, because he was an holy man. The next day this foolish Frier openeth all the matter to the ringleaders of this deuise, beséeching them to assist him, that the miserable soule might be deliuered. The matter was out of hand rumored about the Citie. The Monkes preached openly hereof in the pulpit, commending highly ẏ holinesse of their order, which euen hereby might be séene, for that the spirite craued helpe of them, and not of the wicked drunken Franciscans. At the time appointed, the spirite accompanied with other euill spirits, came againe with great noyse to the Friers Cell, who adiuring and coniuring him, questioned with him touching certaine points. The spirit shewed him who he was, and for what cause he was so miserably vexed: and withall gaue great thanks both vnto him and also to his fathers, for being touched wᵗ remorse of him, adding, ẏ in case there were yet 30. Masses sung, and 4. Vigiles obserued, and ẏ he would yet once again whip himself vntil he bled, thē he shuld be clean deliuered out of most cru-all torments, which he had cōtinually endured a 160. yeers. He had conference with him all of other maruellous matters, which we neede not here to reherse. Afterwards ẏ same spirit appeared again vnto the Frier, and preferred the order of preachers before all others, bearing him in hand, that many of them which had bene aduersaries vnto this order, suffered most horrible torment in purgatorie, and that the citie of *Berna* should be vtterly ouerthrowne, except they banished ẏ Franciscans, and refused ẏ yeerly stipends which they receiued at the French kings hands. He also talked of sundry things which had hapned to the Frier (which thing they had learned before of him by meanes of auricular confession.) Moreouer he hartily thanketh the Frier for the great benefit of his deliuerance, giuing him to vnderstand, that he was now admitted into the eight degree of Angels, and that he should say Masse there for his benefactors.

After these things thus done, an other night one comming vnto him in the apparell of a woman, said he was S. Barraba, whom he deuoutly serued, and told him ẏ the blessed virgin would shortly appear vnto him, and make ful answere vnto those questions which one of the Monkes had writtē in paper for him. This paper Barbara promised that she her self would deliuer vnto our Lady, which they should shortly after find in a holy place sealed & signed miraculously. The Frier vpon this reuealeth the whole matter vnto his fathers, desiring to be confessed of his sinnes, wherby he might be found worthy the apparition or seeing of our Lady. He willed them to search in ẏ halowed place for the scroll, which at the last they found in the Fratry (as they term it) where they had laid it before. Thē they caried it with great reuerēce vnto the high alter, affirming ẏ it was sealed with Christs blood, and that the tapers lightned of their own accord. In the morning the virgin Mary appeared vnto him againe, rehearsing many things which her sonne Jesus commaunded her to tell vnto him: to wit, that Pope Iulius

was

was that holy man, which should reconcile the two orders in friendship againe, and institute and ordaine the feast of the defiled conception of our Lady, for she would send unto the Pope a crosse marked with foure droppes of her sonnes blood, in signe that she was conceiued in originall sinne: and that they should find an other crosse marked with fiue drops of blood in their fratrie, which they must conuey to *Rome*, for the Pope would allowe and confirme it with large indulgences, and after return it to *Berna* again: other things likewise she said, whereof many things were both reported and written to and fro.

But in witnesse of the aforesaid things, the same Mary droue an yron nayle through the hande of the poore Frier, saying: this wounde shall be renewed in the day wherein my sonne was crucified, and in the feast of my sonnes bodie. After they toke a burning water made by Necromancie, by the which they taking away his senses, made foure other woundes in his bodie. And after that he came againe unto himselfe, they bare him in hand that there was a certaine holy thing I wotte not what, which appeared about him. And when they sawe that many men came flocking about him to see this newe Christ, they taught him (for hee was of rude conditions) howe to behaue himselfe. And when they had giuen him a drinke bereauing him of his senses, and causing him to fome at the mouth, then they sayd he striued and wrestled with death, euen as Christ did in the mount Oliuet. After all this, another of them appeared unto him, telling him many things: but ẏ Frier knowing him by his voyce, beganne to suspect and mislike the whole matter, and with violence thrust him from him. The next night the Frier himselfe appeared unto him, saying that he was Mary of whome he had bene in doubt, and to the ende he should be out of all suspition, she had brought him the host of her sonnes bodie (for he brought him an host stipet in poyson) to the ende hee shoulde no more thinke he sawe an euil spirite: he also affirmed, that he had brought a vessel of glasse full of her sonnes bloud, which he would giue vnto him, and vnto his Monasterie. But the Frier, who also had this vision in suspition, answered: If (sayde he) thou be not an euil spirit, rehearse thy Pater noster and thy Aue Maria with me. The Prior sayde the Pater noster, and afterward sayd in the person of our Lady: Hayled am I Mary full of grace, the Lord be with me, &c. The Frier knowing the Priors voyce, caught a knife, and wounded him therewith, and when he defended himselfe, the Frier stoutly resisted, and draue him backe. These things thus done, the Supprior being in good hope to restore all that they had lost, appeared againe to the Frier, saying that he was S. Catherin of *Sena*, and therwith begun to chide him, for that he so discurteously had intreated the holy Virgin: adding moreouer, I am sent (quoth he) to shewe thee, that the wounds which thou hast in thy body, are the very true wounds of Christ, which neyther I, nor yet S. Francis hath, and that he enlarged with many words. Yet notwithstanding, the Frier so entertayned him, that he was glad to saue him selfe with running away. Now bicause the Frier wold no longer be mocked at their hands, they, marueilously troubled, and almost at their wits ende, taking aduise among them selues, brake the matter vnto him, and tolde him, that in verie deede they freely confessed many of those apparitions which he had seene to be fayned, and that for no other cause, but to the ende he should perseuere in his profession and Religion, howbeit the very effect of the matter was most true, and that he ought not to doubt, but that he bare the wounds of Christ in his body. And forsomuch as the matter was nowe knowen abroad, they earnestly besought him, that he would not refuse to go on in the matter, for otherwise their order should incurre open shame, and both he and they fall into present daunger, but in case he woulde persist in his enterprised pur-

 pose,

pose, the thing would fall out to his and their great aduantage. And so with fairer wordes, they perswaded him to make promise to be ruled by them hereafter.

After long instruction and teaching, they placed him on the altar of our Lady, kneeling on his knees within a chappell before the image of the holy virgine: Where one of the Monkes standing behinde a cloath, spake through a cane reede, as if it were Christ talking with his mother, in this wise: Mother why dost thou weepe? haue I not promised thee, y whatsoeuer thou willest, shall be done? Whereto the image made answere. Therefore I weepe, bicause this businesse findeth no end. Then said the image of Christ: Beleeue mee mother, this matter shall be made manifest. This done, the Monke priuily departing, the chappell doores were shut. Assone as these things were scattered about the citie, by & by there was a great thronging of people. Amongst whome also came foure monks, dissembling and fayning, that they knewe not what was there done, and therefore they commanded the doores to be opened, and after asked the Frier howe and after what sorte he came there. He answered them that he was carried by a spirit. And moreouer told them what wordes the image had spoken, and that he could by no meanes moue out of that place before that foure of the chiefest Aldermen were come vnto him, vnto whom he had certaine things to be declared: he also desired to receiue the holy sacrament. The Aldermen were forthwith called, and then the Frier declared vnto them, how the virgin Mary lamented and sorrowed, for that the citie of *Berna* should be shortly destroyed, for receiuing yearely pentiōs of the French king: Also for that they droue not the Franciscans out of their citie, who honoured her with the fayned tytle of vndefiled cōception. Unto this hir talke the Aldermen answered very little. By and by the other Monkes gaue him the host infected with poyson, which when he refused to receiue, they brought him an other,

ther, which he toke, then they led him with greate pompe into the quire, (for so they call the uppermost parte of the churche. The Frier & the other foure Monkes were sone after called before the Aldermen, to testifie the truth whether those things were so or not. But the foure fearing exceedingly least he should bewray something because they knew he suspected the, endeuoured by all meanes to do him some priuie mischief by poyson giuen in his meate, & therefore they gaue him the sacrament dipped in poyson, which he presently cast up againe by vomit: finally they so vexed and tormented him by so many wayes, that in the end he left the Colledge and ran away, and opened the whole matter to diuers and sundry men. In the meane time the Monkes dispatched two Legates or messengers to Rome, to obtaine a confirmation of these things of the Pope, that hereafter it should be utterly unlawfull for any man to contrary or mislike the same. And when these messengers were returned, (and as the Prouerbe is) thought themselues in a safe heauen, the noble Senate had commaunded the foure Monkes to be fast kept in prison: for they had learned the whole circumstance of the matter before of the Frier, whome they had committed to ward. And sparing neither labour nor mony, sent also unto Rome, that they might perfectly knowe, what they should do in this matter. In the end both the Frier & the foure Monkes were all put to torments, and there confessed all the matter. And when they had bin openly conuict of so many guiles, and horrible deeds, by the Popes permission they were first putte from the orders (which they commonly call degradation) and afterwards burned in the fire.

It was commonly reported, that in case the noble Senate of *Berna* hadde not prosecuted the matter with great constancie, and courage, the Cleargie would haue cloaked all the knauerie, and haue sette the authors at libertie. For they had greate cause to doubte, as it after came to passe, lest they should lose their credit and authoritie amongst many of the orders of Monks, and that these things whereon the Popedome resteth, as it were vpon pillers, should now be had in great suspition with all men. For it is most euident, that after the impietie, deceit & wickednesse of these Monkes began to be knowne abroad, the opinion of the Cleargie began to decaie, and to be suspected more and more euery day, of good and godly men: when as they sayd this or that soule required their helpe: that tapers lighted of their own accord: that this or that image spake, wept, or moued it selfe from place to place: that this or that Saint endowed their monasterie with precious reliques: or that Crosses were sprinkeled with the blood of Christ: yea and although they had obteined confirmation of these matters from the Pope, yet notwithstanding many afterwards would in no wise beleeue it to be so. Likewise they would not bee perswaded, that this holy father falling into a traunce, saw any miraculous things: or that Francis and Catherin of *Sena*, bare the markes of Christes fiue woundes in their bodie.

Furthermore, not without great cause, men began to doubt of transubstantiation of bread into the body of Christ, sith they had so often poysoned the Sacrament: and also of those things which they chaunted vpon with open mouth, touching pardons, vigilies, orders, purgatorie, holy water, and satisfaction. For that we let passe many things, it is clearer then the day-light, euen by this historie, that many things haue bene beaten into the peoples heads touching these foresaid matters, which were only deuised and inuented by these idle bellies.

CHAP. VIII.

Of a counterfait and deceiuing spirit at *Orleance* in *France*.

AND that no man thinke the Friers Preachers alone to haue bene so bolde, and wicked, and so readie in deuising so many monsters, let vs hearken a while to a notable historie of the Franciscan Friers, reported by Sleidane in the ninth booke of his Commentaries, concerning the state of religion and the Common wealth in the time of Charles the fifth.

In the yeare (saith he) of our Lord 1534. the Franciscan Monkes played a blodie and deadly pageant at *Orleaunce* in *France*. The Maiors wife of the same Citie, when shee died, commaunded in her will, that she shoulde be buried without any pompe or noyse, solemnely vsed at that time. (So also William Bude, a rare and singular ornament of *Fraunce*, lying on his death bedde at *Paris*, in the yeare of our Lord 1540. in the month of August, left commaundement with his friendes to bury him without any great solemnitie and pompe.) The womans husband, who reuerenced the memoriall of his wife, did euen as she had willed him, and because she was buried in the Church of the Franciscans, besides her father and grandfather, gaue them in rewarde only sixe Crownes, whereas they hoped for a farre greater pray. Shortly after, it chaunced that as he felled certaine woods, and solde them, they desired him to giue vnto them some parte of it frely without money: which hee flatly denied. This they toke very greuously, and whereas before they misliked him, they deuised this meanes to bee reuenged: forsooth to report that his wife was damned for euer. The chiefe workemen and framers of this tragedy were Colimanus, and Stephanus Atrebatensis, both doctors of diuinitie, and Colimannus a great coniurer, hauing all his implements in a readinesse, which he wonted to vse in such businesse: and thus they handled the matter. They place ouer the arche of the church a yong nouice: he about midnight when they came to mumble their praiers (as they were wont to do) maketh a great rumbling & noise: out of hand the Monks began to coniure & charme, but he answereth nothing, then being required to giue a signe whether he were a dumbe Spirit or no, he begins to rumble and stir again: which thing they toke as a certaine signe. Hauing laid this foundation, they go vnto certain citizens, chief men and such as fauored them, declaring that a heauy chaunce had happned at home, in their monasterie, not shewing what the matter was, but desiring thē to come to their mattens at midnight. Whē those citizens were come and that praiers were now begun, the counterfeit spirit beginneth to make a maruellous noise in the top of ẏ church, and being asked what he meant, and who he was, he giueth them signes that it is not lawful for him to speak: Therfore they commaunde him to make aunswere by tokens and signes, to certaine things they woulde demaunde of him. Nowe was there a hole made in the vaute, through the which he might heare and vnderstand the voyce of the coniurer; and then had he in his hande a little borde which at euery question he strake in such sort as he might easily be heard beneath. First therefore they aske him whether he were one of them that had bin buried in the same place, afterwards they reckning vp many by name which had bin buried there, at the last also name the Maiors wife: and there by and by, the Spirit gaue the signe that he was her soule. He was further asked whether he were damned or no, and if he were, for what desert or fault? Whether for couetousnesse, or wanton lust, for pride, or want of charitie, or whether it were for heresie, and for the secte of Luther newly sprung vp? Also what he meant by that noyse and sturre he kept there? Whether it were to haue the bodie

bodie now buried in holy ground to be digged up again, and to be laide in some other place? To all the which points, he answered by signes as he was commanded; by the which he affirmed, or denied any thing, according as he strake the bord twise or thrise togither. And when he had thus giuen them to vnderstand, that the very cause of his damnation was Luthers heresie, and that the bodie must needs be digged vp againe, the Monkes request the citizens (whose presence they had vsed) that they would beare witnesse of those things which they had seene with their eyes, and that they would subscribe to such things, as were done a fewe dayes before. The citizens taking good aduise on the matter, least they should offend the Maior, or bring themselues in trouble, refuse so to do: but the Monkes notwithstanding take from thence the swéete bread, which they call the host, and body of our Lord, togither with all ẏ reliques of saints, and cary them to an other place, & there say their Masse. The bishops substitute iudge (whom they call Officiall) vnderstanding this matter, commeth thither accompanied with certain honest men, to ẏ intẽt he might know ẏ whole circumstances more exactly, & therfore he cõmandeth them to make cõiuration in his presence, & also he requireth certaine to be chosen to go vp to ẏ top of the vault, and ther to sée whether any ghost appeared or not. That Stephanus Atrebatẽsis stifly denied, and maruellously persuading ẏ cõtrary, affirmed, that the spirit in no wise ought to be troubled. And albeit the Officiall, vrged thẽ very much, ẏ there might be some coniuring of the spirit, yet could he nothing preuaile. In the mean while that these things wer a doing, the Maior, whẽ he had shewed the other iustices of the citie, what he wold haue thẽ do, toke his iorny to the king, and opened the whole matter vnto him. And because the Monks refused iudgement vpon plea of their owne lawes and liberties: the king chosing out certaine of the Aldermen of *Paris*, giueth them absolute and full authoritie, to make enquirie on the matter.

The

The like doth the chancelor, maister Anthonius Pratensis, Cardinall and Legate for the Pope, throughout *Fraunce*. Therefore when they had no exception to alleadge, they were conueyed vnto *Paris* and there constreyned to make their aunswere: but yet could nothing be wrong out of them by confession. Whereupon they were put a part into diuers prisons, the Nouice being kept in the house of maister *Fumaus*, one of the Aldermen, who being oftentimes examined & earnestly requested to vtter the truthe, woulde notwithstanding confesse nothing, because he feared that the Monks would afterwards put him to death, for stayning their order, and putting it to open shame: but whē the Iudges had made him sure promise, that he should escape punishment, and that he should neuer come into theire handling, he repped vp vnto them the whole matter, as it was done, and being brought before his fellowes, auouacheth the same to their faces. The Monkes albeit they were by these meanes conuicted, and almost taken tardy with the deede doing, yet did they refuse the Iudges, bragging and vaunting them selues on their priuiledges: but al in vaine: for sentence passed on them, and they were condemned: that they being caried backe againe to *Orleaunce*, and there cast in prison, should finally be broughte forth to the chiefe Church of the citie openly, and from thence to the place of execution, where they should make open cōfession of their trespasses. But there chaunced at the very same time a greeuous persecution against the Lutherans, which was the cause why that sentence, (albeit was too gentle for so great an offence) was neuer put in executiō. For they feared much, because Luthers name was odious euery where, least if any sharpe iudgement hadde passed, they should not so muche haue punished the offenders, as shamed their order: and many supposed that whatsoeuer had happed vnto them, would haue bin a pleasant and ioyful pageaunt and spectacle for the Lutherans. Now the order uen of the Franciscane Friers, hath the opinion of great holinesse with the common people: insomuch, that when they being condemned, were carried to *Orleaunce*, certaine fonde women moued with foolish pittie, followed them to the very gates of the citie, weeping & sighing abundantly. When they were come to *Orleaunce*, and were there cast into diuers prisons, againe they vaunted and bare them-selues very brag on their priuiledges, and liberties: and so at the last when they had lyen long in prison, they were in the end deliuered without any greater punishment. All the while they were in prison, they wanted nothing: for there was bestowed vpon them, especially by women, very largely, for to serue for their liuing, and to purchase to them help and fauour. Except these persecutions and troubles, which we spake of before, had hindred the matter, the king (as many reported) was fully determined, to haue ouerthrowne their house, and made it euen with the ground.

This Historie also doth demonstrate and shewe, that Spirits are not alwayes heard, when some men affirme they are.

CHAP. IX.

Of a certaine parish Priest at *Clauenna*, which he fayned himselfe to bee our Ladie, and of an other that counterfeited himselfe to be a soule: as also of a certaine disguised Iesuite Frier.

TO the ende wee may the better vnderstande this matter, I will yet rehearse an other Historie of a certaine parishe Prieste, which chaunced a yeare before the other I spake of, which is sette foorth briefely, but yet truely, by Ioannes Stumpsius, in the Germane Chronicles of the Heluetians, in the twentieth Booke and eighth Chapter, whereof also many notable men at this day beare sufficient witnesse. Ioannes Stumpsius.

tempted to haue defloured her, but she euer resisted, and put him backe. In the ende when he saw he could not obtaine his purpose, he priuily stole out of the church a blew cloth, beset with sundry starres, and therwith couering himselfe, saue only that he left his armes & fæte naked, which he also berayed with blood, he hideth himselfe without the towne, and there muffling his face with a thinne linnen cloath, méeteth again with the mayd, fayning himself with a counterfeit voyce, to be the blessed virgin Mary. Then in many words he declareth vnto her diuers plages, which were shortly like to fall on the Citie, for the heresies of Luther, (for at other times also hée had bitterly enueyed against Luther, in his open Sermons:) he also commaunded the mayd to shew many things vnto the citizens, touching holy dayes, fastings, generall processions, &c. And amongst other things he added, that there was a certain holy and religious man, whiche had heretofore asked a thing at her hands in the very same place, which she had hitherto denied him, but now it was her pleasure, if he required ẏ same again, she should in any wise grant it, if she would attain euerlasting life: and ẏ aboue all thing, she must conceale and kéep close this latter point vnto her self. The mayde by & by blazed it about al the citie, that our Lady had visibly appeared vnto her, & foretold her of sundry plagues likely to happen vnto the citie. The inhabitants taking good aduise on this matter, at the last for feare of these imminent dangers and plages, gaue commandement, that thrée daies should be kept holy. In the which time, the mayd, supposing she should do high seruice to the virgin Mary, fulfilleth the lust of that wicked knaue. This trecherie and deceit being shortly af-

ter

Erasmus Roterodamus, writeth in his two and twentieth booke of Epistles, unto a certaine Bishop, excusing himself, touching certaine points, which he had moued unto him, to the ende he should be very circumspect: and amongst other things, making mention there of spirits or wandring soules, he reporteth this Historie. There was (saith he) a certaine parish Priest, who had dwelling with him in his house, a Neece of his, a woman well stored with money: In whose Chamber hee woulde oftentimes conuey himselfe, being disguised in a shéete lyke unto a Spirite: And then he cast forth a doubtfull voyce, hoping that the woman would either procure a coniurer for her helpe, or else her selfe make him answere. But she hauing a manlike courage, priuily requesteth one of her friendes to lodge in her Chamber secretly all night. The man being armed with a clubbe insteed of other coniuring tooles, and being well tipped with drinke, to auoyd feare, hideth himselfe in the bedde. Sodainly commeth the Spirit roaring very miserably: The coniurer with his clubbe awaketh, leapeth out of his bedde scant sober, and setteth upon him. Then the Spirit with his voyce and iesture, beginneth to make him afrayd. But the drunken coniurer soone answered him: If (quoth he) thou be the Diuel, I am thy mother: and there with catching holde on him, all to beat him with his club, and would also haue slaine him, if he had not chaunged his voyce, and cryed; O spare me for Gods sake, I am no soule, but I am sir John. Which voyce when the woman heard and knewe, she leapes out of her bedde, and parts the fraye, &c. The same Erasmus writeth in the foresayd Epistle, that this Priest upon Easter eue, put liue crabbes priuily into the churchyard, hauing ware candles on light cleauing to their sides: which when they crawled amongst the graues, séemed to bee suche a terrible sight, that

Margin notes: Erasmus. — Spectrum.

that no man durst approach néere them. Hereof rose a fearfull reporte, wherewith all men béeing amazed, the priest declareth to ẏ people in the pulpit, that they were ẏ soules of deade men which desired to be deliuered out of their torments by Masses & almes déeds. This deceite was espied by these meanes: that at the last one or two of the crabbes were found amongst the rubbish, hauing the candles done out cleauing on their backs, which ẏ priest had not takẽ vp.

Georgius Buchananus.

Georgius Buchananus, prince of all Poets in this our age, reporteth an historie in his Commodie called Franciscanus, of one Langus a priest, who falsly affirming that in a field of Scotland full of Brimstone there were soules miserablie tormented, which continually cried for helpe and succour, suborned a countrie clowne whome he would coniure, as if he had bin one of those soules. Which deceite of his, ẏ husbandmã afterward discouered whẽ he was drunk. I would here repeate his verses, but that his bookes are nowe in euery mans hands. While I was writing these things, it was reported vnto me by credible persons, that in Augusta, a noble citie of Germanie, this present yeare 1569. there was a maide and certaine other men seruants in a great mans family, which little regarded the sect of the Iesuite Friers: & that one of the saide order made promise to their master, that he wold easily bring them to an other opinion: & so disguising himselfe like vnto a Diuel, was hid in a priuie corner of ẏ house: vnto the which place, one of the maides going, either of hir owne accorde to fetche some thing, or being sent by her master, was by ẏ disguised Iesuite made maruellously afraide: which thing she presently declared vnto one of the mẽ seruants exhorting him in any wise to take héede of the place. Who shortly after going to the same place, & laying hold on his dagger, sodeynly stabbed in the counterfeit diuell, as he came rushing on him. This history is written in Duch verses, and put in print, and now almost in euery mans hands.

That

CHAP. X.

That it is no maruell if vaine sightes haue bene in old time, neither yet that it is to be maruelled at, if there be any at this day.

Many other like examples might be brought, but these may suffise to proue euidently, to what point ambition, couetousnesse, enuy, hatred, stubbirnnesse, idlenesse and loue, do most commonly driue men.

We see by common experience, that proude ambitious men dare aduenture any thing. If they may hurt or hinder other men by accusations, slanders, or any other wayes or meanes, whome they suppose may preiudice or let their exalting to honour, they sticke not at all to doe it. What maruell is it then that Monkes and Priests, which desire to be aloft, indeuour now a daies to purchase vnto themselues authoritie by false miracles, vaine apparitions, and such other like trumpery. Ambition.

All men know what a pernitious thing couetousnesse is. For they which are not contented to liue with a litle, but will néeds be rich, neither care for any man, nor yet spare any man. Hungry guttes séeke sundrie wayes to fill themselues: fewe willingly endure hunger. Wherefore it is not to be maruelled at, if amongst Monks and Priests at these our dayes, who haue bene euer reported to be couetous, there be some founde, which by false apparitions of soules, séeke their gaines, inuenting holy pilgrimages, and other baytes to get mony. For what wil not idle and slothfull lubbers attempt to purchase riches? Doth not Saint Paule say, that those which will waxe rich by idlenesse, fall into the snares of the Diuell? Couetousnesse. Paule.

Emulation, wilfulnesse, enuie, hatred, contention, desire to ouercome, what they may doo, what they may bring to passe, daily experience teacheth vs. The Preachers of Enuie.

Berna, when they perceiued they could not ouercome their aduersaries by any other means, yéelded themselues (which is horrible to be spoken) unto the diuel, making him one of their counsell. And who can deny but ỳ priests now adayes are also for the most part, stubborne, and full of contention.

Idlenesse. Idlenesse is the nurse and mother of all mischiefe: what goodnesse then may ye looke for of them, which not only exercise themselues in no labours prescribed by God, neither yet apply themselues to good learning, but day and night play the gluttons? Tell me I pray thée, whether the laboring husbandman, or the idle man, who allwayes spent his time in inuenting pernitious mischiefes, first founde out those cruel instruments of warre which they call gunnes?

Loue. It might be declared in many words what loue is able to do. Now because Monks and Priests liue idlely, abounding in all wantonnesse, and yet are restrained from holy marriage, what maruell is it if at this time also they faine and counterfeit many visions, that they might thereby the easier enioy their loue? And here I wil not say it is to be feared, that there are many amongst them so wicked and villanous, as to exercise & practise magicall Artes, and such like, which are utterly forbidden. Who can then maruell hereafter, if it be sayd, they counterfeyt spirites, affirming they haue let men sée this or that soule? For in what men soeuer these vices be, which we haue rehearsed, surely those dare boldly aduenture any thing.

No kinde of men are more obnoxious to these kinde of things, than those which leade their life in Monasteries, and Colledges: and therefore no man ought to maruell or thinke it a straunge thing, if we say that in times past many false visions haue bene practised, and may also at this day likewise happen. For ỳ world, as all men iustly complaine, waxeth worse and worse. Men are now more impudent, more bold, more couetous, and more wicked, than euer they were in times past.

Moreouer,

Moreouer, the Cleargie of *Rome* haue in many places this prerogatiue aboue others, that most men (especially such as are led by superstition) make much of them, worshipping them with great reuerence, no man so much as suspecteth them to apply their mindes to euill matters, to subtiltie, craft, and deceit: all men looke for other things at their hands. If therefore they addict themselues to euill deuises, they may easily deceiue men, except God miraculously reueale their wickednesse, and bring it to light, as we declared in a fewe examples rehearsed before.

And perchance for this cause also, Priests and Monkes could not bee so well blamed, for their so often deceiuing plaine meaning folkes with craft and subtiltie, in so much as some of their moste holy Fathers, I meane Popes of *Rome*, haue bin very cunning in magicall sciences, as their owne Historiographers affirme, and by meanes of those artes, haue aspired to the high top of Popedome. Beno (or rather Bruno, for so I iudge his name is) who was also a Cardinall, set forth the life of Pope Gregorie the seuenth, in writing, in the which hee sheweth the sayd Bishop to haue bene a proude, arrogant, malitious and couetous Monke, and that hee was throughly seene in the blacke art of Negromancie. Bartholomeus Platina (who being a sworne seruant with the Pope, excusing their faults as much as he can) writeth of Siluester the second, ẏ he gaue himselfe to the diuel, and that by his meanes, his counsell & magical deuises, he atteined ẏ great office of papacie. Do ye think, that it is a hard thing for him ẏ is confederat with the enemy of mankind, to faine spirits & soules, or to cōiure a diuel, to make men beleeue he were a soule, do you thinke such men abhorre to doo such mischiefe? The Historiographers report that Bonifacius the 8. deceiued his predecessor Celestinus, by a voyce sent through a cane reede, as though it had come from heauen, perswading him to giue ouer his office of Popeship, and to institute therein, one Bonifacius a way,

Popes haue fained visions.

Bruno.

Gregorius 7.

Bartholomeus Platina.

Bonifacius.

a worthier man than he, except he would be thrust out of the kingdome of heauen. The poore simple Pope obeying this voyce, ordeined Bonifacius Pope in his steade, in the yeare of our Lord 1294. who first brought in the yeare of Iubile. Of this Boniface, the common people would say: *He came in like a Fox, he raigned like a wolfe, and died like a Dog.* If the very vicar of Christ, who hath all knowledge as it were fast lockt in the Coffer of his brest, could be deceiued, lette no man maruel any more if simple credulous husbandmen and citizens haue ben deceiued, and that it hath bin said to them: God spake this: This soule did aske helpe: and such like things, which are most false and vaine. If this man coulde counterfeit the voyce of God, coulde he not also faine the voice of dead men?

Sometimes Laye men beguile the Priests.

Before I procéede any further, this is also to be obserued, that plesaunt conceited fellowes, may oftentimes deceiue the priests, themselues. For when the priests did brag, that they coulde coniure Spirits and deliuer mens soules, it may be that other being wrapped in shéets, hauing vnderneth them liue coales in an earthen pot, appeared vnto priests, who by and by were persuaded they sawe soules which required their helpe to be deliuered. Erasmus in his Colloquio or talke which he intituled: Exorcismus, vel spectrum, or a coniuration or vision, writeth howe one Polus maruellously deceiued a priest called Faustus. But there is no doubt but that priests being many times deceiued in iest by the lay men for pastimes sake, haue on the other side more often times beguiled them in earnest.

Men walking by night.

I haue spoken hitherto of men being awake, and now I will adde a fewe words of such as sléepe. There be many which haue such a kinde of disease, that they walke in their sléepe: which thing we reade to haue bin true in one Theon a Stoicke, and in Pericles seruant, who in their sléepe climed vp to the top of the house. I haue hearde of some which in their sléepe haue done that which béeing a

wake

wake, they could not do by any meanes. If a man sée such a one walking in the night, either apparrelled or naked, and after here him say he was at the same time in his bed, he will straight thinke, it was his soule that he sawe, the like will he do if he heare such a one at his owne house.

CHAP. XI.

That many naturall things are taken to be ghoasts.

There happen daily many things by the ordinary course of nature, which diuers men, especially they that are timorous and fearefull, suppose to be visions or spirits. As for example, when they heare the crying of ratts, catts, weasels, martins, or any other beaste, or when they heare a horse beate his féete on the plankes in the stable at midnight, by and by they sweat for feare, supposing some bugges to walke in the dead of the night. Somtimes a bittour, or hearne (which birds are seldome séene with vs in *Germany*) or some other straunge birds, make a noise in the aire: many fooles straightwayes dreame, they haue heard I wotte not what. If a worme which fretteth wood, or that bréedeth in trées, chaunce to gnawe a wall of waynescot, or other timber, many will iudge they heare one softly knocking vppon an anduill with a sledge: and sometimes they imagine they heare many hammers at one time. Simple foolish men hearing these things, imagine, I know not how, that there be certaine elues or fairies of the earth, and tell many straunge and maruellous tales of them, which they haue heard of their grandmothers and mothers, how they haue appeared vnto those of the house, haue done seruice, haue rocked the cradle, and (which is a signe of good lucke) do continually tarry in the house. If such dwarfes or elues haue bene séene at any time, surely they were euill spirits. For we reade

Fayries of the earth.

that the Gentiles in time past, had their familiar or houshold gods, whome they worshipped with great deuotion, because (as they thought) they toke care of their house, and defended their family: and vnto these men, euil spirits did sometimes appeare, thereby to confirme them the more in their blinde superstition.

Olaus Magnus.

Olaus Magnus Archbishop of *Vpsalia*, writeth in his historie de Gentibus Septentrionalibus, that euen at this day also, there are spirits séene in these countries, which hauing the shape of men, do men seruice in the night, dressing their horse, and looking to their cattell. The winde in the night, ouerthroweth some thing, or shaketh a casement or lid of the window: many by and by thinke they sée a spirite, and can very hardly be brought from that vaine opinion.

Echo.

This thing is also according to nature, that when a man either crieth or speaketh in the woods, valies, or other hollow places, Eccho wil resound the later word, or sillable, so plainly many times, that a man would verily thinke some liuing bodie made him answere againe. Many would be afraide hereof at all times, but especially in the night season, except he knew very well it were a naturall thing.

Cardanus.

Cardanus in his boke de Subtilitate lib. 18. rehearseth a maruellous historie of one Comensis, who very late in the night, comming to a riuers side, not knowing where he might passe ouer, called out aloude for some bodie to shewe him the forde, and when the Echo made him answere, hée supposing it to be a man, asked him if he might passe ouer here: to whom the Echo answered again in ẏ Italian tong, Here, here. But in ẏ place was a whirlpoole, and a great roring of the water: Therfore ẏ man douting, asketh once or twice againe, whether the riuer might be past ouer in the same place: to which the Echo answered stil that it might. In the end, when he had escaped ẏ passage without danger, he told his friends, how by the persuasiō of the diuel, he had almost throwne himself hedlong into the riuer, and drow-

the noyse of Echo.

There are certain things which shine only in the night, as some precious stones doo, the eyes of certaine beastes, a Glowworme, or Globard, as also some kinde of rotten wood, wherewith many times children so terrifie their play-felowes, that they imagine with themselues, to see euil spirites, or men all burning with fire. Hector Boethius writeth, that a certain King of Scots caused some of his men to be disguised in garments with bright shining scales, hauing in their hands rotten wood insteed of staues, and so to appeare to his nobilitie and Lords in the night, exhorting them to fight coragiously with their enemies, and promising them to obtaine victorie. Whereby the noble men supposing they had seene angels, behaued themselues valiantly, and atchieued the victorie. Things shyning by night. Hector Boethius.

Many times candles & small fires appeare in the night, and seeme to runne vp and downe. And as the yong men in *Heluetia*, who with their firebrands which they light, at the bonfires in Shroftide, sometime gather themselues togither, and then scalter abroad, and againe, meeting togither, march in a long rancke: euen so doo those fires sometime seeme to come togither, and by and by to be seuered & runne abroad, and at the last to vanish cleane away. Sometime these fires goe alone in the night season, and put such as see them, as they trauell by night, in great feare. But these things, and many such lyke haue their naturall causes: and yet I will not deny, but that many times Diuels delude men in this maner. Burning lights

Natural Philosophers write, that thicke exhilations aryse out of the earth, and are kindled. Mynes full Exhalations.

matter, séeking a vent to gush out. Wee reade of the mount *Aetna* in *Cicilie*, that in times past it burnt continually, day and night, casting forth flames of fire, fiery stones and ashes in great aboundance. The lyke is read also at *Vesuuius* a hill in *Campaine*, about a Germaine mile from *Naples*. The same hill in the time of Titus the Emperour, as S. Hierom reporteth, cast forth of it so much fire, that it burnt the country, and cities, and people rounde about it, and filled the fieldes adioyning full of cinders and ashes. These two hilles, euen in our dayes boyling with great heate, haue very much indamaged the people inhabiting thereabout. In *Iseland*, as Olaus Magnus witnesseth, are found fiers which breake out of the earth. And as whole hilles and mountaines may burne, euen so may a litle fire be kindled in the earth, and yet wander very large. They which travelling by the way, or by some other meanes chaunce to sée these things, and know not the naturall causes of them, imagin by reason of feare, that they haue séene men burning like fire, or some other straunge thing, which they haue heard other men talke of. And by means of their great feare, oftentimes they fall into great daungerous diseases.

Glasses. The arte perspectiue doth also worke this wonderfull feate, that diuers and sundrie shapes will appeare in glasses, made and sette togither after a certeine artificial sorte: sometimes they will séeme to goe out of the doores, and resemble men of our familiar acquaintance. Many things in very déed are naturall, although we cannot finde any naturall reason for them.

And yet by the way, they shewe themselues to foolishe,

which labour to bring all things to natural causes. Here I will say nothing of those men, which can beare plaine and rude people in hande, that they, or some other of their acquaintance, haue seene strange things, which they earnestly auouch to be true, when as indeede there was no suche thing. How often I pray you, do we heare things affirmed as true, which afterward proue most false: as that one was caried away bodie and soule, that an other was put to death, and an infinit nomber of such like reports.

CHAP. XII.

A proofe out of the Gentiles histories, that Spirites and Ghoasts do oftentimes appeare.

ALbeit many melancholicke, madde, fearefull, and weake sensed men, do oftentimes imagine many things which in very deed are not, and are likewise deceiued, sometime by men, or by brute beasts: and moreouer mistake things which procede of naturall causes, to be bugges and spirites, as I haue hitherto declared by many examples, yet it is most certaine and sure, that all those things which appeare vnto men are not alwayes naturall things, nor alwayes vaine terrors to affray men: but that spirites do often appeare, and many straunge and maruellous things do sundry times chance. For many such things of this sort, are to be red in diuers graue and auncient Historiographers: and many men of no small credite, haue affirmed, that they haue seene spirites both in the day and in the night also. And here I will orderly declare a fewe histories out of diuers allowed authors, touching spirites which haue appeared and shewed themselues.

Suetonius Tranquillus writeth, that when Iulius Cæsar marching out of *Fraunce* into *Italie* with his army, and comming to the riuer *Rubico*, which diuideth *Italie* from the

Triton appeared to Iulius Cæsar.

the hether *Fraunce*, staying there a while, and reuoluing with himselfe howe great an enterprise hee had taken in hand, as he was wauering in mind whether he shuld passe the water or not, suddeinly there appeared a man of excelling stature and shape sitting hard by, pyping on a rede. (Melancthon in his Phisickes calleth him Triton) vnto whom when not only shepheards, but also very many souldiers from the campe, and amongst them diuers trumpetters had flocked to heare him, he sodeinly snatched a trumpet from one of them, and leaped to the riuer, and with a lustie breath blowing vp the alarum, went to the farther side. Then sayd Cæsar, good lucke mates, let vs goe whither the gods warnings leade vs, and whither our enemies iniquitie calleth vs: The dice are throwne. And so he transported ouer.

Theseus seene in the battaile of Maratho.

Plutarke writeth in Theseus life, that many which were in the battaile of Marathonia, against the Medians, did affirme, that they sawe the soule of Theseus armed, (who long time before died of a fall) before the vauntgard of the Grecians, running and setting on the barbarous Medians. For which cause the Athenians afterward were moued to honor him as a demigod.

Pausanias writeth in Atticis, That in the field of Maratho. 400. yeares after the battaile there foughten, there was heard the neying of Horses, and the encountring of souldiers, as it were fighting euery night: And that they which of purpose came to heare these things, could heare nothing, but those that by chaunce came that way, heard it very sensibly.

The same Plutarke writeth in the life of Cimon, that when the citizens of Cherouesus, had by faire words called home their captaine Damon, (who before for diuers murthers departed the citie) afterwards they cruelly slew him in a Hotehouse, as he was bathing himselfe, and from that time forth, there were many strange sightes seene in the

the same place', & many times also most gréeuous gronings were there heard, insomuch that they were euer after constreined to stop vp the hotehouse doores.

Also in ẏ life of Dion, he reporteth that the saide Dion being a stoute & a couragious man without any feare, sawe notwithstanding a great and maruellous horrible sight. For when he chaunced to sit alone in the entry of his house in the euening (those are Plutarks owne words, as Xilander interpreteth them) musing & discoursing many things with himselfe, being sodeinly moued with a great noyse, he arose and looked backe to the other side of the gallerie, and there he espied a monstrous great woman, who in apparell and countenaunce nothing differing from a Tragicall furie, swept the house with a broome. With the which sight being amazed & terribly afraide, he called his friends and acquaintance vnto him, and declaring vnto them what he had séene, desired thē to remaine with him al that night: for béeing as it were stricken dead with feare, he doubted least it would appeare vnto him againe, if he were alone, which indéede neuer hapned after. But a fewe daies after, his sonne threwe himselfe headlong from the top of the house, and died, and he himselfe being stabbed through the bodie, ended his miserable life.

The same author writeth in the life of Decius Brutus, how when Brutus was determined to transporte his army out of Asia into Europe, being in his tent about midnight, the candle burning dimly, and all the host quiet and silent, as he was musing and reuoluing with himselfe, he séemed that he hearde one entring the Tente into him, and looking backe vnto the doore, he sawe a terrible and monstrous shape of a bodie, which farre excéeded the common stature of men, standing fast by him without any words, wherewith he was sore afraid: and yet he ventured to aske it this question. What art thou (saieth hée) either a God, or a man? and why commest thou

vnto

vnto me? Whereto the image answered: I am (quoth he) O Brutus, thy euill ghoast, at Philippos thou shalt see mee. Then saith Brutus, being nothing amazed: I will see thee. When the sight was vanished, he called his seruants, who tolde him, that they neither sawe any such thing, neither heard any voyce at all. All that night Brutus could not sleep one winke. In the morning very early he goeth vnto Cassius and sheweth him his straunge vision. Cassius who despised all such things (for he was an Epicure) ascribed the whole matter to naturall causes. For his disputation hereof, is yet extant in Plutarke. Afterward Brutus (being vanquished by Augustus, and Anthony, in the field of Philippi) slew himselfe because he would not bee deliuered into the hands of his enemies.

Caius Cassius sawe Iulius Cæsar.

Valerius Maximus, in his first booke and sixt chap. writeth, that Caius Cassius sawe Iulius Cæsar in the battaile of Philippi, (in a shape of greater maiestie, than any man hath) setting spurres to his horse, and running on him with a terrible threatning countenance: which when Cassius sawe, he turned his backe to the enemy, and fled, and shortly after murthered himselfe.

Drusus sawe a woman excelling all mortall creatures in maiestie.

Dio Cassius Nicæsus, in his Roman historie from the beginning of his 55. booke writeth of Drusus, who by spoyling *Germany* far and neere on euery side, came euen to the riuer Albis, where when he could not get ouer, erecting monuments of victorie, departed back againe: For he there saw a woman, exceeding the state of mortall creatures, which met him, and sayd vnto him: Drusus, which canst finde no end of thy greedie desire, whither goest thou? It is not lawfull for thee to see al these things: but rather get thee hence, for the ende both of thy life and worthie deedes is nowe at hand. When Drusus heard these things, he sodeinly chaunged his course, and being on his iourney, before he came to the riuer of Rein, he sickned and dyed. Other like foretokens the same author reporteth to haue hapned before his

death,

death, all the which notwithstanding, he nothing regarded. For two yong men appeared on horsebacke vpon the rampiers, and the shriking of women was also hearde, with many other such like. &c.

Plinius secundus citizen of Nouocomensis, hath an Epistle of Spirits appearings, written vnto his friend Sura in the vii. booke of his Epistles, which we haue thought good to set downe whole in this place: Leisure (saith he) graunteth me libertie to learne, and giueth thee leaue to teache. Therfore I am very desirous to knowe whether thou thinke fantasies are any thing, and whether they haue any proper figure of their owne, and be some kinde of diuine power, or else whether they take vppon them some vaine & variable shape, according to the feare which we haue of them? That I should so beleeue, I am especially moued thereto by that which I heare saie happened to Curtius Rufus, who was as then, companion to the Proconsul of *Affrica*, bothe poore, and also of small reputation. And as he walked one day in a Gallerie towardes the euening their meeteth with him the shape of a woman, more great & beautifull, than any liuing creature. Wherat he beeing amazed, she telleth him that she is *Affrica*, and is come vnto him to foretell him of good happe to followe: First that he should go to Rome, and there take on him the state of great honoure, and afterwarde, that he should returne into the same prouince with full and high authoritie, and there end his daies. Which things came all to passe. And moreouer, the same figure (as it is saide) mette with him againe on the shore side, as he entred out of the ship, and came towardes *Carthage* to take his charge and regiment in hande. Afterwards falling sick, when no man dispayred of his healthe, coniecturing things to come by those that had passed, and comparing aduersitie with his former prosperitie, he vtterly cast away all hope of recouerie. Is not this also more terrible, and no lesse marvellous

Plinius secundus writing of Spirits.

uellous, whiche I will now repeate as I haue heard it tolde?

The spirit of Athens.

There was in *Athens* a goodly and a very large house, but euill reported, and counted as an infortunate and vnluckie house. For about midnight, there was heard the noyse of iron, and if one marked it well, the ratling of chaines, as it were a farre off at the first, and so, nearer and nearer: shortly there appeared an image or shape, as it were an olde man, leane and loathsome to beholde, with a long beard and staring haire: on his legges he had fetters, and in his hands carried chaines which he alwaies ratled togither. By meanes whereof, those that inhabited the house, by reason of their feare, watched many heauie and pittifull nights: after their watching folowed sicknesse, and soone after, as feare increased, ensued death. For in the day time also, albeit the image were departed, yet the remembrance thereof, was euer present before their eyes: so that their feare was longer than they had cause to feare. Upon this the house stood desert and solitarie, wholly lefte vnto the monster whiche haunted it: yet was it proclaimed to be solde, if happily any man whiche was ignorant of this great mischiefe, would either buy it or hire it. Athenodorus chanced to come to *Athens*, and there readeth the writing on the doore: And when he had learned the price, because he suspected the good cheapenesse thereof, enquiring further, vnderstoode the whole matter, and notwithstanding any thing that he heard, he hired the house, so much the rather. When it waxed night, he commaundeth his seruauntes to make his bedde in the vtter part of the house: he taketh his writing tables, his writing wier and a candle, and sendeth all his seruaunts into the inner part of the house. He himselfe setleth his minde, his eyes and hand to write, least his mind being vnoccupied, should imagine it heard straunge figures, and should breede vaine feare. In the beginning of the night, there was silence as is is in all other places, but not long after the iron began to ring, and the chaines to moue: but yet he would not looke vp, nor let ceale his writing, but hardned his hart, and stopped his eares. Then the noyse increaseth & draweth neare, and séemeth sometimes to be without the porch, sometimes within. Thē he looketh back, and seeth and acknowledgeth the shape whereof he had heard before: the image stood still and beckned with his finger as though he had called him, the philosopher on the other side signifieth with his hand, that he should stay a while, and falleth againe to his writing. The image shaketh his chaines ouer his head, as he sate writing. He looketh about againe, and seeth him beckning, as he did before. And so rising vp without delay, taketh the candle in his hand and foloweth: the image goeth before with a softly pace, as though he were heauily laden with chaines: After he had turned aside into the court of the house, sodeinly vanishing away, leaueth his walking mate alone. He being forsaken, laieth hearbes and leaues gathered togither vpon the place. The next day he goeth to the rulers of the citie, and willeth them to commaund the place to bée digged vp, whiche done, they finde bones wrapped and tyed in chaynes: which the bodie béeing putrified and consumed with long lying in the earth, had left lying in bandes: those bones being gathered togither, were buried solemnely: The house, after they were orderly laide in the ground, was euer after cleare of all such ghostes.

In these things I must beléeue other mens reports, but that which followeth, I can boldly affirme on mine owne knowledge.

I haue one with mée, sometime my bondseruaunt, but nowe enfraunchized and set at libertie, a man not vtterly vnlearned: with him my yonger brother lay togither in one bed. He in his owne imagination séemed that he saw a certaine personage sitting vpon the bedde where he laie, putting knives unto his head, and therewith polling off his haires. When it was day light, the haires were found on the ground, he being in very déed notted about the crowne of his head. Shortly after the like happened unto him, which made all men beléeue the first was true. The boy amongst a great many of his fellowes chaunced to sléepe in the schoole, and being in sléepe, there came certaine in at the windowes (as he sayd) cloathed in white garments, and shore of his haire as he laie, and so departed againe as they came. This polling, and also his haires scattered abroad, were founde when it was day. No notable matter ensued hereof, except it were, perchaunce, that I was not accused of treason, as I should haue bene, if Domitianus, who died about this time, had liued longer. For there was a libell found in his coffers, giuen unto him against me, written by maister Carus. By which it may well be coniectured, that in so much as those which are accused, doo use to let their haire growe very long, the cutting of my friends haire, was a sure signe of escaping the great daunger, which then hung ouer my head. Wherefore I hartily require you to straine your learning. The matter is worthie, wherein ye may use long and déepe consideration: and I surely am unworthie to whom ye shuld open your knowledge. You may therfore (if it please you) dispute the matter on both sides, as ye are accustomed, but yet I pray you handle it more throughly on the one side, least ye sende me away wauering and hanging in doubt, whereas the cause of my séeking counsel, is to the ende I might be quite out of doubt. Fare ye well.

What answere maister Sura, (who as it appeareth, was well learned) made unto maister Pliny I do not finde. But to say the truth, what sound answere could he, being a Gentile make herein: The like history is to be red in the collections of Iohn Manlius common places, who (as Philip Melancthon reporteth) doth write, that Theodorus Gaza

Manlius.

had.

had a lordship or manour place in *Campania*, giuen him by Nicholas Pope of *Rome*. In the manour, when by chaunce, one of his farmers had digged vp a coffin with dead mens bones in it, there sodeinly appeared a spirit vnto him, commaunding him to bury the coffin againe, or else his sonne should shortly after die. Which when the farmer refused to doo, shortly after his sonne was found slaine in the night. A fewe dayes after, the Spirit appeared againe vnto the husbandman, menacing and threatning him, that in case he did not bury the aforesaid bones, he would kill his other sonne also. The man taking warning by his losse, and seeing his other sonne fallen sicke, goeth vnto maister Theodorus and sheweth him all the matter. He vnderstanding it, goeth with him to the manour, and there in the same place where the farmer had before digged vp the coffin, casting a new graue, they bury the coffin with the bones. Assoone as the bones were laide in the graue, the husbandmans sonne immediatly recouered his health.

Dion writeth, that the Emperour Traianus was ledde out of the house, where he had taken vp his Inne, in the time of an earthquake, into a more safer place.

Iulius Capitolinus, which setteth out a fewe liues of the Romane Emperours, reporteth, that Pertinax for the space of thrée dayes before he was slaine by a thrust, sawe a certaine shadow in one of his fishponds, which with a sworde readie drawne threatened to slaie him, and thereby much disquieted him.

Flauius Vopiscus writeth, that wheras Tacitus fathers graue opened it selfe, the sides therof falling downe of their owne accord, and that his mothers soule appeared both to him and Florianus day and night, as if she had bene liuing, it was a most sure and infallible signe, that he should die shortly after.

Ammianus Marcellinus, writing of the signes or prognostications of Constantius death, saith that he was troubled and terrified in the night season with shapes and figures.

The same Author affirmeth in his 25. booke, that a little before Iulianus died, as he sate writing in the tents, following the example of Iulius Cæsar, he sawe the image of the publicke Genius, or god of the place (which was wont to be painted with Amaltheas horne in his hand) departing from him, more deformed and ill fauoured, than when it began to mount up to the narrow top of the tent.

Lucan. Lucanus as well an excellent Historiographer, as also a most learned Poet, reckneth up many fore warnings, in his first booke of the battaile of Pharsalia, which chaunced before the great conflict betwéen Iulius Cæsar, and great Pompeius: and amongst other things, he writeth thus.

The trumpets blew, and locke euen as the battaile ioynd apace,
So did the night with silent shaades increase her darkish face.
And then the ghosts of Sylla *fierce, were plainly seene in field,*
Thereby declaring euil signes, of blood that should be spild.
And by the floud of Anien, the husband did spie
Great Marius, *out of broken graue his head aduauncing hie.*

CHAP. XIII.

A proofe out of the histories of the auncient Church, and of the writings of holie Fathers, that there are walking Spirits.

Sozomenus. If we reade ouer the Ecclesiasticall histories, we shall finde many of these examples. Sozomenus writeth in his Ecclesiasticall historie, the firt booke and 28. chapter, of one Apelles, a black Smyth by occupation (whose name was at that time very famous throughout *Egipt*, for the gift of working miracles, wherwith he was indewed) who as he was one night hard at his work, had appearing unto him, a vision of a Diuel in the likenesse and attire of a very beautifull womã, mouing & intising him to the vice of lechery. But he sodenly catching ŷ iron which he wrought on, glowing hot out

out of the fire, thrust it in ye diuels face, and scorched his visage. Wherat he fretting & crying out, in al hast fled away.

Like wise in his 7. booke and 23. chap. writing of the sedition raised at *Antioche*, for the immoderat action and tribute which Theodosius layd on the citie in the time of warres, whereby the people being offended, ouerthrew the images of the Emperour and his wife, dragging them in roapes about the citie, and reporting all kinde of villany and dispite against them, thus he saith. But in the night before, assone as the rebellion began, immediatly at the breake of the day, it is certainly reported there was a straunge sight seene, of a woman hauing a huge stature and most horrible looke, running vp and downe the citie through the streetes aloft in the aire, whisking & beating the aire with a whip, rendring a fearefull sound. That as men are wont to prouoke wilde beasts to anger, which serue for publike spectacles: euen so it seemed, some euil angell by the craft of the diuell stirred vp that commotion amongst the people.

Theodorus Lector, in his first booke of Collectanies, out of the Ecclesiasticall historie writeth, that as Gennadius Patriarch of *Constantinople*, came downe to the high aultar to make praiers and orizons, there appeared vnto him a certaine vision or spirit in a most horrible shape and figure, which so soone as he had sharply rebuked, straightwaies he heard a voice crying out aloud, yt so lõg as he liued he would giue place & cease, but when he was once dead, he would surely ransack and spoyle the Church. Which when ye good father heard, he ernestly praied for ye preseruation of the church, & soone after departed this life. There are many things to be read in Gregorius Nicephorus, who setteth forth Ecclesiasticall matters at large, & Abdias in the liues of the Apostles, concerning visions, dreames, miracles of saints, and also appearings of spirites. For wise men iudge, they were more diligent & ready in describing such things, than in other matters, which might haue bin to greater purpose

Theodorus.

Nicephorus.

and

and much more profitable for the readers to understand.

He that readeth ouer the Histories, which in times past haue bene written, (and that especially by Monkes) shall méete with an innumerable company of these sorts: Yet by the way I must néedes say this, that verie many things haue bin written by them, which the Readers may iustly suspect, and stand in great doubt of.

Ludouicus Viues, Beatus Rhenanus, and many other learned men of our time, in describing other things, do finde great fault with the Chronicles written by Monkes, for that they were gathered togither by vnlearned dolts without any iudgement. But let euery man estéeme of them as he list. For albeit there are diuers things in them very foolish and ridiculous, yet it may be well thought that many things were so in very déed, as they haue committed them to writing.

A man shall méete with many places concerning visions and appearings of spirits, euen in the old fathers also.

Ambrose. S. Ambrose in his 90. Sermon, writeth of a noble Virgin named Agnes, who was crowned with martirdome for the professiō of christian religion. And as her parents watched one night by her graue, they saw about midnight, a goodly company of Virgins cloathed in golden vayles, amongst whome also was their daughter, arraied like vnto the rest: who willing the other Virgins to staie awhile, turning her selfe towards her parents, willed them in any case, not to bewaile her as if she were dead, but rather to reioyce with her, for that she had obteined of God eternal life. Which as soon as she had spoken, she immediatly vanisht out of sight.

Augustine. S. Augustin declareth in his booke, De cura pro mortuis agenda, that when the Citie of *Nola* was besieged by the Barbariens, the citizens saw Felix the martyr plainly appearing vnto them. Touching S. Gregorie, who in his Dialogues writeth many such things, we will entreate hereafter when his turne commeth.

Felix appeared at Nola.

Gregorie.

Ye

Ye shall read of many such like, in the liues of the auncient Fathers, which al are not to be reiected as vain & fabulous, for some part of them written by graue and learned men, whereof letting the rest passe for breuitie sake, I will rehearse one short historie.

It is to be seene in the life of Ioannes Chrysostom, that Basiliscus Bishop of *Comane* (who suffered as a Martir with Lucianus the priest at *Antioch*, vnder Maximianus the Emperour) appeared vnto Saint Chrysostome, when hee was in exile, and sayd vnto him: Brother Iohn, be of good comfort, for to morrow we shall be togither. But first he appeared to the priest of that Church, and sayd vnto him: prepare a place for our deare brother Iohn, who will shortly come hither. Which things the euent proued afterwards to be true. Basiliscus appeared to Chrysostome.

CHAP. XIIII.

That in the Bookes set foorth by Monkes, are many ridiculous and vaine apparitions.

WE made mention a litle before, of Chronicles written by Monkes. Now as touching their legendes of Saintes (as they terme their storehouses of examples, and liues of auncient Fathers, in the which are many apparitions of diuels & spirits,) verily there is no cause at all why we should ascribe much vnto them, for the most part of such stuffe as is set forth in them, haue no shewe nor likelihood of truth: perchaunce their minde was to bring men to great feare and Religion by those their counterfeited and imagined histories. But concerning these, this place now serueth not to intreate.

The like may be sayd, of many superstitious Popish writers, who following these mens steppes, haue written many vpon other mens credit and reports, which least any man thinke I write, being moued with enuie or hatred of the persons, I will shewe you one onely historie or fable amongst so many, that you may thereby haue as it were a taste of that which I sayd euen now.

S. Seuerine Bishop of Coln.

Petrus Damianus, who first was a Monke after the order of S. Benedict, and afterward Bishop of *Hostia*, a man of great estimation among Papists, as well for the opinion they had of his learning, as for the shewe of his vpright liuing, telleth a storie of a certaine Monke of *Colein*, who on a time passing ouer a Riuer on horsebacke, espied Saint Seuerinus sometime Bishop of *Colein* on the Riuer, who not long before was departed this life, and being buried at that time, was much renowmed for doing sundrie miracles. The Bishop catcheth holde on the Monkes bridle, and would not let him passe any further: wherewith the Monke was sore afraide, and diligently enquired of him, why he being so notable a man, was there withholden in that place. The Bishop then required him to lende him his hand, that hée might vnderstand by féeling how it was with him, which when he had done, and that the Bishoppe had dipped the Monkes hande downe into the water, sodeinly in one moment all the flesh of his hand, by reason of the extreame heate, was scalded off, so that the bones only remained al bare. Unto whom then the Monke, sith (quoth hée) thou art so famous a man in the Church, how commeth it to passe that thou art so gréeuously tormented? The Bishop aunswered: only sayd hée for this cause, for that I haue not sayd ouer my Canonicall houres in due time distinctly as I should haue done: for I was in the Emperours Court busied and occupied with matters of his priuie Counsell, in the morning hudling vp all my prayers at once, all the rest of the day I was troubled with other businesse: and for that cause do I now suffer this punishment of miserable heat. But let vs both

togither.

together call unto Almightie God, that it may please him to restore thy hand againe, which came presently to passe assone as they had thus saide. And then spake he to the Monke saying: Go my sonne and desire the brethren of our Church, as also al other of the Clergie there, to poure out their praiers for mée, to giue almes to the poore and néedie, and to perseuere incessantly in offring vp continuall sacrifice for me, for so sone as these things shalbe fulfilled, I shal be deliuered out of these my torments, and shal be ioyfully translated to the fellowship of those blessed Citizens of heauen, which vs earnestly desire my company. Out of this historie, this argument or reason they make: If that good and godly Bishop, who being ouercharged with affaires of the Emperour leading to publike wealth, could not dispatch his taske of prayers in due time, and therefore is so miserably vexed and tormented, what punishment may they looke for, which hauing no necessarie businesse, say ouer the Canonicall houres very coldly, or else leaue them cleane vnsayd, that they may the better followe their owne lustes and vaine deuises? And héere note by the way, they make no mention at all of omitting those things which God hath expresly commanded vs. But in case the Popish Bishoppes do verily beléeue this story to be true, let them thinke with themselues, howe they can be able to excuse themselues before the iudgement seate of Almightie God, for that they are content to be created Bishops of those Churches, whereof notwithstanding they haue no care or regarde, but either wholly intangle themselues with worldly matters, or if they do deale in matters of the Church, their whole study is directed to this end, to stop the sincere preaching of Gods word, and to tread those vnder foote, whose mindes are occupied day and night, to the aduancing and setting forth of Gods glory. Of this stampe and sort, are most of those thinges wherewith the Monkes inferred and stuffed their bookes.

CHAP. XV.

A proofe by other sufficient writers, that Spirites doo sometime appeare.

Alexander ab Alexandro.

As touching other notable writers, they also make mention of spirites which do oftentimes appear. Alexander ab Alexandro, an excellent Lawier, born at *Naples*, in his secōd booke *Genialium dierum*, and ninth chapter, writeth that a certain familiar friend of his, of good credite, did celebrate ẏ funeral of one of his acquaintance, and as he returned towards *Rome*, he entred into an Inne fast by the way, because it was night, and there laide himselfe downe to rest. As he laie there alone broad awake, sodeinly the image of his friend lately deceased, came before him maruellous pale and leane, euen as he was when he sawe him last on his death bedde, whome when he beheld, being almost besides himselfe with feare, he demaunded of him who he was? But the ghost making no answer, but slipping off his cloathes laide him downe in the same bedde, and drew neare, as if he would haue embraced him. The other gaue him place, and keeping him off from him, by chance touched his foote, which seemed so extreemly cold, as no Ice in the world might be compared vnto it. Whereat the other looking very lowringly vpon him, tooke vp his clothes againe, and rose out of the bed, and was neuer afterwards seene. He reporteth other histories in the same place, which hapned in his time. He liued aboue foure score yeares ago, or neare that time.

Baptista.

Baptista Fulgosus, Duke of *Genua*, in his booke of worthy sayings and doings of Emperors, Princes, Dukes, &c. (which he wrote being in exile to auoyd idlenesse: Touching straunge and monstrous things) writeth that in the

the Court of Mattheus, surnamed the great Shiriffe of the Citie, in the euening after Sunne sette, there was seene a man farre exceeding common stature, sitting on a horse in complete armour: who when he had bin there seene of many, by the space of an houre, in the end vanished away, to the greate terrour of those that beheld him. About three daies after in like maner, two men on horsebacke of the same stature, were seene in the same place, about three houres within night, fighting togither a long season, and in the ende vanished away as the other didde before. Not long after, Henry the seuenth Emperor, departed this life, to the vtter vndoing of all the Shiriffes.

Immediately after this Historie, he putteth an other more worthie memorie than the foremost. Lodouicus father to Alodisius, ruler of *Immola*, not long after he died, appeared vnto a Secretarie, whom Louodicus had sente to *Ferraria*, as he was on his iourney, riding on a horse with a Hauke on his fist, as he was wonte when he liued, and willed the Secretarie (albeit wonderfully afraid) to bid his Sonne the nexte day to repaire vnto the same place, for he had matter of greate importance to declare vnto him. Which when Lodouicus heard, partly because he could not beleeue it, partly for that he doubted some body laye in waight for him, he sent an other to answere in his roome. With whome the same soule meeting as it did before, lamented very much that his Sonne was not come thither, for if he had so doone, he saide, he would haue opened many other things vnto him. But as then he willed the messenger to tell him, that twentie two yeares, one month and one day being passed, he should loose the rule and gouernment whiche he nowe possessed. As soone as the time foreshewed by the ghost was expired, albeit he were very circumspect and careful, yet the same night, the souldiours of Philip Duke of *Millen*, with whom he was in league (& therfore stood in no feare of him) came ouer the ditches hard frozen with Ice vnto the walles, and raising vp ladders, toke both Citie and Prince togither.

Phillip Melancthon, writeth in his boke *De anima*, that he himselfe hath séene some Spirits, and ye he hath knowne many men of good credit, which haue auouched not only to to haue séene ghostes themselues, but also that they haue talked a great while with them. In his boke which he intituleth *Examen Theologicum*, he rehearseth this historie. Which was, that he had an aunt, who as she sat very heauily by the fire, after her husband was dead, two men came into her house, whereof the one being very like, said he was her husband deceased, the other being verie tall, had the shape of a Franciscan Friar. This that séemed to be the husband, came neare the chimney saluting his heauy wife, bidding her not to be afraide, for (as he said) he came to commaund her certaine things: then he bid the long Monke to go aside a while into the stoue hard by. And there beginning his talke, after many wordes, at the last he earnestly beséecheth, and most hartily desireth her, to hire a Priest to say Masse for his soule, and so being readie to depart, he biddeth her giue him her right hand: which thing (she being sore afraide) abhorring to doo, after he had faithfully promised she should haue no harme, she giueth her hand, which albeit indéed it had no hurt, yet did it séeme to be so scorched, that euer after it remained blacke. This being done, he calleth forth the Franciscan, and hastily going forth togither, they vanish away. Ioannes Manlius, in his collectanies of Common places, writeth concerning other spirites which he and other men also did sée, the first tome in the Chapter *De malis spiritibus & ipsorum operibus*, and also in the Chapter *De satisfactione*.

Melancthons Aunt.

Ludouicus Viues, saith in his first boke *De veritate fides*, that in the new world lately found out, there is nothing more common, than not only in the night time, but also at none in the midday, to sée spirits apparantly, in the Cities

Ludouicus Viues.

and

and fieldes, which speake, commaund, forbid, assault men, feare and strike them. The very same do other report which describe those nauigations of the great Ocean.

Hieronimus Cardanus of *Millen*, excellently séene in Philosophie & Phisicke, remembreth a great many of these apparitions, in his booke *De subtilitate, & varietate rerum:* which who so listeth to reade, I referre him to his bookes, for I am desirous to be bréefe. Hieronimus Cardanus.

Olaus Magnus, Archbishop of *Vpsalia* in *Sueneland*, declareth in his historie *De Gentibus Septentrionalibus*, the second booke and third chap. that spirits appeare in *Iseland*, in the shape & likenesse of such, as men are acquainted withal: whom the inhabitants take by the hand in stead of their acquaintance, before they haue heard any word of those their acquaintãce death, whose similitude and likenesse they take on them, neither do they understand that they are deceiued, before they shrinke and vanish away. These things haue I brought togither both out of the olde and also new writers, that it might plainly appeare, that spirites do oftentimes walke and shewe themselues unto men. Olaus.

CHAP. XVI.

Daily experience teach vs, that spirits do appeare to men.

TO all the premisses before handled, this also is to be added, which no man can deny, but that many honest and credible persons of both kindes, as well men as women, of whome some are liuing, and some already departed, which haue and do affirme, that they haue sometimes in the day, and sometimes in the night séene and heard spirits. Some man walketh alone in his his house, and behold a spirit appeareth in his sight, yea and sometimes the dogs also perceiue them, and fal down at their masters féet, and wil by no means depart fro them, for they are sore afraid themselues too. Some man goeth to bed, and laieth him downe to rest,

and

being of a fierie shape, knowne vnto diuers men, & such as died not long before. And it hath come to passe likewise, that some eyther slaine in the warres, or otherwise deade naturally, haue called vnto their acquaintance béeing aliue, and haue bene knowne by their voice.

Spirites requiring helpe.

Many times in the night season, there haue béene certaine spirits heard softly going, or spitting, or groning, who being asked what they were, haue made aunswere that they were the soules of this or that man, and that they nowe endure extreame tormentes. If by chaunce any man did aske of them, by what meanes they might be deliuered out of those tortures, they haue aunswered, that in case a certaine number of Masses were song for them, or Pilgrimages vowed to some Saintes, or some other such like déedes doone for their sake, that then surely they shoulde be deliuered. Afterwardes appearing in greate light and glorie, they haue said that they were deliuered, and haue therefore rendred greate thankes to their good benefactours, and haue in like manner promised, that they will make intercession to God and our Ladye for them. And hereby it may be well proued, that they were not allwayes Priestes, or other lewde and wicked men, which haue fayned themselues to be soules of men deceased, as I haue before saide: in so much that euen in those mennes chambers when they haue bene shut, there haue appeared such things, when they haue with a candle diligently searched before, whither any thing haue lurked in some corner or no. Many vse at this day to search and sifte euery corner of the house before they go to bed, that they may sléepe more soundly: & yet neuerthelesse, they

heare

heare some scriking out, and making a lamētable noise, &c.

It hath many times chanced, that those of the house haue verily thought, that some body hath ouerthrowne the pots, platters, tables and trenchers, and tumbled them downe the staires: but after it waxed day, they haue founde all things orderly set in their places againe.

It is reported, that some spirits haue throwne the doore off from the hookes, and haue troubled and set all things in the house out of order, neuer setting them in their due place againe, and that they haue maruellously disquieted men with rumbling and making a great noyse.

Sometimes there is heard a great noyse in Abbeis, and in other solitarie places, as if it were Coopers hooping and stopping vp wine vessels, or some other handicraftes men occupied about their labour, when it is most certaine, that all in the house are gone to bedde, and haue betaken themselues to rest.

When houses are in building, the neighbours many times heare the Carpenters, Masons, and other Artificers handling all things in such sort, as if they were busily labouring in the day time. And this straunge wonder is ioyfully receiued as a sure token of good lucke. Builders hear spirits in the night.

There be some which iudge it commeth to passe naturally, that we suppose we heare these things in the night, which we heard before in the day time. Which question I leaue to be discussed of better learned than my selfe.

Pioners or diggers for mettal, do affirme, that in many mines, there appeare straunge shapes and spirites, who are apparelled like vnto other labourers in the pit. These wander vp and down in caues and vnderminings, and seem to besturre themselues in all kinde of labour, as to dig after the veine, to carry togither oare, to put it into baskets, and to turne the winding wheele to drawe it vp, when in very deed they do nothing lesse. They very sildome hurt the labourers (as they say) except they prouoke them by Diuels are in Mines.

A certain godly and learned man wrote once vnto me, of a siluer mine at Douosium in the *Alpes*, vpon the which Peter Buol a noble man, the Schultish of the same place, (whom they call Landammanus,) had bestowed great cost a fewe yeres before, and had gathered therby good store of riches. In the same myne was a spirite or Diuell of the mountaine, who when the laborers filled the stuffe they had digged into their vessels, he seemed, for the most parte, euery Fridaye, to be very busie, pouring the mettals of his owne accord out of one basket into an other, Wherewith the Schultish was not offended: and when he would eyther descende into the pit, or come vp againe, blessing himselfe with the signe of the Crosse, he neuer receiued hurt. It chaunced on a time that while the saide spirit was too busie intermedling himselfe with euery thing, one of the miners being offended therewith, began to raile at him very bitterly, and with terrible cursing wordes, bid him get him thence in the diuels name. But the spirit caught him by the pate, and so writhed his necke about, that his face stode behinde his backe, yet notwithstanding he was not slaine, but liued a long time after, well knowne vnto diuers of his familiar friends, which yet liue at this day, howbeit he died within a fewe yeares after.

Agricola. Georgius Agricola, whose learned workes which he wrote of mettalles, be yet extant in the end of his booke of creatures liuing vnder the earth, he maketh two kindes of Diuels haunting in certayne Mynes abroade. For hee saith, there are some cruell and terrible to behold: which for the moste parte, doo very much annoy and hurt the labourers digging for mettall.

Suche a one was hee which was called Annebergius, who

ground, and set him in the brinke of a certaine exceeding deepe place, where had sometime bene great store of siluer, not without greeuous brusing of his bodie.

And againe he saith, there be some very milde and gentle, whom some of the Germanes call Cobali, as the Grecians do, because they be as it were apes and counterfeiters of men: for they leaping and skipping for ioy do laugh, and seeme as though they did many things, when in very deed they do nothing. And som other call them elues, or dwarfes of the Mountaines, thereby noting their small stature, wherein they commonly appeare. They seeme to be hoare, wearing apparell like the mettall Finers, that is, in a peticoate laced, and an aperne of leather about their loynes. These hurt not the labourers, except they misuse them, but do imitate them in all their doings. And he saith, they are not much vnlike vnto those whom the Germanes call Guteli, because they seeme to beare good affection towards men, for they keep horses, and do other necessary businesse. They are also like vnto them whom they call Trulli, who taking on them the feined shapes of men and women, to serue as it is sayd, like seruants, both amongst other nations, and specially amongst the Suetians.

Touching these spirits haunting Mines of mettal, there is somewhat to be read in Olaus Magnus de Gentibus Septentrionalibus, the first booke and tenth Chapter.

They which saile on the great Ocean sea, make report, that in certaine places, where the Anthropophagi do inhabit, are many spirits, which doo the people there very much harme.

VVhich are people that eate and deuoure men.

Here many straunge things might be brought concerning visions appearing unto men in their sleepe: and also of them, which being in a traunce, haue lyen a whole day and more without mouing, lyke unto dead men: and after being restored to themselues againe, haue told many miraculous things which they haue seene.

Cicero.

Cicero writeth of maruellous things in his booke of diuination, or soothsaying. And so do many other men also.

Augustine.

Augustine himselfe reciteth in many places of his bookes, that some after they were dead, haue warned many their friends of diuers matters, and haue disclosed unto them secrete things, which were to come, and haue shewed sicke folkes good remedies for their diseases, and haue done many such like things.

Auenzoar Albumato, a Phisitian of *Arabia*, writeth, that he receiued an excellent medicine for his sore eyes, of a Phisitian lately deceased, appearing unto him in his sleep:

Marsilius.

as Marcilius Ficinus doth testifie, writing of the immortalitie of the soule. Lib. 16. cap. 5.

The holy Scriptures also teach us, that God hath re-

Mat. 1. & 2.

uealed many things unto men by dreames. S. Mathew in his first and second chapter writeth, that the Angell of God appeared many times unto Ioseph, our Sauiour Christes foster father in a dreame, and commaunded him to beware of those which laie in wayt to destroy Christ Iesus.

Acts.

We reade in the tenth Chapter of the Acts of the Apostles, that S. Peter fell into a traunce, sawe the heauens open, and sawe a vessell, as it were a great sheete, descend downe unto him from heauen, knit togither at the foure corners, wherein were all maner of foure footed beastes of the earth, and wilde beasts, and creeping things, and foules of the heauen. And there came a voyce unto him: Rise Peter, kill and eate.

Acts 16.

And in the 16. Chapter, as S. Paul was yet in *Asia*, comming downe towardes *Troada*, this vision appeared unto

him:

him: There stoode a man of *Macedonia* and prayed him, saying: Come into *Macedonia* and helpe vs. Hereby Paule gathered, it was the will of God, that he should passe the sea, and should preach the Gospell in *Macedonia*.

But I purpose not to write of spirites and visions appearing vnto men in their sleepe, least my Booke grow vnto an huge volume: but only of those which we sensibly see when we are awake.

CHAP. XVII.

That there happen straunge wonders and prognostications, and that sodein noyses and cracks and such like, are heard before the death of men, before battaile, and before some notable alterations and chaunges.

IT hapneth many times, that whe̅ men lie sicke of some deadly disease, there is some thing heard going in the chamber, like as the sicke men were wont, when they were in good health: yea & the sicke parties themselues, do many times hear the same, and by and by gesse what will come to passe. Oftentimes a litle before they yeeld vp ẏ ghost, and sometime a litle after their death, or a good while after, either their own shapes, or som other shadowes of men, are apparantly seen. And diuers times it commeth to passe, that when some of our acquaintaunce or friends lie a dying, albeit they are many miles off, yet there are some great stirrings or noises heard. Sometimes we think ẏ house wil fal on our heads, or ẏ some massy & waighty thing falleth down throughout all ẏ house, rendring and making a disordered noise: and shortly within fewe moneths after, we vnderstand that those things happened, the very same houre ẏ our friends departed in. There be some men, of whose stock none doth die, but that they obserue and marke some signes and tokens going before: as that they heare the doores and windowes open and shut, that some thing runneth vp the staires, or walketh vp and downe the house, or doth some one or other such like thing.

But here I cannot passe this in silence: that there are many superstitious mẽ, which vainly persuade themselues that this cousin, and this or that friend of theirs will shortly die. For in the end, the falling out of the matter it selfe, sheweth it was a vaine and foolish persuasion, that they vnderstood such things by any signes.

Cardanus. Cardanus in his booke *De veritate rerum*, writeth, that there was a certaine noble Familie at *Parma* in *Italy*, out of the which so often as any one died, there was seene an olde woman in the chimney corner. On a certaine time shee appeared, when a mayden of the same family laie very sick, and therfore they cleane dispaired of her life: but soone after she recouered again, and in the meane while, an other, which was then in good health, sodainly died.

There was a certaine parish priest, a very honest and godly man, whome I knew well, who in the plague time, could tell before hand, when any of his parish should die. For in the night time he heard a noyse ouer his bed, lyke as if one had throwne downe a sacke full of corne from his shoulders: which when he heard, he would say: Now an other biddeth me farewell. After it was day, he vsed to inquire who died that night, or who was takẽ with ẏ plague, to the ende he might comfort and strengthen them, according to the dutie of a good pastor.

It hath bin often obserued in Guilde Halles where Aldermen sit, that when one of those Aldermen was at the point of death, there was heard some ratling about his seate, or some other certaine signe of death. The same thing happeneth beside pewes and stalles in Churches, or in other places where men are often conuersaunt, or accustomed to exercise their handie labour.

In

In Abbies, the Monkes seruants or any other falling sicke, many haue heard in the night, preparation of chestes for them, in such sort as the Coffin-makers did afterwards prepare in déed.

In some country villages, when one is at deaths doore, many times there are some heard in the Euening, or in the night, digging a graue in the Churchyard, and the same the next day is so founde digged, as these men did heare before.

There haue bin séene some in the night when the Moone shined, going solemnely with the corpes, according to the custome of the people, or standing before the doores, as if some bodie were to bee carried to the Church to burying. Many suppose, they sée their owne image, or as they say, their owne soule, and of them diuers are verily perswaded, that except they die shortly after they haue séen themselues, they shall liue a very great time after. But these things are superstitious. Let euery man so prepare himselfe, as if he should die to morrow, least by being too secure, he purchase himselfe harme.

There happen other straunge things also. For when some lye in the prison in chaines, readie to suffer punishment for their offences, many times in the night season, there is heard a great noyse and rumbling, as if some bodie were breaking into ẏ gaile to deliuer the prisoners. When men come to vnderstand the matter, they can neither hear, nor sée any bodie, and the prisoners likewise say they heard no maner thing.

Some executioners or hangmen do report, that for the most part, they know before hand whether any man shall shortly bee deliuered into their handes to suffer: for their swordes will moue of their owne accord. And there are other that say, they can tell before, after what sort the prisoners shall suffer.

Many wonderfull and straunge things happen about

those

those which wilfully cast away themselues. Somtime their corpses must be carried a great way off, before they being thrust in a sack can be throwne into the sea: and being laid in a waggon or cart, the horse could scant draw them downe the hill, but vp the hill they néed not labour at all, for the cart would runne very fast of his owne accord.

Some men being slaine by théeues, when the théeues come to the dead bodie, by and by there gusheth out freshe blood, or else there is declaration by other tokens, that the théefe is there present. Plato writeth in the first booke of his lawes, that the soules of such as haue bene slaine, do oftentimes cruelly molest & trouble the soules of those which slew them. For which cause Marsilius Fiscinus doth thinke it chaunceth, that the wound of a man being slaine, while the carkasse lieth on the ground, doth send out blood against him, which wounded him, if he stand neare looking on his wound. Which thing both Lucretius affirmeth to come to passe, and also Iustices haue diligently obserued. Dido in Virgil thus threatneth Aeneas.

De animorum immortalitate li.16. cap.5.

Virgil.

And when the cold of death is come, and body voyd remaines,
Each where my haunting spirit shall pursue thee to thy paines.

The like place is in Horace & in other Poets. As a théefe sitteth at the Table, a cuppe being ouerthrowne, the wine pearceth through the whole and sound wood of the Table, to all mens admiration.

Touching these and other such maruellous things, there might be many histories and testimonies alleaged. But whosoeuer readeth this booke, may call to their remembrance, that they haue séen these and such like things themselues, or that they haue heard them of their friendes and acquaintance, and of such as deserue sufficient credit.

Before the alterations and chaunges of kingdomes and in the time of warres, seditions, and other dangerous seasons, ther most commōly happen very strange things in the aire, in ẏ earth, and amongst liuing creatures clean cōtrary to to the vsuall course of nature. Which things men cal, wonders, signes, monsters, and forewarnings of matters to come. There are séene in the aire, swords, speares, & suche like, innumerable: there are heard and séene in the aire, or vppon the earth, whole armies of men encountring togither, and when one part is forced to flye, there is heard horrible cries, and great clattering of armour. Gunnes, launces and holberdes, with other kindes of weapons and artillerie, do often times moue of their owne accord as they lye in the armories. When as souldiers marche towards their enimies, and their ensignes will not displaie abroade but fold about the stander-bearers heads: if the souldiours be therewith amazed, they surely perswade themselues there is some great slaughter towardes. It is saide also, that horses will be very sad and heauie, and will not lette their masters sit on their backes, before they go to the battaile wherin they shall haue the ouerthrow: but when they are coragious and lustilie neighing, it is a sure token of victorie. Suetonius writeth, that the company of horses which Iulius Cæsar let run at libertie, neuer to be put to labour againe, did wéepe aboundantly when Cæsar was slaine. Suetonius.

When Miltiades addressed his people against the *Persians*, there were heard tirrible noyses before the battaile, and certaine spirits were séene, which the Athenians afterwards affirmed to be the shaddowe of Pan, who cast suche a feare on the *Persians*, that they turned their backs and fled. Thereof Terrores Panici tooke their name, being spoken of sodayn feares vnlooked for, and terrours, suche as Lymphatici metus are, which driue men out of their wits being taken therewith.

Before the *Lacedæmonians* were ouerthrowne in ye battaile at Leuctris, the armour moued, & made a great noise in the temple of *Hector*. At the same time the dores of Hercules temple at Thebes being fast shut with barres, opened sodainly of their owne accord: and the weapons and ar- Cicero de diuinatione.

mour which hong fastned on the wall, were found lying vppon the grounde. These things are to be read in Cicero his first booke De diuinatione.

In the second warres of *Carthage*, the standerd-bearer of the first battaile of pikemen, could not remoue his ensigne out of his place, neither yet whē many came to helpe, they could any thing preuayle. These and suche other signes of euill lucke, Caius Flaminius the Consull, nothing regarded, but soone after his army was discomfited, and he himselfe slaine. Concerning which matter, Titus Liuius writeth at large. In the beginning of the warres waged with the people called Marsi, there was heard out of secrete places, certaine voyces, and noyse of harnesse, which foreshewed the daunger of the warres to come.

Liuie.

Plinie writeth in his. 2. booke and 59. chapter, that in the warres with the *Danes*, and many times before, there was heard the clashing of armour, and the sound of trumpets out of Heauen.

Plinie.

Appianus declareth what signes and wonders went before the ciuill warres at *Rome*: what miserable cries of men clashing of armour, and running of horses were heard, no man seing any thing.

Appianus.

Valerius Maximus in his firste booke and 6. chapter of straunge wonders, writeth how Cneius Pompeius had warning before, not to fight the fielde with Iulius Cesar: for as he launced off, at Dirrachium, his souldiours were taken with a sodayne feare: and in the night likewise before the battaile, their hearts and courages sodainly failed them. And after, the same author addeth that which Cesar himselfe rehearseth in his 3. booke De bello ciuili: how that the very same day wherin Cesar fought his fortunate battaile, the crying of the armie, and the sound of trumpets was heard at *Antiocche* in *Syria*, so sensibly, that the whole citie ranne in armour to defend their walles. The very same thing he saith, happened at Ptolemais, and that at

Valeri. Max. li. 1 cap. 6.

The historiographers reporte, that Castor and Pollux haue bæn often sæne in battailes sitting on white horses, & valiantly fighting against ÿ enemies campe. Plutarch writeth in Coriolanus life, that they were sæne in the battaile against Tarquinius, and that immediatly after, they bare tidings to *Rome* of the victory. The selfe same writeth Titus Liuius also in his 8. boke of his first decade. We may reade in the history of the siege of the noble citie of *Magdeburge* in *Saxonie*, that the enimie which laide siege to the towne, so often as the citizens issued out to skirmish with them, supposed that one vpō a white horse came riding before the citizens battaile, when as the citizens themselues sawe no such man. Iosephus in his bokes of the warres in *Iurie*, recordeth what straunge signes happned before the destructiō of Ierusalem: which were, that a brasen gate being fast rampierd with barres, opened in the night time of his owne accord. And that before the Sunne set, there were sæne chariots in the aire, and armies of men well furnished, enuironing the citie rounde about. And that at Whitsontide, as the priests entred the temple to celebrate diuine seruice, they heard a great noise, and by & by a voice crying Migremus hinc. Let vs depart hence. He reckeneth vp other like things, which we næde not repeate in this place. The same night that Leo of Constantinople was slayne in the temple, the trauellers by sea heard a voice in the aire which said: that Leo had roared out euen to the same place.

Castor and Pollux.

Plutarch.

Iosephus.

Felix Malleolus doctor of both ÿ lawes, master of Solodor, & canon at Tigurū, a mā of great reading, as it may easily apeare by his lerned writinge which ar yet extāt. (For he liued about ÿ time whē ÿ Coūcell of Basil was holdē) writeth in his boke de nobilitate, c. 30. ÿ it is to be sæn in ÿ historie

Felix Malleolus.

L 2 of

of Rodulphus king of the Romanes, that when the said Rodulphus had vanquished Othotarus, King of *Boemia*, continuing on the place all night, where the battell was fought, about midnight, certain Spirits or Deuils, with horrible noise and tumulte, troubled and disordered his whole armie. And that those were spirits walking by night, it appeared hereby, that they sodeynly vanished away like smoake.

The same Author writeth in his xxvi. chapter, That in the yeare of our Lord 1280. as one of the Plebans (as they call them) belonging to the churche of *Tigurine* preached to the people, the graue stone of the tumbe or sepulchre of the two martires Felix and Regula, patrones of the same place, violently brake asunder, no man meuing or touching it, giuing a horrible sound like vnto thunder, so that the people were no lesse astonished and afraide, than if the vaute of the Churche had fallen downe. And he saith, that the same yeare, the third day of October, the greater part of the citie of Tigurum was brent with fire, and moreouer, that sedition was moued amongst the Citizens, for certaine Ecclesiasticall disciplines, and for the Imperiall Banne (as they terme it.) In the yeare of our Lord. 1440. the twelfe day of December, at ye dedication of the foresaid churche, about midnight, there was the like noise hearde, and immediatly after followed ciuill warres, which the *Tigurins* held with vncertaine successe against the other Heluetians, for the space of seuen yeares and more.

The same writer in the. 33. Chap. hath, that at the same time in the yeare of our Lorde. 1444. before that valiaunt battaile, which a feawe Heluetians fought against the innumerable companie of Lewes Dolphin of Fraunce, fast by the wals of Basill, in the time of the generall Councell, there was hearde certaine nightes about those places, the alarme of Souldiours, the clattering of harneys, and the noyse of men encountring togither. &c.

Here

Here I purposely omit many such like examples, for there are many bookes, both of auncient and also of newe writers, touching straunge signes and wonders, wherein these may be redde.

CHAP. XVIII.

It is proued by testimonies of holy scripture, that spirites are sometime seene and heard, and that other straunge matters do often chaunce.

Yet perchaunce it will be obiected vnto vs, that we bring no testimony out of holy scripture, touching this matter: especially to proue, that Spirits do oftentimes appeare vnto men. I answer, that truth it is, There are fewe things hereof in the scriptures, and yet notwithstanding somewhat is to be redde in them. It is read in S. Matthew his fourteenth Chapter, of Christs Disciples, that when in the night season, by reason of a contrary wind, they were in great danger of drowning in the lake of Genazareth, and that in the dawning of the day, the Lord walked on the water, they being afraide, cried out, supposing they sawe a Spirit. Hereof we gather, Luke 14.
that they knew well inough, that Spirits appeared vnto men vpon sea and land.

Likewise when the Lord being risen from death, appeared vnto his Disciples, meaning to assure them of his resurrection, they thought at the first, that they sawe a Spirit. In the which place, Christ denieth not but there are Spirits and straunge sightes, and that they are sometimes seene, but he rather confirmeth the same by putting a difference betweene himselfe, and Spirits of vaine apparitions. But as touching these two testimonies, we wil speak more in another place.

2.Samuel. It is a notable historie which we reade in the seconde Booke of Samuel concerning Saule, who, at what time the Philistians warred vppon him, and that he was in verie great daunger of them, he came to a woman, who was a witch, and desired her to raise Samuel from death, that he might know his counsell touching the successe of the wars. She raised him vp one, whom Saule tooke to be Samuel in deede, who also tolde him what euente shoulde come of the warres. But whether hee were a true Samuel or a counterfait, wee will dispute the matter more at large in his conuenient place.

2.Samuel. 1.Paral.14. As concerning other maruellous things, there is somewhat to be read in the Scriptures: In the seconde of Samuel & the fift chap. Also in the first of Paralipomenon, and the xiiii. chap. we reade, that the Philistines went vp the seconde time into Iurie, to make warres on David: Hee went vnto the Lord, and shewed him the matter, who commaunded him, that he shoulde embushe himselfe behinde the wood with his armie, and when he heard a rustling or noise in the toppes of the trees, he should immediatly sette vppon them. This sounde they say was a strange and supernaturall sound.

2.Reg.6.7. It is written in the second booke of the Kings the. vi. and vii. chapters, that God deliuered the citie of *Samaria* from great famine, when it was fiercely besieged by Benhadad king of the *Assirians*, for in the night season their enemies did heare the noise of the chariots, the neighing of horsses, and shreeching of a huge armie, as it were in their owne pauillions and tentes, supposing therefore, that the kyng of Israel had gathered togither his footemen and horssemen, and had nowe sette vppon them, they soughte to saue themselues by flighte, leauing theyr victuall and other prouision behinde them in their tentes.

1.Samu.7. In the first of Samuel and the seuenth chapter, God caused a wonderfull greate noyse to sounde ouer the Philistians,

listians, and so destroyed them. I meane they were so affrighted with a kinde of straunge feare, that it was an easie matter to vanquish them.

In the fifth Chapter of Daniel ye may reade, that king Balthasar in his roysting banquet, espied right against the candle, a hand writing upon the wall what his end should be. *Daniel 5.*

It is redde in the third Chapter of the seconde of the Machabees, that there appeared a horsse unto Heliodorus, seruant unto Seleucus king of *Asia*, as he was about to destroy the temple of *Hierusalem*: and upon the horsse séemed to sit a terrible man, which made towards him to ouerrun him. On eache side of him were two yong men of excellent beautie, which with whippes scourged Heliodorus. *2. Macha. 3.*

The second of the Machabees and tenth chapter, Iudas Machabeus encountred with his enemies, and when the battaile was hotte, there appeared unto the enemy out of heauen, fiue men sitting on horses, rayned with notable bridles of gold, who ledde the Jewes hoste, and two of them defended Machabeus from all his enemies. And unto Machabeus appeared a horsman in a shining garment, his armour all of gold, and shaking his speare. Whereby it was signified, that he should obtaine a notable and famous victorie. 2. Macha. 11. *2. Mach. 10.* *2. Mach. 11.*

I alleadge not these examples, for that I adiudge the bookes of Machabees, of as good authoritie as the Canonicall bookes of the new and old Testament: but only for that they are ioyned togither with them, and may be read of euery one: and they were alwaies read of the auncient people. For albeit they neuer went about to approue any doctrine by them, yet were they of great authoritie amongst them.

Chap.

CHAP. XIX.

To whome, when, where, and after what sort, Spirites do appeare, and what they do worke.

By all these examples we may plainly perceiue, that many strange things are obiected to mens senses, and that sometimes Spirits are séene and heard, not only (as some haue thought, as Plutark witnesseth in the life of Dion) of children, women, sicke folkes, dottards, and otherwise very plain and simple creatures, but also to men of good courage, and such as haue bin perfectly in their wits. Yet it may not be denied but that there appeare many more vnto some, than vnto other some, as vnto trauellers, watchmen, hunters, carters, and marriners, who leade all their life not only in the day time, but also in night, in iourneying, in the water, woods, hills and vallies. You shall méete with some one who neuer sawe nor heard any of this geare in all his life time, and contrariwise, there be other some which haue séene and heard very many such like things.

So there are some which very siloom chance vpon Serpents, and againe, many there are which oftentimes méete with them in their iourney. The common people say, that those whose natiuities chance vpon the Angaries (for so they terme the foure seasons of the yeare) do sée more store of spirits, than those which are borne at other times, but these are méere trifles. Those which are stedfast in true faith, sée or heare such things more sildome than superstitious people, as in all other things. He that is superstitious, vseth some blessing (as they call it) to heale his Horsses disease, and it taketh good effect: he enchaunteth a Serpent, and it cannot once moue out of the place. He applieth a blessing to staunche bléedyng, and it stoppeth presently:

he

He taketh a hollie rod, or twisted wand inchaunted, & it will moue where a mettle mine is: but he that is of a sounde fayth and doth despise these things, (for he knoweth well they are contrary to the word of God, and also to the Popes decrées) albeit perchaunce he practise such things, yet notwithstanding he can bring nothing to passe. And so also it chaunceth that he seeth spirites and vaine visions, a great deale more seldome than superstitious men do, for hée knoweth well what hée ought to déeme and iudge of them. There are some kinde of men, who thinke it a gay thing, if many such straunge sights appeare vnto them.

There were farre many more of these kindes of apparitions and myracles séene amongest vs, at such times as we were giuen vnto blindnesse and superstition, than since that the Gospell was purely preached amongest vs: the cause whereof I will shewe hereafter.

And moreouer it commeth oftentimes to passe, that some one man doth heare or sée some thing most plainly, when an other which standeth by him, or walketh with him, neyther seeth, nor heareth any such matter.

We reade in the historie of Heliseus, that he sawe chariottes of fire, and many horsmen vpon the toppe of the Mountaine: and yet his seruaunt sawe nothing vntill the Prophet prayed vnto the Lord, that he would vouchsafe for his confirmation and consolation, to open his eyes that he might also beholde this notable miracle. So likewise we reade in the 9. chapter of the Actes of the Apostles, that Christ ouerthrew Paule before *Damascus*, and that he spake vnto him, and his companions also hearde the voice. Afterwardes in the 22. chapter, Paule himselfe shewing vnto the people in the presence of Lycias, in the Castle at *Hierusalem*, what had happened vnto them, saith that they heard not the voice of him that talked with him: which two places are not repugnant, for the meaning is, that they heard a voyce or sounde indéede, but they vnderstood

Some men see things which other men see not.

Actes.9.

Actes.22.

derstood not what the Lord had sayd vnto him.

Socrates familiar. Plato writeth in his dialogue called *Theages*, that Socrates had a familiar spirit, who was woonte to put him in mynd to cease from labouring, when that which he attempted should haue no happie successe. This spirit he himselfe sawe not, and other men hearde not. They say that sometimes Children doe see certaine things, which other men see not, and by a certaine peculiar operation of nature, some men behold that which others in no wise can perceiue.

At what time spirits appeare. As touching the time when spirits appeare, we reade in histories that it shall be after a thousand yeares which God hath appoynted, in the which time Sainte John prophesied in the Apocalips, that Sathan shoulde be lette loose, that is to saye, errours and superstition, and al kinde of mischeefe shuld abound, and many spirits appear euery where: for men gaue them more credite, than the Scriptures. If a spirit appeared, or was heard to say in case these or those things be decreed, to wit, vowed Pilgrimage, and erecting Chappelles, and that this shall be an acceptable kinde of worship vnto God, the Bishoppes and paryshe Priestes weighed not whether those things were agreeable to the word of God or no, &c. Spirits appeared in old time, and do appeare still in these dayes both day and night, but especially in the night, and before midnighte in our first sleepe. Moreouer, on the frydayes, satterdayes, and fasting dayes, to confirme superstition. Neither may we maruell, that they are heard more in the night, than in the day time. For he who is the author of these things, is called in the holye Scriptures the Prince of darkenesse, and therefore he shunneth the light of Gods word.

Apocalips.

In what place spirits are seen. And albeit these are heard or seene in al places, yet are they most especially conuersant in the fieldes where battels haue bene fought, or in places where slaughters haue bene made: in places of execution; in woods into the which they haue coniured deuils being cast out of men: in Thurches,

ches, Monasteries, and about Sepulchers, in the bounds of countries, and buts of lands: in prisons, houses and towers, and sometime also in the ruines and rubbish of Castles.

God threatneth the Babilonians in the 13. chap. of Esay, that Spirits and Satyres shal daunce where their magnificent houses and Pallaces were, where they were wont to lead their daunces. And in his 34. chapter, where he threatneth destruction unto all nations and enemies of God, he saith: In the ruinous and tottering Pallaces, Castles, and houses, horrible spirites shall appeare with terrible cries, and the Satyre shall call unto her mate, yea and the night hags shall take their rest there. For by the sufferaunce of God, wicked divels worke straunge things in those places where men haue exercised pride and crueltie. *Esay 13.* Monsters of the desert. *Esay 34.*

The maner of appearing of spirits, is divers and manifold, as it appeareth by those things which I haue alleaged before. For they shewe themselues in sundry sorts: sometimes in the shape of a man whom we knew, who is yet aliue, or lately departed: and otherwhile in the likenesse of one whom we know not. After what sort spirites appeare.

I heard of a graue and wise man, which was a Magistrate in the Territorie of *Tigurie*, who affirmed, that as he and his seruant went through the pastures, in the sommer very early, he espied one whome he knew very well, wickedly defiling himselfe with a Mare, wherewith being amazed, he returned back againe, and knocked at his house, whom he supposed he had seen, and ther understood for a certaintie, that he went not on foote out of his chamber ye morning. And in case he had not diligently searched out ye matter, the good & honest man had surely bin cast in prison, and put on the rack. I reherse this historie for this end, that Judges should be very circumspect in these cases, for ye divell by these means doth oftentimes circumuent ye innocent. Chunegunda wife unto Henry the 2. Emperour of ye name, was greatly suspected of adultery, and thereuppon many false

 rumors

rumors scattered, that she was too familiar with a certaine yong man in the Court, for the Diuell in the likenesse of the same yong man, was oftentimes séene come out of the Empresse Chamber. But she afterwards declared her innocencie by treading vppon hotte glowing ploughshares, (as the custome was then) without any hurting her féete, as witnesseth Albertus Cranzius, in his fourth booke, and first Chapter of his *Metropolis*.

We reade that many spirites haue appeared vnto certaine Hermites and Monkes in the shape of a woman, alluring and intising them to filthie lust. They appeare also in the fourme of brute beastes, sometime foure footed, as of a Dogge, a Swine, a Horsse, a Goate, a Catte, or a Hare: and sometimes of foules, and créeping wormes, as of a Crow, a night Owle, a schritch Owle, a Snake, or Dragon, whereof the Gentiles had great plentie in their Temples and houses, and nourished them, as we may reade euery where in the Poets. Spirits haue sometimes appeared in a pleasaunt fourme, and sometimes in a horrible shape. At one time some hath bene séene ryding on horsebacke, or going on foote, or crawling vppon all foure. At an other time hath appeared a man all burning in fire, or beraide with blood: and somewhile, his bowelles haue séemed to traile out, his belly being as it were ripped vp. Sometimes a shadow hath onely appeared: sometimes a hand, sometimes an instrument, as a staffe, a sworde, or some such lyke thing which the spirite helde in his hande. Sometimes he appeared in maner of a bundle of hey, burning on fire: another while onely a hoarse kinde of voyce was heard. Sometimes a spirit hath bene heard walking in the inner parte of the house, turning the leaues of a Booke, or telling money, or playing at dice, or bounsing against the wall. And sometimes there is heard a terrible noyse or clappe, as if a peale of Gunnes were discharged hard at hand. And spirits sometimes, taking a man by the

arme

arme or by the haire of the head, haue walked with them.

Olaus Magnus in his third booke and eleuenth Chapter Olaus.
De Gentibus Septentrionalibus, writeth, that euen in these our dayes, in many places in the North partes, there are certaine monsters or spirites, which taking on them some shape or figure, vse (chiefly in the night season) to daunce, Daunces of after the sounde of all maner of instruments of musicke: Spirits. whom the inhabitants call companies, or dances of Elues, or Fairies. Some what also is to bee reade touching this matter in Saxo Grammaticus, in his historie of *Denmarke*. Saxo. Such like things are those which Pomponius Mela reporteth Pomponius in his third booke of the description of *Aethiopia*, that in Mela. *Mauritania* beyonde the Mount *Atlas*, many times in the night season are seene great lightes, and that tinkling of Cymballs, and noyses of Pipes are also heard, and when it is daylight no man appeareth. Solinus writeth in his thirtie Solinus. eight and fortie foure chapters, that in this same Mountaine, Ægiptians vse euery where to leade their daunces: of whom also Plinie maketh mention in his first booke and first Chapter. Men holde opinion, that they are Panes, Faunes, and Satyres, of whom the olde writers haue mentioned many things.

Saint Hierome writeth in the life of Paule the Hermit, Hierome. that an Hippocentaure, appeared vnto S. Anthonie, in the A Fable out same shape which is described of the Poets. In a stonie Hierome, of valley (saith he) he espied a Dwarffe of a small stature, ha- a Centaure, uing a crooked nose, and his forehead rough with hornes: A Monster the hinder part of his bodie, and his feete like vnto a Goate. hauing the Anthony nothing amazed with this sighte, taketh vnto forepart like him the shield of faith, and the brestplate of hope, lyke a a man, the good warriour. Notwithstanding the foresayde creature hinder like a presented him with Dates, to refresh him in his iourney, horse. as witnesses of peace and friendship. Which when Anthonius vnderstood, he staide, and enquiring of him what he was, receiued this answere. I am (quoth he) a mortall creature, and one of the inhabitants of this desart, whome the Gentiles, being deceiued with many errors, doth worship, calling vs Faunes, Satyrs, and night Mares.

And I am sent as Embassador from our company, who earnestly beseech thee, that thou wilt pray vnto the God of all creatures for vs, whom we acknowledge to be come into the world, to saue the same, &c.

Plutarch. And here we may in no wise ouerpasse in silence, that notable historie which Plutarch in his booke *De fectu oraculorum*, (translated by that learned man Adrianus Turnebus) reciteth in these words. Touching the death of diuels, I haue heard a certaine historie of one who was neither foolish, nor accustomed to lye. For it was Epitherces, my countrey man, a professour of Grammer, father vnto Æmilianus the Rhethoritian, of whome some of you also haue heard the same: He told me, that when he once tooke ship, meaning to go into *Italie*, because he carried with him not only great store of marchandise, but also very many passengers, in the euening when they were about the Ilands Echinadæ, the wind quite ceased, and that the shippe driuing in the Sea, being brought at the last vnto *Paxe*, many then waking, and many also quaffing after they had supped, sodeinly there was heard a voyce of one which called Thamus, in such sort that euery man marueiled. This Thamus was a Pilotte borne in *Egipt*, vnknowne vnto many which were in the ship. Wherefore being twice called, he held his peace, and the third time answered: then the other with a louder voyce commaunded him, that when he came vnto Palodes, hee should tell them that the great God Pan was departed. When this was heard, euery man was amazed with feare, as Epitherces affirmed vnto vs: And being in consultation whether they should do as was commaunded or not, Thamus thus iudged of the matter: that if the winde did blowe, they must passe by with silence, but if it were calme without winde, he must vtter

that

that which we had heard. When therefore they were come to *Palodes*, and no wind stirred, nor waue moued, Thamus looking out of the sterne towards the lande, cryed out as he had heard, that the great God Pan was deceased: Hee had scant ended those wordes, when immediatly there followed a great groning, not of one man, but of many, being admixt as it were with great admiration. And because many were present in the ship, (they said) the same hereof was speedely spred abroad at *Rome*, and Thamus sent by Tiberius ŷ Emperour, who gaue so much credit vnto the matter, that he diligently enquired, and asked who that Pan was. The learned men whome he had in great number about him, supposed that Pan was he, who was the sonne of Mercurie and Penelope, &c.

These and such like things, (Eusebius who also reciteth this historie) affirmeth to haue chaunced in that time of Tiberius, in the which Christ being conuersant amongst men, expelled all maner of diuels from the societie of them. De preparatione Euang. li.5. chap.9.
Other most godly professours of our Religion, affirme, (as namely Paulus Marsus, in his Annotations vppon the first of Ouids Fasti) that this voyce was heard out of *Paxe*, the very same night ensuing the day wherein our Lorde suffered, in the 19. yeare of Tiberius, which was the same yeare that Christ was crucified in: by the whiche voyce being vttered in a wildernesse of solitary rockes, it was declared that our Lord and God had suffered for vs. For the word Pan in Greeke, signifieth all: and then the Lord of al the world was crucified. Paulus Marsus.

He addeth moreouer, that Theodosius doth say, that the *Archadians* do worship this God, calling him τὸν τῆς ὕλης κύριον, meaning thereby to signifie a Lorde and Ruler, not of wordes, but of all manner of materiall substances: whose power is suche, that it is able to create the essence and substaunce of all bodies, whether that they be heauenly, or earthly. And albeit he referre this vnto the Sunne,

yet

yet if a man marke diligently, his mysteries haue a higher meaning, &c.

Hereunto belongeth those thinges which are reported touching the chasing or hunting of diuels, and also of the daunces of dead men, which are of sundry sortes. I haue heard of some which haue auouched, that they haue séene them.

Hunting of Diuels.

No man is able to rehearse all the shapes wherein spirits haue appeared, for the diuell, who for the most part is the worker of these things, can (as the Poets faine of Proteus) chaunge himselfe into all shapes and fashions.

These walking spirites sometimes stoppe the way before men as they trauell, and leade them out of their way, and put them in suche great feare, that sometimes they become grayheaded in one night. I remember I haue heard the like historie of my olde friende Iohn Willing, a godly and learned man, of one in the Countie of *Hannow*, who not many yeares ago, méeting with a walkyng spirite in the night season, was so much altered, that at his returning home, his owne Daughters knewe him not.

Spirites oftentimes awake men out of their sléepe, and cause many to forsake their owne houses, so that they cannot hire them out to any other. Sometimes they ouerthrow somewhat, or strike men, or cast stones at them, and hurt them either in their bodies or in their goods: yea and sometime God doth suffer them to bereaue men of their liues. It often chaunceth that those mens faces and heads do swel, which haue séene, or heard spirits, or haue bene blasted with them: and some are taken mad, as we sée by experience. I remember well it hath happened, that some supposing they haue séene armed men, who were ready to take them, haue therefore assaied to slaie themselues: which thing may be by craft of the diuel. Spirites do also trouble cattell in the night time, in the pastures.

Thus

Thus much concerning the first part of this worke, wherein (I trust) I haue proued, and made it euident, that albeit there be many which vainely perswade themselues they haue séene wandring spirits, or haue beheld one insteed of an other: yet notwithstanding that there are walking spirits, and that other strange things do sometime happen.

I haue also shewed vnto whome they appeare especially, and where, when, after what sort, or in what fourmes they shewe themselues, and what things they worke and bring to passe.

Whosoeuer dare flatly deny these manifold and agréable testimonies of the olde and new writers, he séemeth vnworthie in my iudgement, of any credit, whatsoeuer he say. For as it is a great token of lightnesse, if one by and by beléeue euery man which saith, he hath séene spirits: so on the other side, it is great impudency, if a man rashly and impudently contemne all things which are auouched, of so many, and so credible Historiographers, and auncient Fathers, and other graue men of great authoritie.

The seconde parte of this

Booke doth shewe, that those Spirits and other straunge sights, be not the soules of men, but either *good or euil Angels, or else some secret and hid operations.*

CHAP. I.

The opinion or beliefe of the Gentiles, Iewes, and Turkes, concerning the estate of Soules seperated from their bodies.

IN the second part of this booke we haue to consider, what those things be which (as wee haue before shewed) are both heard and seene, in the day time and in the night, whether they be the soules of dead men or no: also what the olde writers haue iudged of them, and what the holy scriptures, do teach vs herein.

Platos opinion.

Plato doth think, that Heroicall and excellent soules, as being of the pure sort, do mount aloft: but that other base and viler soules, that are defiled with the pleasures & lustes of the bodie, do wander below on the ground, and the same he deemeth to be those spirits which are eftsones seene.

Also other heathen and prophane writers say, they are heereby moued to thinke that the soules of men do liue after death, for that it is most cleare and euident, that many spirits wander and raunge hither and thither, and are oft times heard and séene, and founde to talke with men: for they suppose that most of these are mens soules. Tertullian a very auncient writer, in his booke *De anima*, saith, that the wise Heathens, which did define the soule to be immortall, (for some of them, as namely the Epicures, thought that the soules died with their bodies) thought that the soules of the wise, if they departed from their bodies, hadde their abiding on high: but the rest were throwne downe into Hell. Tertullian.

Furthermore, the Heathen thought the Soules should stray continually abroade before they founde rest, vnlesse the bodies from which they were seuered, were rightly buried in the earth. Wherefore (as we may reade in Poets) it was a gréeuous crime to caste forth any bodie vnburied. Hector in Homere, besought Achilles that he woulde not cast forth his carcasse to be deuoured of Dogs and birds, but that he would deliuer the same to be enterred by olde Priamus his father, and Hecuba his mother. Patroclus appeared in a vision by night after his deathe vnto Achilles, and requested him to bestowe vppon him all funeral solemnities. For otherwise he saide the soules of those that were buried, woulde thrust him backe, that he should not be able once to enter in at Hell gates. Which example Tertullian aledgeth, and therwithal cōfuteth this vaine opinion of the heathen. Palinurus in Virgill, besought Æneas, that he woulde cast earth on him, when he was dead, and erect vnto him an hearse, for so did they call those Monuments of the deade, in whiche albeit no man was layde, yet were they vsed in the honour of the deceassed. Virgill writeth, that Deiphobus his Ghost wandred abroade, vnto the whiche Æneas erected an Horse. Homer. Virgil.

For the Gentiles were of suche an opinion in those dayes, that they thought an emptie and counterfeyted buriall profitted very much. Moreouer the heathen were perswaded that the soules which died before their naturall time (especially of those whiche perished by violent death, whom they call βιοθανάτους, as by hanging, drowning, or beheading, &c.) did straie abroade so long time as they should haue liued, if they had not bin slain by violent death. Which opinion Tertullian also confuteth. Plato in his ninth booke *De legibus*, writeth, that the soules of those which are slain, do pursue their murtherers so farre, that they do hurt them: the which, except it be understood by way of a Metaphor, is likewise to be reiected.

Plato.

The Iewes opinion.

The Catholike faith amongst the Iewes was, that the soules of the dead did not returne into this earth, but either were at rest, which was when they died in the faith of the promised Messias, or were cōdemned if they departed hence in their sinnes without repentance. For Iob in his seuenth Chapter saith: Euen as the cloude vanisheth and fadeth away, so he that goeth downe to the graue shall come vp no more, nor returne into his house, &c.

Iob.7.

But if thou wilt say that Iob was an Ethnicke, it may be alleaged of Dauid, that when he was in very great danger, and death euen present before his eyes, he praied in the 31. Psalme. Into thy hands O Lord I commend my spirit. The Preacher also in his 12. Chapter saith: The spirite shall returne to God that giueth it. In the booke of Wisedome (which of olde writers is attributed to Philo Iudeus) the third Chapter thereof, it is written: the soules of the righteous are in the hande of God, and no torment shall touch them. And on the other side, the soules of the wicked go downe into hell. In the 49. Psalm it is written of those wealthie worldlings, which for lucres sake, depart from God and his Commaundements: They are laid as shéepe in Hell, Death shall consume them, and Hell is their habitation, &c.

Psal.31.
Eccle.12.
Wisd 3.
Psal.49.

If the Iewes had beléeued, that the soules after this life

were

were tormented in Purgatorie, no doubt amongst so many diuers kinds of sacrifices, which they offered for the sinnes of the liuing, they would at least haue some one kind of sacrifice wherby to redéeme soules, or in some part to asswage and mitigate their paines. And that soules do returne after death, do offer themselues to be séene and beheld of men, and require aide of them, we finde no where in the old Testament, but rather the contrary. In the 2. of Samuel 12. Dauid speaketh this of his yong childe, that he begat by Bersaba, that he could not bring him into life againe, that hee would go to him, and the childe should neuer returne vnto him againe. And Jesus the sonne of Syrach, in his 38. chapter saith: There is no returning from death. Of the vision which was shewed to Samuel, we will straightway speake in his proper place. 2. *Samu*. 12. *Eccle*. 38.

And that in latter ages, long after Christ came in flesh, there were some amongst the Jewes, who thought that the soules separated from their bodies, did straie and raunge abroad: it may hereby be gathered, for that certaine of the Rabbines write, that the soule of Naboth (which was slain, because he would not sell his Vineyard to Achab) was that spirit that promised his helpe to seduce Achab, being as it were one that coueted his death.

The Turkes also beléeue that the soule is immortall, and that assone as they are losed from the bodie, they come either into a place of rest, or of torment. But whether that they did thinke, that soules returned againe into the earth, and roue there to and fro, I could finde no plaine mention thereof in their *Alcaron*. The Turkes' opinion.

CHAP. II.

The Papists doctrine touching the soules of dead men, and the appearing of them.

Papists.

THe Papists in former times haue publikely both taught and written, that those spirites which men somtime sée and heare, be either good or bad angels, or els the soules of those which either liue in euerlasting blisse, or in Purgatory, or in the place of damned persons. And that diuers of them are those soules that craue aide and deliuerance of men. But that this doctrine of theirs, and the whole state therof may be the more euidently perceiued, we will more largely repeate the same out of their owne bookes. Iacobus de Cusa, a *Carthusian* Friar, and Doctor of diuinitie, wrote a booke of ỹ Apparition of soules, after they were seperated fro the bodies: which worke of his, hath in it many superstitious toyes, and was Printed in a Towne belonging to the dominion of *Berna*, named *Burgdrofe*, in the yeare of our Lord, 1475.

Iacobus de Cusa.

Popish writers commenting on the 4. booke of the Master of Sentences, do appoint foure places to receiue soules, after they are departed from the bodies. Thrée of the which places they say are perpetuall, and one which lasteth but for a time already limitted.

Foure places for soules. Heauen. Hell. Limbus puerorum which is a place wher the Papistes imagine the soules of yong childrē to be, which departed without Baptisme. Purgatorie.

The first place or receptacle is *Cœlum Empireum*, the firie heauen, so termed of his passing great brightnesse and glory, which they say is the seate ordeined for ỹ blissed sort: this place by an other name in scripture is called Paradise. The second place is Hell vnder the earth, being the Mansion of Diuels and Infidels, departing hence in deadly sinne, without repentance. The third place they tearme *Limbus puerorum*, which is prouided as well for the children of the faithfull, as of the vnfaithfull; who (they say) shall

shall continually abyde there without any sense of payne, being only depriued from the fruition of Gods presence. And therefore they say, that after their death, they ought not to be buried in holy buriall. The fourth place is Purgatorie, which is prepared for them that departe hence without deadly sinne, or if they committed any such sinnes, did some penance for them, but yet made not full satisfaction for them, or else went hence only stained with venial sin.

Of this place, to wit, Purgatorie, Popish writers teach maruellous things. Some of them say, that Purgatorie is also vnder the earth as Hell is. Some say that Hell and Purgatorie are both one place, albeit the paines be diuers according to the deserts of soules. Furthermore they say, that vnder the earth there are more places of punishment in which the soules of the deade may be purged. For they say, that this or that soule hath bin seene in this or that mountaine, floud, or valley, where it hath committed the offence: and that these are particuler Purgatories, assigned vnto them for some speciall cause, before the day of Iudgement, after which time all manner of Purgatories, as well general as particuler shall cease. Some of them say, that the paine of Purgatorie is all one with the punishment of hel, and that they differ only in this, that the on hath an end, the other no ende: and that it is far more easie to endure all the paynes of this worlde, whiche all men since Adams time haue susteined, euen vnto the day of the last Iudgement, than to beare one dayes space the least of these two punishmentes.

Further they holde that our fire, if it be compared with the fire of Purgatorie, doth resemble only a painted fire. Seeke their Doctours in this pointe, on the fourth booke of Sentences, the 20. distinction.

This question also they moue, by whome the Soules in Purgatorie are tormented. Wherefore their opinions are very diuers, and disagreeable among themselues. B: S: m: g:

Richardus

Richardus de Media Villa a *Franciscan* Frier, writeth vpon the Maister of Sentences, and saith, he verily beléeueth that soules are caried by good Angels, into the places of torment, but yet that they themselues do not torment them, because they shall become at length fellow citizens with them. Neyther yet are they punished by Deuils (who after this life do no longer tempte men) but only by the mére iustice of God. And yet (saith he) it may so come to passe, that the Deuils be present at the doing thereof, and reioyce at their tortures. I thought good to repeate these things of Purgatorie somewhat at large, the rather for that the reader might sée, that their Doctours do disagrée in a matter of great weight, by which they haue both robbed men of their wealth, and plunged them into very great miserie.

Papists feigne that soules returne to earth againe.

Héervnto they adde, that the spirits, as well of the good, as the ill, do come and are sent vnto men liuing, from hell. And that by the common lawe of iustice, all men at the day of Iudgement shall come to their trial from hell: and that none before that time can come from thence. Farther they teache, that by Gods licence and dispensation, certaine, yea before the day of Iudgement, are permitted to come out of hell, and that not for euer, but only for a season, for the instructing and terrifying of the liuing. Héervppon they recite diuers kindes of visions, that certaine Clarkes, and Laye persons being damned, bothe men and women, haue appeared to their ghostly fathers, and others, and haue opened vnto them the causes of their damnation: all which to rehearse héere were lost laboure. And that the soules which be in euerlasting ioye, or in Purgatorie, do often appeare, it may be séene in Gregories Homelies and Gregories Dialogues, who writeth that Peter and Paule, and other Saintes, did not onely appeare vnto holie men, but did also conducte their Soules vnto Celestiall ioye. Moreouer that God doth licence soules,

soules to return from those two places, partly for the comfort and warning of the liuing, and partly to pray aide of them. And yet that those soules do not here represent themselues to be séene of men, when, and how often soeuer they list themselues. No doubt these men shewe themselues to haue a sharpe wit and profound knowledge.

These Doctors moreouer moue this question, whether we may request without offence, that the soules of such as are departed, may shewe themselues to be beheld and séene of the liuing.

VVhether we may wish to see spirits.

To riue asunder this crabbed knotte, they bring this wedge: that if this request procéede of some good intent, without the spot of lightnesse & vanitie, that a man might understand the state of some friend, neighbour, benefactour, or of his parents, or some other, therby to helpe and relieue them spéedily of their torments, it is no offence at all: because dead mens soules do of their owne accord shew them selues unto the liuing, to receiue helpe of them, and therefore nothing can let us to aske this thing at Gods hand. Of this opinion is Thomas of Aquine.

But as concernyng the time and place, when and where Spirites do proffer themselues to be séene, they say, no certaine rule can be giuen: for this standeth wholly in Gods pleasure, who if he list to deliuer any, suffereth him to make his appearaunce forthwith, euen in such places as he may be well heard in. And that spirits do not alwayes appeare under a visible shape, but sometimes inuisibly, in so much that sometime nothing else is heard of them but snéesing, spitting, sighing, and clapping of hands &c. Of which point I haue noted somewhat before, when I spake generally of ghostes, because they appeare in sundry sorts. And wheresoeuer these spirits be, they say, that they endure punishment. Besides that soules do not appeare, nor answere unto euery mans interrogatories, but that of a great number they scantly appeare unto one.

How a man ought to use himself when spirits appeare according to the Papists. *Dan.* 10. 11.

And therefore they teache. Whensoeuer such visions of spirits are shewed, men should vse fasting and praier or euer they demaunde any question of them: which (say they) in the tenth and eleuenth Chapters of Daniell, is read to haue bene done by Daniell himself. Besides this, shrift, and massing should be vsed ere we question with them: farther, that we should not giue credit assone as we heare but one sign, but waite to heare the same thrice repeated, which in the first booke of Samuel and third Chapter, is read to haue bin done by Samuel being yet a childe: for otherwise the diuell may delude and deceiue vs, as he doth very often. And so soone as these thinges are dispatched and performed, that foure or fiue deuout priests are to be sent for, which should come to the place where the spirit was wont to shew himselfe, and that they should vse certaine ceremonies, as to take a candle that hath bene halowed on Candlemasse day, and light it: also holy water, the signe of the Crosse, a censor in their hand, and when they light their candle, should pray ouer it (as I remember) the seuen penitential psalms, or read the Gospell of S. Iohn. And when they come to the place, they should sprinkle it with holy water, and perfume it with Frankincense, casting about their neckes a holy stoale, and then that one of them kneeling on his knees, should rehearse this praier following. 1. *Samu.* 3.

O Lord Iesu Christ, the searcher of all secrets, which art alwaies wont to reueale healthfull and profitable things vnto thy faithful people and litle ones, which hast permitted some certaine spirit to shew himselfe in this place: we humbly beseech thee of thy great mercy, by thy death & passion, and by the sheading of thy most precious bloud for our sinnes, that thou wilt vouchsafe to giue in charge to this spirite, that he may declare and open what he is, without any fraying or hurting of vs, or of any other creature besides: shewing vnto vs thy seruants, or to other sinners as we be, who he is, why he is come, and what he desireth, so

that

that hereby thou maist be honoured, he comforted, and thy faithfull people also holpen and succoured. In the name of the father, the sonne, and the holy ghost. Amen.

Yet do they teach, that a man may chose to use this or some other forme of praier, and ceremonies: because that without these, spirites haue often appeared, & shewed what they required. This done, we should (as they teach) fall to questioning with them, and say: Thou spirite, we beséech thée by Christ Jesus, tell us what thou art, and if there be any amongst us, to whome thou wouldest gladly make answere, name him, or by some signe declare so much? After this, the question is to be moued; eache man there present being recited whether he would answere unto this or that man. And if at the name of any, hée speake, or make a noyse, all other demaunds remaining, should be made unto him: As these and suche lyke. What mans soule he is? for what cause he is come, and what he doth desire? Whether he require any aide by prayers and suffrages? Whether by Massing, or almes giuing he may be released? Farther, by how many Masses that may be compassed, by thrée, six, ten, twentie, thirtie. &c. Furthermore, what manner of priests should say Masse for him, Monks, or secular priests. Then if he aske for any fasting, by what persons, how long, and in what sort he wold haue it done: If he require almes déeds, what almes déeds they should be, how many, and on what persons bestowed, whether on him that lacketh harbour, or that is diseased of the leprosie, or on some other sort of people.

Furthermore, by what signe it may be perfectly knowne that he is released, and for what cause he was first shut up in Purgatorie. And yet they hold, þ no curious, unprofitable, or superstitious questiōs shuld be demanded of þ spirit, except he wold of his own accord reueale and open thē. And þ it were best, þ sober persons shuld thus questiō wᵗ him, on som holiday before diner, or in þ night seasō, as is commōly accustomed. And if the spirite will shewe no signe at that time, the matter should be deferred unto some other season, untill the spirit would shewe himselfe againe: and yet that the crosse and holy water should bee left there, for that by the secret iudgement of God, it was ordeined, that they should appeare at certaine houres, and to certaine persons, and not unto all men. And farther, they say that we neede not to feare, that the spirite would doo any bodily hurt unto that person, unto whome it doth appeare. For if such a spirit would hurt any, he might iustly be suspected that he were no good spirit.

By what tokens good spirites may be discerned from euil.

Moreouer, popish writers teach us to discerne good spirits from euill, by foure meanes. First they say, that if he be a good spirit, he will at the beginning, somewhat terrifie men, but againe soone reuiue and comfort them. So Gabriel with comfortable words did lift up the blessed Virgin which before was sore troubled by this salutation. They also alleage other examples. The second note is to discerne them by their outwarde and visible shape. For if they appeare under the forme of a Lyon, Beare, Dog, Toade, Serpent, Cat, or blacke ghoste, it may easily be gathered that it is an euil spirit. And that on the other side, good spirits doo appeare under the shape of a doue, a man, a lambe, or in the brightnesse, and cleare light of the Sunne.

Luke 1.

We must also consider whether the voyce whiche we heare be sweete, lowly, sober, sorrowfull, or otherwise terrible and full of reproach, for so they terme it.

Thirdly we must note, whether the spirit teache ought that doth varie from the doctrine of the Apostles, and other Doctors approued by the Churches censure: or whether he utter any thing that doth dissent from the faith, good maners, and ceremonies of the Church, according to the Canonical rites or decrees of Councels, and against the lawes of the holy church of *Rome*.

Fourthly, we must take diligent heede whether in his

words,

good spirits that desire any helpe or deliueraunce. Other signes also they haue to trie the good Angels from the bad; but these are the chiefe.

How we may helpe and succoure soules.

Now touching the suffrages or waies of succour, wherby soules are dispatched out of Purgatorie, Popish doctors appoint foure meanes: That is, the healthfull offering of the sacrifice in the Sacrament of the aultar, almes giuing, prayer, fasting. And vnder these members, they comprise all other, as vowed pilgrimages, visiting of Churches, helping of the poore, and the furthering of Gods worship and glory, &c. But aboue all, they extoll their Masse, as a thing of greatest force to redeeme soules out of misery: of whose wonderfull effect, and of the rest euen now recited by vs, they allege many straunge examples.

Of these things they moue many questions, the which who so lust to see, let him search their bookes which haue bin written and published of this matter.

A notable deede to relieue soules.

Neither only in their writings, but in open pulpit also they haue taught, how excellent and noble an act it is, for men touched with compassion, with these foresaid workes to ridde the soule that appeareth vnto them and craueth their help, out of the paines of purgatorie; or if they cannot so do, yet to ease and asswage their torture. For say they, the soules after their deliuerance, ceasse not in moste earnest maner to pray for their benefactors, and helpers. On the other side, they teach that it is an horrible and heynous offence, if a man giue no succoure to suche as seeke it at his hands, especially if it be the soule of his parents, brethren and sisters. For except by them they might conueniently be released of so manifolde miseries, they woulde not so earnestly craue their helpe. Wherefore say they, no man should be so voyd of naturall affection, so cruell and outragious, that he should at any time deny to bestowe some small wealth, to benefit those, by whom he hath before by diuers and sundry waies bene pleasured.

If they were not the soules of the dead which craue helpe and succour, but diuellish spirits, they would not will them to pray, fast, or giue almes for their sakes: for that the diuels do hate those, as also all other good workes.

CHAP. III.

What hath followed this doctrine of the Papists, concerning the appearing of mens soules.

BY these means it came to passe, that the common sort were of opiniō, that those spirits which wer séen and heard, were the soules of the dead, and ẏ whatsoeuer they did say, was without gainsaying to be beléeued. And so the true, simple, and sincere doctrine of ẏ calling vpō God in the name of Christ Iesus only: of the confidence in Christs merits, and redemption from sin and damnation: of ẏ true déeds of Christian charitie, was daily more and more impugned and oppressed. So that when men by litle and litle, forsooke holy scripture, and cast it aside, mens traditions and precepts began straightway to be had in great price and estimation, yea, they were more regarded than Gods owne word. A great offence was it taken to be, if any would presume once to breake mens traditions. On those apparitions of spirits, as on a sure foundatiō of their Purgatory is chiefly builded. For by talke had with them, Popish writers taught that men atteined vnto saluation, by their owne, and by other mens merits: which opinion so blinded them, that they became retchlesse, secure, and sluggish. For if a-

and tenne virgins, of whom mention is made in the 25. of Matthew. By these apparitions of spirits, masses, images, satisfaction, pilgrimages for religion sake, relikes of saints, monasticall vowes, holidaies, auricular confession, and other kinds of worshippings and rites, and to be short, all things which haue no grounde in holy scripture, by little and little grewe into authoritie and estimation. So that the matter came at the last to that extremitie and excesse, that many deuoute, and simple soules, pinched and nipped their owne bellies, that they might ẏ better haue by these meanes, wherewithall to finde and mainteine idle monks and priests, and to offer vnto images. They founded chappels, alters, manasteries, perpetuall lights, anniuersaries, frieries, and such like, to release their friends out of the torments of Purgatorie. And this did the walking spirits will them to do. And sometime also by their councell, mens last willes & testaments were altered. Hereby priests and monks increased daily, their parishes, colleges & monasteries with yerely reuenewes, & got into their hands ẏ best farmes, vineyards, lands, medowes, pondes, parkes, bondmen, iurisdictions, great lordships, and the authoritie of the sword. For after ẏt this opiniō once tooke firme roote in mēs harts, ẏ mens soules did walke after their death, & appeare on ẏ earth, the greatest part did whatsoeuer they commanded thē. And ẏ it may more plainly be perceiued how much mē esteemed those visions & such like pelf, & how in memorial of thē they deuised & framed to thēselues new kinds of worshippings, I will recite vnto you one or two histories.

Monkes by their doctrine of spirits haue heaped infinite riches.

Martinus Polonus Archebishop of Consentine, and the Popes Penitētiarie, writeth in his Chronicles, that Pope Clement.

Martinus Polonus.

Clement the fourth did canonize for a Saint at *Viterbe*, one Eduergia, Duchesse of *Polonia*, a widdow of great holinesse, who (among many notable things that are written of her) when her canonization had bene many yeares delaied, at length appeared her selfe in a Vision to her Proctor in the Court of *Rome*, being heauie and pensiue about this matter, and certified him, both of the spædie dispatching of this businesse, and also of the day wherin it should be dispatched. Canonization amongst the Ethnicks, from whence it tooke his originall, is named ἀποθέωσις. that is, deification, or making of a God.

All soules day whéce it took originall.

Ioannes Tritenhemius Abbotte of *Spanheim*, a man of great authoritie, in his booke of Chronicles teacheth, that the memorie of all faithfull soules, termed All soules day, had his originall obseruation by this meanes: that when a certaine Monke returned from *Ierusalem*, and lodged in a certaine Hermits house in *Sicill*, about the mount *Aetna*, which flasheth forth fire, hée learned of the saide Hermit, that many soules of the dead were tormented there by fire, out of which again through the praiers of the faithful, they were released, as it was taught him by the testimony euen of the spirites themselues. Hereof also writeth Polydore Virgil, in his first booke, and 9. Chapter, *De inuentione rerum*, that the feast of All hallowes had the very same originall, which they shall finde in *Petrus de natalibus* his tenth booke, and first Chapter. Wherby thou maist gather, that Feastes were first ordeyned by the tales of spirites appearing vnto men. The like fable is founde in Damascene, who writeth of Macharius thus: When according to his maner he prayed for the dead, and was desirous to vnderstande whether his prayers did profitte them ought, and whether they receined any comfort thereby, God willing to reueale so muche to his seruaunt, inspired a drie scull with the word of truth, so that the dead scull brake forth into these words: When thou praiest for the dead,

Polydore.

we

we receiue comfort by thy praiers.

Of the like roote sprung the order of the Carthusian Monkes, which of the common sort is iudged to be the most holiest and straightest order: of the which the Monks them-selues of this broode haue put forth a booke. For as Polydore Virgil recordeth, they began vpon this occasion in the Vniuersitie of *Paris*, in the yeare of our Lord 1080. A certaine Doctor which for his learning and integritie of life was very famous, chaunced to die, when he should haue bene buried in a certaine Church, he cried out with an horrible voyce: I am by the iust iudgement of God accused. Wherupon they left the Coffin in the Church by the space of three dayes, during which time the people flocked togither out of sundry places, to behold this straunge sight. The second day he cried againe: By the iust iudgement of God I am iudged. The third day likewise he cried: I am by the iust iudgement of God condemned. And as Vincentius Bellonacensis saith, some adde hereunto, that he rose vp thrice vpon the beere, which perchaunce they faine of their owne heads. Now because no man suspected that so notable and famous a man was vtterly condemned for euer, euery man was sore astonished thereat.

The begin-ning of the order of Carthusians.

Polydore.

Wherfore Bruno, a Doctor of diuinitie borne in *Coleine*, forthwith forsooke all that he had, and taking to him sixe other godly companions, gat him into a desart called *Carthusia*, in the diocesse of *Grationopolis*: where he erected the first monasterie of that order, which drawing his name of the place, was called the Carthusian order. For this cause also, or for the like, many other monasteries at the first beginning, were both founded and endowed with great liuelihood.

Testimonies out of the word of God, that neither the soules of the faithfull, nor infidels, do walke vpon the earth after they are once parted from their bodies.

Soules go either to hell or to heauen.

NOw that the soules neither of the faithfull nor of infidels do wander any longer on the earth, when they be once seuered from the bodies, I wil make it plaine and euident vnto you by these reasons following. First, certaine it is, that such as depart hence, either die in faith, or in vnbeliefe. Touching those that go hence in a right beliefe, their soules are by and by in possessiō of life euerlasting, and they that depart in vnbelief, do straightway becom partakers of eternal damnatiō. The souls do not vanish away & die with the bodie, as ŷ Epicures opinion is, neither yet be in euery place, as som do imagin: touching this matter I wil alleage, pithie & manifold testimonies out of the holy scripture, out of which alone this questiō may and ought to be tried & discussed. Our Sauiour Christ Iesus which could well iudge

Iohn 3. of these misteries, in the 3. of Iohn saith: So God loued the world, ŷ he wold giue his only begotten son, ŷ who so beleeueth on him, shuld not perish, but haue life euerlasting. For, god sent not his son into ŷ world to cōdemn ŷ world: but that ŷ world by him might be saued. He ŷ beleeueth in him is not cōdemned, & he ŷ beleeueth not, is cōdemned alredy, because he beleeued not in ŷ name of ŷ only begotten son of god. And

Iohn 5. in ŷ 5. of Iohn he saith: Verily verily I say vnto you: he that heareth my word, & beleeueth on him ŷ sent me, hath euerlasting life, & shall not come into iudgemēt or cōdemnation, but hath passed alredy frō death to life: he doth not say ŷ his sins shuld first be purged in purgatorie. And in the 6. cha. he

Iohn 6. saith: This is ŷ wil of him ŷ sent me, that euery one ŷ seeth the son, and beleeueth on him, should haue life euerlasting, and I will raise him vp at the last day againe: verily I say vnto you, he that beleeueth on me hath life euerlasting.

Iohn 14. In the 14. of Iohn, also our Sauior Christ Iesus saith, that he wil take vs vp to himselfe, that where he is, there should

we

we be also.&c. When Christ sent forth his disciples to publish his gospel in ye 10.of Mat.he said unto them:Go ye into the whole world,and preach ye gospel to euery creature: he yt beleeueth and is baptized, shalbe saued, and he yt beleeueth not shalbe cōdemned:& in the 5.cha.of ye 2.to ye Cor ye apostle S.Paul saith: we know yt if the earthly house of this tabernacle be destroied, we haue a building of God, yt is, a house not made wt hands,but eternal in ye heuens,&c. By these places it may be euidently gathered, yt the soules of the faithful are takē up into eternal ioy:and the soules of the unfaithful assone as they are departed frō their bodies are condemned to perpetual torment. And yt this is done straightway after death,may be perceiued by the words yt Christ spake to the theefe on the crosse,when he hong on his right hand:This day shalt thou be with me in paradice. And in the 14.cha.of the Apoc.it is written,And I heard a voice yt said unto me, Write,Blessed ar ye dead yt die in the lord,ἀπάρτι amodo,as the old trāslatiō readeth, yt is by & by,out of hand,without delaie. Steuē in the very point whē he looked to be stoned,cried lord Jesu receiue my spirit. He douted nothing,but was assuredly persuaded yt his soul shold straitway be translated to eternal ioy. Paul in the 1.chap.of his epist.to the Philip.saith: I desire to be losed, or I couet to depart hence, and to be with Christ. Here is no mentiō at all of purgatory, in which the soules should be first purged. If thou wilt here obiect that the persons afore alleaged were saints and martirs, we say farther,that paradice was opened also to the theef,assone as he became repentant. And that the soules both of the faithful & unfaithful,which presently after their death are translated to heauē or hel,do not return thence into the earth before the day of the last iudgement,may wel be perceiued by the parable of the rich man cloathed in purple,and Lazarus, as we read in the 16.of Luke. For when the rich man praied Abraham that he would send Lazarus unto him, to coole his tong, Abraham gaue him this answere: Betwixt the

Mat.10.

2.Cor.5.

Luke 23.

Apo.14.

and vs, there is a great gulfe set, so that they which would go hence (from Abrahams bosome) to you (in Hell) cannot: neither can they come from thence to vs. And when he besought him, that he would send Lazarus to his fathers house to admonish his fiue brethren, least they also should come into that place of torment: he saide vnto him; They haue Moses and the Prophets, let them heare them. And again: If they heare not Moses and the Prophets, neither will they beléeue though one rose againe from the dead.

CHAP. V.

Testimonies of the auncient Fathers, that dead mens soules parted from their bodies, doo not wander heere vppon earth.

August. This matter was also thus vnderstood by the holy and auncient Fathers. For Augustine in his 18. Sermon *De verbis Apostoli*, hath, that there be two mansions, the one in euerlasting fire, the other in the euerlasting kingdome.

Idem. And in his 28. Chapter of his first booke, *De peccatorum meritis & remissione contra Pelagianos*, in the seuenth tome of his workes, he saith: Neither can any man haue any middle or meane place, so that he may be any other where than with the diuel, who is not with Christ.

Idem. And in his notable worke *De ciuitate Dei*, the 13. booke and 8. Chapter, he saith: The soules of the godly so soone as they be seuered from their bodies be in rest, and the soules of the wicked in torment, vntil the bodies of the one be raised vnto life, and the other vnto euerlasting death, which in scripture is called the second death.

Iustine. Iustine also an auncient Father, writeth in *Responsione ad Orthodoxos, quest. 75.* that the difference of the iust and vniust, doth appeare euen assoone as the soule is departed from

from the body. For they are carried by the angels into such places as are fit for them: that is, the soules of the iust are brought vnto Paradice, where they haue the fruition of the sight and presence of Angels, and Archangels: and moreouer the sight of our Sauiour Christ, as it is conteined in that saying, whiles we are straungers from the bodie, we are at home with God. And the soules of the vnrighteous on the other side, are carried to Hell, as it said of Nabuchodonozor the king of *Babylon*: Hell is troubled vnder thée, being readie to méete thée, &c. And so till the day of resurrection and reward, are they reserued in such places as are méetest for them.

Saint Hillarie in the ende of his exposition of the second Psalme, writeth: that mens soules are straightway after death, made partakers of rewards or punishments. Hillarie.

And touching the soules of the old Patriarkes, that died before the natiuitie of Christ, Austin, Hierom, Nazianzen, and other holy Fathers teache, that God in certaine places by him chosen out for that purpose, hath preserued the soules of al those that are departed from this life in the true faith of the Messias to come, in such sort that they féele no griefe, but yet are depriued of the sight of God. This place they call Abrahams bosome, and Hell (for Hell doth not alwaies betoken a place of torment, but also generally the state that soules are in after this life.) And that our Lord Iesus Christ did visit and release them, and when he ascended, carried them with himselfe into heauen. Albeit certain of the Fathers, as Ireneus, Tertullian, Hilarie, & others, think that they shall at the last day ascend to heauen. Some also there be of our time which maintaine this fonde opinion, that the soules sléep, vntil the day of the last iudgement, in which they shall be again coupled with their bodies: but this assertion hath no ground in holy scripture, of the which point diuers haue entreated. But especially Iohn Caluin, that worthie seruant of God, in a proper Treatise that he Dormitantii. Caluin.

wrote of the same matter, in which he doth learnedly confute their reasons that maintein the contrary opinion.

Wherefore sith holy scriptures, as the Fathers understand and interpret them, teache that the soules of men, as soone as they departe from the bodies, do ascende up into heauen if they were godly, descende into hell if they were wicked and faithlesse, and that their is no thirde place in which soules should be deliuered, as it were out of prison, & that soules can neither be reclaimed out of heauen or hel. Hereby it is made euident, that they cannot wander on the earth, and desire aide of men. For first the soules of the blessed néed no aid or help that men cã giue them: & on the other side, the damned sort can no way be releued: the which S. Ciprian the martir in his oration against Demetrian, doth plainly witnesse in these words: when we be once departed out of this world, there is afterward no place left for repentance, no way to make satisfactiõ: here life is either won or lost, & so forth. Albeit the testimonies alredy alleged on this point of doctrine, may well suffise those that loue the truth, and are desirous to come to the knowledge therof: yet to increase the number, I wil recite other testimonies also out of ẏ fathers, to proue manifestly, ẏ the soules departed, do not againe return, & wander on the earth, so that all they which haue not yet stopped their eares that the truth might not pierce & enter into them, may euidently perceiue, that those anciẽt times taught a far better doctrine of those spirits and ghosts, than other latter times under poperie haue cõmended and allowed. Tertullian a very auncient writer, in the end of his boke De anima, saith, the soules do not any longer abide on the earth, after they be once losed from their bodies: & that neither by their owne accord, nor other mens cõmandement, they do wander at all after they haue descended into hell, but he saith, that euil spirits do use this kinde of deceypt, to faine themselues to be the soules of suche as are deceased. And that Hell is not open to any soule, that

[Margin notes: Ciprian mar. — Soules do not walke. — Tertullian.]

that it should afterward at any time depart thence, Christ our Lorde in the parable of the poore man that was in rest, and the rich glutton that was in torment, doth plainely ratifie vnder the person of Abraham, that there can be no man sent backe to shewe or tel ought of the state of hel. And albeit the fathers haue noted certaine errours and scapes in Tertullian, yet there was neuer any that reproued him for this opinion. Athanasius in his booke of questions, the xiii. questiō, doth giue a reason wherfore God will not suffer that any soule deceased, shuld returne vnto vs, and declare what the state of things is in hel, and what great misery is there: herehy (saith he) many errors wold easily spring vp among vs: for many diuels might so take on thē the shape of men, and be transformed into ẏ likenesse of the dead, and say, that they arose frō the dead, and so publish many lying tales, and false opinions of things there don, therby to seduce and hurt vs. Weigh these wordes of Athanasius, I pray thée. Athanasius.

Saint Chrysostome in his nynetéenth Homilie on the eight chapter of saint Matthewes Gospell, hath in maner the same wordes, for hée moueth this question: Why suche as were possessed with Spirites, liued in graues? Therefore (sayeth he) they abode there, to put this false opinion in mens heads, that those persons soules whiche by violent death departed, were turned into Diuels, and so did seruice vnto witches and sothsayers. The which opinion the diuell first broughte in, thereby to diminishe the Martyrs prayse and glorie, that so the Sorcerers might slea those persons, whose wicked trauell and help they vsed; and those matters saith he, are far from truth. For he proueth by the Scripture, that the spirits of the godly are not vnder the power of the Diuels, nor yet do stray abroade after death: then that they woulde retourne vnto theyr owne bodies, if they mighte wander whether they listed. And further, if they didde any seruice to theyr Murtherers, by that meanes they should at their handes Chrisostome.

receiue

receiue a reward for an ill déed and displeasure. By naturall reason also it cannot come to passe, that a mans bodie should be turned into an other bodie, and therefore also the spirit of a man cannot be changed into a diuel.

But among other things which properly belong to our purpose, he saith: If we heare a noyse that saith, I am such a soule, we must thus thinke, that this talke procéedeth of some sleight and subtiltie of the diuel, and that it is not the soule of the dead bodie that speaketh these things, but the diuell that deuiseth them to deceiue the hearers. And by and by he saith, that these are to be counted old wiues words, or rather doting fooles toyes to mocke children withall. For the soule when it is parted from the bodie cannot walke any longer in these parties. For the soules of the iust are in the hands of God. And on the other side, the soules of the wicked after their departure hence, are straightway ledde aside and withdrawne from vs, which may euidently be séene by Lazarus and the rich man. And in another place also the Lord saith: This day will they take thy soule from thée, wherefore the soule cannot heere wander when it is departed from the bodie.

A little afterward he addeth, that it may be proued out of many places of scripture, that the soules of the iust do not here wander after death. For Steuen said, Lord receiue my spirit, and Paule desired to be losed and to depart hence, and to be with Christ.

Also the scripture, as touching the Patriarks death, vseth this phrase, he is laide vnto his fathers, growne vp vnto a good olde age. And that the soules of sinners and wicked men, cannot after their departure, here abide any longer, we may learne by the riche mans words, if we will weigh and consider with our selues what he demanded and could not obtaine. For if after death mens soules might any longer haue their conuersation heere on earth, no doubt the riche man himselfe woulde haue returned as his desire

was

was, and certified his friendes of hell torments. Out of which place of scripture it is most cleare, that soules immediatly vpon their departure from their body, are carried vnto a certaine place, whence they cannot of themselues returne, but néedes must waite there for that terrible day of iudgement.

Also in his second Homily of Lazarus, amōg other things, he saith; It is most plaine, not only by that we haue before rehearsed, but also by this parable, that soules parted from the bodie, haue their abiding here no longer, but are forthwith lead away. For it came to passe (saith he) that he died, and was carried away by the Angels. And not onely the soules of the iust, but of the vniust and wicked, are hence led away, and carried to their proper places, which doth euidently appeare, by another rich man, of which mention is made in the 12. of Luke, to whom the Lord said: Thou foole this night will they take thy soule from thée.

And in his fourth Homily of Lazarus, he plainly teacheth, that we should giue more credite to holy scripture, than to one that came from the dead, or an Angell from Heauen. Herewithall he also sheweth, that the dead do not only make no appearance vnto men liuing, but yeldeth reasons wherefore they do not returne hither, in these words. If God had knowne that the dead being raised might haue profited the liuing, he would neuer haue let passe so great a benefit, who otherwise doth giue and prouide vs al things profitable.

Furthermore he addeth, that if it were requisite still to raise vp dead men, to make relation vnto vs of such things as there are done, this no doubt in continuaunce of time would haue bene neglected: and so the Diuell very easily would haue broached and brought in damnable opinions into the world. For he might often haue made counterfeit sightes, or suborne suche as should faine their selues to be dead and buried, and by and by to present themselues before men, as if they had bin in déede raised from death, and by suche manner of persons might so haue bewitched simple soules, that they would beléeue whatsoeuer he would haue. For if now when there is indéed no such thing, the vaine dreames as it were of men deceased, that haue bin shewed to men in sléepe, haue deceiued, peruerted & distroied many: surely much sooner would the same haue fallen out, if it had bin a thing truly don, & this opinion had preuailed in mens heads. For if many dead persons had retourned backe again into this life, the wicked spirit the diuell would easily haue deuised many sleights and wiles, and brought in much deceit into the life of man. And therfore God hath clean shut vp this dore of deceit, and not permitted any dead man to returne hither & shew what things be don in ẏ other life, least the diuel might gréedily catch this occasiō to plant his fraudulent policies. For when the prophets were, he raised vp false prophets: when the Apostles were, he stirred vp false Apostles: and when Christ apeared in flesh, he sent thither false Christs or antechrists: And when sincere & sound doctrine was taught, he brought into the world corrupt & damnable opiniōs, sowing tares wheresoeuer he came. And therfore although it had come to passe, ẏ dead mē shold return again, yet would he haue counterfeited ẏ same also by his instruments, by some fained raising of the dead through the blinding and bewitching of mens eyes: or otherwise by subborning of some which should feine themselues to be dead (as I said before) he would haue turned all things topsituruie and vtterly haue confounded them. But God who knoweth all things, hath stopped his way, that he should not thus deceiue vs, and of his great mercie towards vs, hath not permitted that at any time any shuld return from thēce and tel vnto mē liuing, such things as there are don, hereby to instruct vs that we should be of this opinion & iudgment, that the scriptures ought to be beleeued before other things whatsoeuer, because that God in them hath most clearly taught

taught vs the doctrine of the last resurrection. Further, by them he hath conuerted the whole worlde, banished errour, brought in truth, and compassed all these things by vile and base fishers, and finally in them hath giuen vs euery where plentifull arguments of his diuine prouidence, &c.

S. Cyril in his 11. booke & 36. ch. vpon S. Iohns gospell saith: We ought to beleeue, that when ẏ soules of holy men are gone away from the bodies, they are commended vnto the goodnesse of God, as into the handes of a most deare father, and ẏ they do not abide in ẏ earth, as some of the Heathens beleeued, vntill such time as they abhorred their graues: neither that they are carried as the soules of wicked men, vnto a place of exceeding torment, which is hel, Christ hauing first prepared this iourney for vs, but that they rather mount vp aloft into their heauenly fathers hands, &c. Cyrillus.

And in the Popes canon law, *Causa 13 quæst. 2. Fatendum*, we read, that many do beleeue that some come from ẏ dead to the liuing: euen as on the other side holy Scripture doth witnesse that Paule was caught vp from the liuing into Paradice. Vpon these wordes the glose saith, that some doo indeed so beleeue, but falsly, sith they be but fansies and vain imaginations, as it is in *Causa. 26. quæstione. 5. Episcopi.* The Glosse of the canō law. *Deut.* 18.

What farther may bee saide to those men that knowe these things, and neuerthelesse do beleeue that soules straie on the earth, I know not: and yet that I may laie out all thinges plainly, I will heere confute their chiefest arguments.

CHAP. VI.

A confutation of those mennes arguments or reasons, which affirme, that dead mens soules doo appeare: And first that is aunswered whiche certaine doo alleage, to witte, that God is omnipotent, and therfore that he can worke contrary to the ordinary course of nature.

FIrst our aduersaries do laie against vs, that by the vsuall and common course of things, the soules of the godly abide in heauen, and the soules of the wicked in hell, vntill the last day, and do not walke at all: but yet that God may dispence with them to appear here sometimes, therby to instruct and admonish vs: And then Samuel did appeare after his death vnto king Saule, and Moses also which forsooke this life many yeres before: Likewise Elias, who was taken vp into heauen in a firie charet, appeared vnto Christ our sauior & his thrée disciples, whom he tooke with him at his transfiguration in the mount. Lazarus also of *Bethanie*, returned from death into ẏ earth, and many other also were raised from death by Christ, his Apostles, and Prophets.

Farther they alledge this, ẏ Christs Apostles beléued, that ẏ spirit or soule either of Christ, (as som of the fathers vnderstand it) or of som other person did appear vnto them. Besides to proue this matter, they alledge places out of the fathers, decrées of councels, & the common report ẏ hath bin bruted of those ẏ returned frō the dead. To al these reasons by Gods assistance, we will briefly and orderly answere.

The soules do returne to instruct men contrary to the common course of nature, by the omnipotent power of god.

As touching ẏ first obiection, ẏ al things are possible vnto God, we deny it not. We graunt then, that God can bring soules out of heauen or hel, and vse their trauell & seruice to instruct, comfort, admonish, & rebuke men. But for ẏ no text or example is found in holy scripture, that euer any soule came from ẏ dead, which did so scoole & warn men: or ẏ the faithfull learned or sought to vnderstand any thing of the soules deceased, we cannot allow ẏ sequele of their reason. We may not of Gods almightie power inferre conclusions to our plesure. For this is a principle holdē in schooles, ẏ the reason doth not truly folow, ẏ is fet from ẏ power of doing, to the déed done. For God doth nothing against himself, or his word writen, to warrāt their reson: they shuld first haue proued, that it was gods wil, ẏ soules shuld return into the erth: for so do holy fathers intreat of gods almightie power.

Tertul-

But first wee ought to make enquirie whether hee hath done them.

S. Ambrose in his first booke of epistles, and 37. epistle, writeth unto Cromatius in this wise: Therefore what is there unpossible unto him? Not that thing which is harde to his power, but that which is contrary to his nature. It is unpossible for him to lye, and this impossibilitie in him, procéedeth not of infirmitie, but of vertue and maiestie. For truth receiueth no lye, neither doth the vertue of God entertaine the vanitie of errour. Reade farther that which followeth in the same place. Ambrose.

Hierome writing to Eustochia, of the preserving of her virginitie, saith: I will boldly auouch this one thing, that though God can do all things, yet can he not restore a virgin after her fall. Hierome.

Augustine in the tenth chapter of his fifth booke *De ciuitate dei* hath: That God is sayd to be omnipotent in doing that he will, and not in doing that he will not. Againe he addeth: Gods power is not hereby any whit diminished, when we say, that God cannot die or be deceiued. And immediatly, therefore he cannot do some things because he is omnipotent, &c. Augustine.

Theodoret also teacheth us, that it may not absolutely without exception be pronounced, that all things are possible unto God. For who so doth precisely affirme this, doth in effect say this much, that all things both good and bad are possible unto God, &c. Wherefore féeble is that obiection of theirs: God can sende soules unto men, to teache and admonish them: therefore these spirites that praye ayde, bee soules that come out of Heauen or Hell. Theodoret.

Deut.18. which the Lorde thy God giueth thee, doo not thou learne to doo after their abhominable rites, and vsages of those nations. Let none bee founde among you, that maketh his sonne or his daughter to passe through the fire: nor a diuiner that doth foreshew things to come, nor a sorcerer, nor a witche, nor a charmer, nor one that consulteth with spirits, nor an inchanter, nor a Magitian, nor one that raiseth vp the dead. For the Lorde doeth abhorre all that doo such things: and because of these abhominations, the Lord thy God hath cast them out before thee. Be thou therfore sound and perfect before the Lord thy God: and by and by he promiseth to send them that great Prophet whom they should heare.

Esay 8. In the 8. of Esay, it is written: If they say vnto you, enquire of them which haue a spirite of diuination, which whisper and murmure softely in youre eares to deceiue you. Should not euery people or nation enquire at their God? what shall they go from the liuing to the dead? Let them goe vnto the lawes testimonie, suche as haue no light, should they not speake according to this word, which who so should contemne, shall be hardened and hunger, &c. Hereby we doo vnderstand, that vnder a great penaltie God hath precisely forbidden, that we shoulde learne and searche out any thing of the dead. He alone woulde be taken for our sufficient scholemaister. In the Gospell we

Luke.22. read: They haue Moses and the Prophets, let them heare them. Vnto these may be added testimonies out of the Apostles writings, that God doth not send vs soules hither to informe vs. The common and ordinarie way whereby it pleaseth God to deale with vs, is his word. Therwithall

should

[illegible]
more in his proper place.

CHAP. VII.

That the true Samuell did not appeare to the Witch in Endor.

Now touching yͤ examples by them commonly alleaged, which do think that the souls of yͤ dead do return again unto the liuing upō the earth: I wil first intreat of Samuels apparition, of which matter now adaies there is great contentiō and reasoning. And (as I trust) I shall proue by strong arguments, that very Samuell himselfe did not appeare in soule and bodie, neither that his bodie was raised up by the sorcerers, which perchance then was rotten & consumed unto dust in the earth, neither yͭ his soule was called up, but rather some diuellish spirit. First the author of the two bookes of Samuel, saith: that Saule did aske counsell of the Lord, and that he would not answere him, neither by Visions, nor by Vrim, nor by his Prophets. Wherefore if God disdained by his Prophets yet liuing, and other ordinary wayes to giue answer unto him, whom he had alreadie rejected, we may easily coniecture, that he would much lesse haue raised a dead Prophet to make him answere. And the rather, for that as we haue a little before said, the lawe of God hath seuerely by a great threatning, forbidden to learne ought of the dead, and would not haue us to searche for the trueth of them, nor that any man use diuination by Spirites, and suche other diuellishe Artes. Secondly, if verie Samuell indeede appeared, that muste of necessitie haue come to passe, either by the

will

will of God, or by the worke of arte Magike. But Gods wilt was not that Samuel should retourne. For he hath condemned Necromancie, and would not haue vs to aske counsel at the dead: and that the spirit of God did that which was contrary herevnto, or did permit the Saints to do it, or was present with them that did ought contrary thereto, it may not be graunted. And that those things were done by the force and operation of Art Magike, wée can not affirme. For the wicked spirit hath no rule or power ouer the soules of the faithfull to bring them out of their places when he lust, sith they be in the hand of God, and the bosome of Abraham, nay (which is lesse) he hath no power ouer filthy and vncleane swine, for he was driuen (as we
Math 8. reade in the viii. chapter of Mathew) to beg leaue, before he could enter into the heard of swine: and how then should he haue any power ouer the soule of man? yet can it not be denied, that God somtimes for certain causes doth giue the Diuell and his seruants, Magitians & Necromancers, power to do many things, as to hurt and lame man and beast, and to worke other straunge things. But that God doth giue the Diuell leaue to raise dead bodies, or to call, bring forth, or driue away soules especially out of Heauen, it hath no grounde at all in Scripture, neither can there be any reasonable cause alledged, wherefore God would or should giue the Diuell licence to do these things contrary to the vsuall and common order, yea and againe his owne expresse commaundement. For vayne and childishe is the cause heereof that is giuen of some men, that Samuell shoulde appeare to terrifie and astonishe Saule: as if God coulde not haue feared him by other waies and meanes. Was he not before vtterly abashed and dismayed? Thirdly, if Samuell were brought backe, the same was done either by his will and consent, or without the same, but that he did fréely and of his owne accord obey the sorcerers, no man I thinke is so blinde to imagine.

For

For that were utterly repugnant to the Lawe of God, that hee shoulde confirme Witchcraft and Sorcerie by his example. If the Witch had called for Samuell, whilest he liued, doubtlesse he would not haue approached unto hir. And how then can we beléeue that he came to hir after his death? We may not so say, that the Witch compelled him to resort to hir against his will: for the Diuel hath no power ouer the soules of the godly, and Magike of it selfe is of no force. Heathenish superstition no doubt it is, that wordes uttered by Magitians, after their peculiar manner, or figures drawne, should haue suche a secret and hidden operation. For the Heathens beléeued that they could with a certain set stile & number of words, bring and draw downe Iupiter out of Heauen. Wherfore they termed him Iupiter Elicius. There are also certaine superstitious persons in these our daies, which go about to cure diseases by certaine rites of blessings, and by coniurings. Some hang aboute their neckes certaine scrolles of Paper, in which ther are written diuers strange words, but whether wordes of themselues haue any force at all, reade Plinie in his 28. booke, and 2. chapter, and Cælius Rhodiginus in his 16. booke and 16. chapter of Antiquities.

Wordes of themselues haue no force.

Iupiter Elicius.

Plinie.

Fourthely, if very Samuel himselfe had appeared, hée would not haue bene worshipped of Saule. For we reade in the 19. and 22. chapter of the Reuelation, that Iohn would haue worshipped the angell, whiche had opened unto him great misteries, but the Angell of God forbad him so to do. Some héere aunswere, that Saule ment not to giue unto the Prophet, the honor that was due unto God, but onely a certeine outward and ciuill worship, such as we are wont to yéelde unto honest men, and suche as haue well deserued of the Churche and common weale. For they say, that the Hebrue word Schachah there used, doth signifie to bend the knée, and to fall downe at a mans féete: which kinde of worship we reade, that Abigael and

Apoc. 19. 21.

Nathan the Prophet gaue vnto King David. And Paule also in the 12. Chapter of his Epistle to the Romanes teacheth, that we should honour one another. Thomas of Aquine intreating of those two places that I euen nowe recited out of the Reuelation, saieth, that Iohn ment not to worship the Angell, with the worship properly called Latria, but with an other kind of worship termed Dulia, that is to say, that Iohns will was not to withdrawe from God, the honor due vnto him, but to worship the Angell that was sent from God, only with a ciuill and outward homage: and yet the Angell would not so far condiscend vnto him. In the new Testament the 10. chap. of the Acts of the Apostles, we read that Cornelius met with Peter, fell downe at his feet and worshipped him, yet, so as he had bene an embassadour from God and not God himselfe, and yet Peter lifted him vp & said, Arise for I my selfe am a man also. He said not to Cornelius thou doest well herein: nor as his worthie Vicare (with a mischiefe) is wont to do, proffered his foote vnto him to kisse. We may read also that Elias disciples worshipped Elizeus that succeeded into his office, to which place the word to bowe the knee, or fall downe, is vsed. But whether the Prophet did except and allowe this kind of reuerence or no, there is no expresse mention. Breefly, it is not likely that the Prophet would haue suffered the King to fall downe at his feete.

Rom. 12.

Actes. 12.

Fiftly, if he had bin the true *S*amuel, he would no doubt haue exhorted *S*aule to repentance, and willed him to wait for aide from God, to put his whole confidence in him, or at least way, to haue giuen him some comforte, or counselled him to fight againste his enimies with more courage. For though the Prophets do often chide and threaten men, yet do they againe reuiue and solace them. Now because this *S*amuel doth beate no other thing into his heade, but that God was displeased with him, and had alredy forsaken him, we may not beleeue that he was the true, but a meere counter-

Testimonies out of the Fathers touching

counterfeit Samuel. Sixtly, the auncient Fathers write, that the true Samuel was not séene. Samuels appearing.

Tertullian in his booke *De anima* saith, that the Diuill did there represent Samuels soule, God forbid (saith he) that we should beléeue that the diuel can drawe the soule of any Saint, much lesse a Prophet, out of his proper place, sith we are taught that Sathan doeth transfourme himselfe into an Angel of light, and much sooner into a man of light: who also will auouch himselfe to be God, and doo notable signes and wonders to seduce, if it were possible, the very elect. S. Augustine is not alwaies of one iudgement touching this apparition: in his second booke to Simplician Bishop of *Millaine*, and the third question thereof, hée graunteth that by the dispensation of Gods will, it might so come to passe, that the spirite of some holy Prophet, should consent to present it selfe in the sight of the King, to come out of his owne place, and to speak with him, but not to doo this by constrainte, or by the vertue of Arte Magike, which might haue any power ouer it: but thereby to shew it selfe obedient to the secret dispensation of God: and yet he doth not dissemble, that a better answer may be giuen, to witte, that the spirite of Samuel was not truly and indéed raised vp from his rest, but rather some vain vision and counterfeit illusion, that should be brought to passe by the diuels practise, which the Scripture therefore doth tearme by the name of Samuel, because the same is woont to call the images and similitudes of things, by the names of the things themselues. For who is he (saith Augustine) that will be afraid to call a man painted, a man, considering that without staggering, we are accustomed to giue eache thing his proper name, assoone as we behold the picture of the same: as when we take the viewe of a painted table, or wall, we say straightway, this is Tullie; this is Salust, hée Achilles, that other Hector, this is the floud called *Symois*, that place tearmed *Rome*, whereof these

Tertullian.

Augustine.

an Angell of light, and fashioneth his ministers like vnto the Ministers of righteousnesse.

In his booke *De octo Dulcitij questionibus*, the 6. question therof, he vttereth all this in as many wordes, & in his booke *De cura pro mortuis gerenda*, he writeth that some are sent, from the deade to the liuing: as on the other side, Paule was rapt vp from the liuing vnto Paradice: hée addeth there the example of Samuel being dead, which did fore-shewe to Saule, things, that afterwardes should come to passe. He saith further, that this place may otherwise be vnderstanded, and that certaine faithfull men haue bene of this iudgement, that it was not Samuel, but that some spirit fit for such wicked practises, had taken vpon him his shape and similitude. And in other places, as we will shew hereafter, he affirmeth, that there is a figure conteined in those wordes, because the name of the thing is giuen vnto the Image that doth but represent the same: and that it was not Samuel that appeared, but some diuellish spirit.

Other Fathers of the Churche haue written nothing particularly of this storie, so far as I know, but in certaine places of their workes, they teache generally that good spirites are not pulled backe into the earth by Magicall Art. Of Iustine and Gregorie I will speake anone. In the very Papall decrées, 26. question 5. chapter, *Nec mirum*, it is written that it was not Samuel, but rather some wicked spirite that appeared to Saule: And that it were a great offence that a man should beléeue the plaine wordes of the storie without some farther meaning, for how saith he could it come to passe, that a man from his byrth holie

The Popes decrees.

and

This is the Diuels legerdemaine, to make [illegible], as though he had power ouer good men, thereby the rather to deceiue many. He there farther addeth, that the Historiographers doo set forth both Saules minde, and Samuels state, and also those things which were sayd and seene, omitting this, whether they were true or false. And other words followe, which who so list to see more of that matter, may there reade.

But here Nicolas Lyras iudgement (which in his Commentaries on the bookes of the Kings, mainteineth the contrary opinion) should bee little weighed and regarded of vs. Where he noteth, that the place by vs euen now alleaged, is not written according to the censure of the Church, though it be found in the Popes lawe, for otherwise saith he, they which ensued in latter times, wold not haue written contrary to ye same, for many of those things concerning which men haue written otherwise in latter times, were neuerthelesse set forth to the world, to be beleeued, as the very expresse and sound iudgement of the whole Christian Church, because they were put in the Popes booke of Decretalls. Lyra.

CHAP. VIII.

A Confutation of their arguments, which would haue Samuel himselfe to appeare.

WE will now come to the Confutatiō of their Arguments, which maintaine, that very Samuel himselfe appeared to the Sorcerers, for he that rightly ouerthroweth his aduersaries arguments, is supposed by the same meanes to confirme his owne cause. The cheefest

Eccle.46. 46. chapter of Ecclesiasticus, where these wordes are found. Samuel before his death made protestation before God, and before his annointed, that he tooke from no man his substance, no not so much as the value of a shoe, and no man could then reproue him. And after his death he prophesied, and tolde the King of his ende. From the earth he lift vp his voyce, and shewed that the wickednesse of the people should perish.

This place somewhat troubled S. Augustine, and other godly Fathers. For if the Diuell onely appeared, and not Samuel, howe is it there saide that he slept, that is, died, for the Diuel neyther sléepeth nor dieth. Hereunto I may shape this answere, that this booke is not to be nombred among the Canonicall bookes of the olde Testament, and that Doctrine in controuersies, cannot bee proued by the authoritie thereof, the whiche Saint Augustine, also confesseth in his booke *De cura pro mortuis agenda.*

But howsoeuer that be credited as true or false, I answere them plainly, that Iesus the Sonne of Syraches intent was, to alleage the Storie literally, as the wordes lye, and not by reason to debate the matter, whether Samuel truly appeared or no. Hée speaketh there according to the opinion of Saule and the Witche, which thought that Samuel himselfe was raised. Further they say, that hée which appeared vnto Saule, is sometimes expresly and in plaine wordes called Samuel. And an vnséemely matter it were, making much for the reproach of so great a Prophet, if his name had bene applied vnto the Diuel. If say they, it had not bene Samuel, but some wicked spirite, the scripture would in some one word or other, haue noted the same.

To

To this Argument first I aunswere, that euen in our common spéeche, it is an vsuall phrase by the figure *Metonymia*, to terme the Image by the name of the thing, that it presenteth. So we terme the Armes and Ensigne of a Noble man, by the name of that Lord himselfe, that giueth those Armes. We say, this is Iulius Cæsar, Nero, Saint Peter, Saint Paule, or here thou maist sée the Cities of *Tigurine*, and *Argentorat*, also the Duke of *Saringe*, whereas in déed they are only their counterfeits, or Armes, and signes of honour.

In a Comedie or Tragedie, we call this man Saule, that Samuel, an other Dauid, whereas they do but betoken and represent their personages. So saith Virgil, in his first booke of Æneidos: They wonder at Æneas gifts, and haue Iulius in admiration. And yet was it not Iulius or Ascanius, but Cupid feining himselfe to be Iulius, whereby he might the easiler pearce the heart of the ignorant Quéene, with his dart of Loue.

Sainte Augustine in his seconde Booke and ninthe chap. *De mirabilibus scripturæ* saieth, that holie Scripture doeth sometimes applie the verie names of thinges to the Images and similitudes of the same. Hée alleageth there this example, that the foule spirit is called Samuel, because hée did falsely beare Saule in hande, that hée was Samuell: whiche fraude of the Diuell, coulde no waies turne to Samuels reproach. For who would say, that it should be a reproach for an honest man, if some knaue would terme himselfe by his name, as if he were he himselfe.

The false prophets sayde, they were true Prophets, and Gods seruauntes, yea (which is more) they feined themselues to be the verie Messias, the Sonne of God. And that Scripture doth not so muche as in one word make mention, that this was verie Samuell in déede, but

but rather some spirite; we must thinke that it so came to passe, for this cause, that all men by the Lawe of God might vnderstand, that Magike and enquirie of things at the dead, did much displease God. Saule himselfe before by the counsell and motion of Samuel, slewe all the Magitians that he could any where finde. And God is not accustomed in this wise to interprete Figuratiue spéeches: for many of them are soone descried by such as giue diligent héed to them. A vaine and superfluous spéech it were, if a man woulde say that is Peter, this is the Image of Peter, whiche by a Figure, is called by the name of Peter.

Furthermore, holie Scripture doth vse to speake of things, rather according to the opinion and iudgement of men, than according to the substaunce and true béeing which they haue indéede. So Jesus is called the Sonne of Ioseph, and Iosephe named his father, whereas notwithstanding, our Sauiour Christ Jesus, was borne of a chaste and vnspotted Uirgine, without any helpe of man. And yet neuerthelesse many of the Jewes, imagined, that

1.*Cor*.1. he was the Sonne of Ioseph. In the 1.Cor.1. the Gospel it selfe is named foolishnesse, because that men did account the great wisedome of God but as méere foolishnesse. So in the

1.*Cor*.10. first Epistle to the Corinthians, and tenth chapter, the scripture tearmeth them gods, which be nothing lesse than so

Iere.10. *Psal*.96. indéed. And that for this cause onely, for that the Heathen tooke them for gods, and so did worship them. Euen so the scripture doeth tearme the Diuell Samuel, because Saule thought him to be Samuel in very déed.

An other reason they vse, that Samuel foreshewed vnto

VVhether the diuel forknow of thinges to come.

Saule suche thinges as afterwardes should come to passe: as that the Philistians should in battayle ouerthrowe his Armie, and he and his sonnes togither be slaine. And all these thinges came to passe according to his Prophesie. And say they, the Diuel knoweth not, neither can he foretell

sultations, priuie practises, and warlike preparation on both sides. He sawe that the Israelites were slenderly addressed vnto battaile, and vtterly daunted of courage. Besides this, Samuel had a little before threatned Saule with Gods heauie wrath and vengeance, and that Dauid should be aduaunced to the kingly throne, whereby he might easily gather what would ensue, and that Saule must néedes giue place to Dauid. And if the euent had bene otherwise, yet he knew that Saule with this prophesie would be quite dismaied, and driuen to dispaire: which thing must néedes well content and please Sathan, who laieth his baites day and night to intrappe men.

The Diuell doth not presently vnderstand things to come, and therefore he giueth doubtfull answeres to such as séeke oracles of him: As when he said, Which being doubtfully spoken, may be vnderstood either of subuerting other kingdomes, or loosing his owne.

Crœsus perdet Halin transgressus plurima regna.

That is, Cresus passing ouer the riuer, Halis shall ouerturne many kingdomes. And yet oftentimes he gathereth one thing no otherwise than by an other. Hereof writeth Augustine in the 26. 27. 28. Chapters of his Bóke *De Anima*. The Diuel is one which hath bene long beaten in experience, the which thing in all affaires and matters is of very great force. For olde and practised souldiours doo by and by foresée to what issue things will come, but yoong men, and such as want experience, doo not forthwith espie out the euent of each enterprise. Moreouer, the Diuels are very actiue, and can sóne dispatch their matters. The Marriners knowe when windes and stormes will arise. Husbandmen also are not destitute of their prognostications. The skilfull Astronomer can many yeares before ex-

 actly

actly foretell when there will happen an Eclipse of the Sunne and Moone. The Phisitian by the criticall dayes, pulse, and urine, can lightly iudge whether his patient shall liue or no: builders see before hand when an house will fall, and a practised souldioure can straightwayes iudge who shall winne the victorie. And what maruaile then may it be, if the Diuell an olde trained souldiour, can sometimes forshew some certaine thing? Shall we be of this minde, that so many yeares experience hath broughte them no knowledge at all? Otherwhiles he telleth things which be true indeed, and yet to no other end, but that he may thereby purchase a certaine credite unto his lying, to seduce the ignorant.

For euen that counterfeit Samuell, made wise, as if he had taken it in very ill part, that Saule did so molest and disquiet him, and that he should be forced to talke with him: he useth farther the words as it were of Samuel himselfe. And hereof it commeth, that many gather, he was the true Samuel indeede. But what doth not Sathan deuise, to deceiue men, and to force them unto desperation? Here I could alleage examples of suche as haue bin perswaded, that they sawe and heard this and that man, and moreouer knewe them perfectly by their speeche: whereas they haue afterwards had euident intelligence, that they were at that time many miles distant from them. So craftie is the Diuell, and knoweth how to worke these and many other feates.

There are farther, diuers places alleaged out of the auncient Fathers, that seeme to make for them, whiche affirme that true Samuell appeared unto Saule. But these places wee haue before for the moste parte aunswered. For albeit Augustine in some places moue a doubte, whether it were the true Samuel or no, yet in certaine other places hee lyketh and beste alloweth their opinion, who denie Samuel to haue appeared at all,

all, taking rather that kinde of speech, for tropicall and figuratiue.

Iustine the Martir, who is one of the most auncient Fathers, reasoning against Trypho a Jewe, writeth in his *Colloquio*, that the couetous Sorceresse at Saules commaundement raysed vp *Samuels* soule. And no man shoulde maruaile hereat, sith that the selfesame Author doeth by and by adde, that he is of this iudgement, that all the soules of Prophettes and iust menne are subiect vnto suche power as a man may in verie deed beleeue, to haue bene on this greedie and subtile Witche. But this none of the Fathers will graunt him. Other Greeke writers also, whiche in their tender yeares applied their mindes to Philosophie, and not to the studie of holy Scriptures, and afterwardes were conuerted to Christianitie, do sette forthe in their writings certaine opinions which are not agreeable to the word of God. Wherefore it neede not seeme a straunge thing to any manne, that Iustine the Martire in some pointes had his errors. Iustinus.

The same Authour in *Responsionibus ad Orthodoxos*, question 52. mainteineth the contrary assertion. For, saith he, whatsoeuer things were done by that hungry Witche, were indeede the workes of the Diuell, who did so dazle the eyes of such as beheld him, that it seemed vnto them, they sawe Samuel himselfe, when in verie deede he was not there. But the truth of his wordes proceeded from God, who gaue the diuel power to appeare vnto the Sorceresse, and to declare vnto her, that which should afterwards come to passe, &c.

If any man obiect that this worke is not rightly ascribed vnto Iustine, (for so muche as he doth make mention of Origen, and Ireneus the Martire, whereas notwithstanding hee him selfe was martyred before them. And farther, speaketh of the Manichees,

who were in their ruffe long after this time. Hereunto we answere, that if this booke were not written by Iustine, yet (as may appeare) some other learned Clarke wrote that worke, whose authoritie might carry away as great credit as Iustines, sith that the same doth fully agree with holie scripture. Furthermore we may set against Iustine, other holy Fathers, as Tertullian and Chrysostome, of whom we haue before spoken, who haue by holy scripture instructed vs, that it was not Samuell indeede whiche appeared vnto
Gregorius. Saule. We will hereafter say somewhat of Gregorie, who no doubt was a learned and godly Father, but yet too simple and light of beleefe.

And the Fathers themselues deny, that a man should subscribe vnto their opinion in ought that they doo maintaine and auouche without the warrant of Gods word. The Popes out of Augustine written in their Decrees, Quest. 9. ca. Noli, that a man should credit none of the Fathers except he proued his saying out of holy Scriptures. But in these dayes many cull nothing out of their bookes but errours, and whatsoeuer they maintaine by good testimony of the holy scriptures, that they reiect and disanull: in which point they do fitly resemble those children, who only in things wicked and euil, imitate their good parents: for good men also haue their faultes.

CHAP. IX.

Whether the Diuell haue power to appeare vnder the shape of a faithfull man?

BUt thou doest demand whether the Diuill can represent the likenesse of some faithfull man deceased? Hereof we neede
2. Cor. 11. not doubt at all. For in the 2. Cor. 11. S. Paul witnesseth, that sathan transformeth himselfe into the shape & fashion of

of an Angell of light. Sathan by nature is a spirit, and is therefore tearmed an Angel, because God vseth to send him to bring that thing to passe which he thinketh best. So in the second of Kings. 22. Chapter, an euil angell was sent forth to Ahabs destruction, to be a lying spirit in the mouth of 400. false prophets. This was an angell of errour and darkenesse: who yet in outwarde shewe could resemble a good Angell, that he might so guide the counsell of Baalls worshippers, who no doubt vaunted themselues, as if they had bene gathered togither by Gods holy spirit. If sathan be then so skilfull, can he not counterfait and faine himselfe to be some holy man, by resembling his wordes, voyce, iesture, and such other things? 2. Reg. 22.

Amongst the Gentiles he hath done miraculous Actes, perswading them to thinke, that soules by Arte Magicke were called vp, and compelled to giue answere of secrete and hidden things that were to come. And therefore not only in publike, but also priuate affaires, if they seemed to be any thing hard vnto them, they consulted with Magitians and Sorcerers, and had moreouer recourse sometimes vnto Oracles.

Tertullian in his booke *De Anima* mentioneth; that there were some euen in his dayes, which professed they could raise vp and reclaime soules from the hellishe habitation. And he calleth Arte Magike, the second Idolatrie, in the whiche the diuels do as well fayne themselues to bee dead men, as they do in the other to bee Gods. So do these subtle spirites larke, and do many straunge things vnder the pretence of deade men. He addeth, that Magike is thought to conuey soules out of Hell which lye there in rest, and to represent them vnto our sighte, by reason that it sheweth a vaine vision, and counterfeiteth the shape of a bodie. Neither is it a harde matter for him to bleare and beguile the outward eyes, who can easily darken and dazell the inwarde sighte of the minde. The Serpents that Tertullian.

were brought forth by the inchaunters rods, seemed to the *Egiptians* to be bodies, but the truth of Moises deuoured vp the Magitians lye. *Simon* also and Elimas the Magitians, did many signes and wonders against the Apostles &c. He addeth, that euen in his time those heretikes named properly Simonistes of *Simon* the Magitian, the first author of that sect, did with suche greate presumption aduaunce their arte, that they professed they coulde rayse from the dead, euen the soules of the Prophets. &c.

Lactantius. Lactantius in the 2. booke & 17. chap. De origine erroris, writeth, that euill angels lurking vnder the names of the dead, did wound and hurt the liuing, that is, they toke vnto themselues the names of Iupiter and Iuno, whome the heathens toke to be gods, or as we now say, they toke vnto them the names of S. Sebastian, Barbara, and others.

Idem. In the 7. booke and 13. chap. he saith, that the Magitians with certaine inchauntmentes did call soules out of hell. But this may not so be understood, that Lactantius was of this iudgement, that they by their wicked arts did bring the soules back again into their dead bodies: but that they did so vaunt and boast that they had raised vp this and that soule. He also confuteth the opinion of the Ethnikes, prouing by the testimonie of the very Magitians, whom they highly reuerenced, that the soule was immortall. These men affirmed and taught, that they did call vp soules from the dead; the which point, euen those of the Gentiles beleued, who notwithstanding thought, that the soule did straightway die with the bodie.

Iustine the Martire, in the second Apologie which he wrote in the defence of Christians, hath these wordes: I will (saith he) say the truth: In times past wicked angels through vain visions deceiued women, and children, and with straunge and monstrous sightes made men afraide, by whiche meanes they often wrong that oute of folishe and rude persons, which by reason they coulde neuer get of of them. And therefore not knowing that these were the Diuels engines and policies tending to delude them, they by one consent termed the workers of these slie conueyances, by the name of Gods, assigning to eache of them their proper names, as best pleased themselues. &c.

Afterwardes in the same Apologie hee exhorteth the Heathens, that they would not deny mens soules after this life to be endued with sense, but at the least way, would giue credit to their owne Necromancers, who teach that they call vp mens soules. Also let them beleeue those y affirme they haue bin vexed with spirits of dead men, which persons the common people term furious & frantike bodies. In Augustin *De ciuitate dei*, many such things be cōteined.

Now what dreadfull, strange, and maruellous ceremonies they vsed when they went about by their Magicall Artes to call vp the soules of the dead, a man may see in the sixth booke of Lucan the Poet: where he setteth forth how Erictho, a famous Witche in *Thessaly*, reuiued and restored a souldiour to life againe, who was lately slaine before. Which act he did at the request of *Sextus* Pompeius, that so he might by him learne what would be the issue of the battaile fought at *Pharsalia*.

This kind of Magike they properly terme Necromancie, or Phycomancie, which is wrought by raising vp the spirits and soules of the dead. Of which there were diuerse sorts. For sometime appeared vnto men the whole bodies of the dead, but at an other time onely ghostes and spirits: and often nothing was heard; sauing onely a certaine obscure voyce.

Plutarch in the life of Cimon, (as hee is translated by Ioachimus Camerarius, in the Preface on Plutarches bookes, *De oraculis quæ defecerint, & de conscriptia figura, Ei, Delphis*) writeth, that Pausanias, when he had taken the Citie of *Bizance*; sent for Cleonice, a mayden of noble parentage, to haue vnhonest company with her.

Whom

stumbled on the candlesticke,and ouerthrew it against her will , as he laie a sleepe in his bedde , who being troubled with the sodaine noyse, drew a sword that laie by him, and therewith slewe the virgine ; as she had bene his enemie, which went priuily to set vpon him. But she being thus slaine with that deadly stroake, would neuer suffer Pausanias to take his quiet rest , but in a vision appearing vnto him in the night season , denounced sentence of hatred against this noble captaine,in these wordes.

Στεῖχε δίκης ἆσσον, μάλα τοι κακὸν ἀνδράσιν ὕβρις.

which is,

Answere to the lawe , for wrong is an euill thing vnto all men. This heinous deede of Pausanias was verie greeuously taken of all his companions, who therefore vnder the conduction of captaine Cymo sette on him, and chased him out of *Thracia*. And thus hauing lost the Citie of *Bizance*, when (as it is reported) the sight continued in troubling him , he fledde vnto *Necyomantium* , at *Heraclea*, where the soule of Cleonices being called vp , hee by intreatie pacified her displeasure. Shee did there both present her selfe vnto his sight , and also told him, it should shortly come to passe , that the euill towardes him should cease, assone as he came to *Sparta*. Hereby priuily intimating his death, &c. This Pausanias did at the first soberly and discreetely demeane himselfe, but afterwardes beeing pussed vp with such victories as he had obteined, he ruled and raigned lyke a verie Tyraunt. Wherefore when the Magistrates called Ephori, would haue committed him to prison, he tooke Sanctuarie in a Temple, where he was shut

> Ephori amõgest the Lacedemonians were Magistrates, who in certaine cases were

that vp vntill he famiſhed through hunger.

I might here heape togither many ſuch like Hiſtories, to proue euidently what this Samuel was. In other matters alſo, if God licence him, the Diuel is not deſtitute of power, and how craftie and readie he is for all aſſaies, experience doth well declare.

aboue kings, vnto whom appeales were made from kings: euen as amongſt the Romans, they appealed from the Conſuls to the Tribunes.

Furthermore graunt that, wherin the pith and ſtrength of the queſtion doth conſiſt (which can neuer be proued by ſcripture) that God did permit *Samuell* to returne and to propheſie of things to come after his death, yet will it not thereof follow, that ſuch viſions ſhould now be ſhewed alſo, or that thoſe things ſhould be out of hand credited and done which they commaund.

God in times paſt, did often in viſible ſhape ſend his Angels vnto men, but now we heare not that many are ſent vnto men, neither indeed is the ſame neceſſary. When the Apoſtles liued here, many notable miracles were done, but now for certaine good cauſes, they ceaſe and fall away, for whatſoeuer is neceſſary for our ſaluation, is expreſly conteined in the word of God. Theſe notes touching Samuels appearing, may ſuffiſe.

CHAP. X.

Moyſes and Elias appeared in the Mounte vnto Chriſt our Lord: many haue bene raiſed from the dead both in bodie and ſoule, and therefore ſoules after they are departed, may returne on earth againe.

IN like manner they obiect vnto vs, out of the 17. of Matthew, that Moſes and Helias were ſeene in the Mount, (which is called by the olde Writers *Tabor*,) with our Lord Ieſus, by the Apoſtles whom he had choſen for the ſame purpoſe, and that they did ſpeake with him. Luke telleth of what matters they com-

Mat. 17. Moſes & Elias appeared.

communed with him, to wit of his death, that is ꝧ death of the crosse. Thereupon they gather, that the soules of dead men may come againe into earth & appeare unto men: we haue graunted before that God is able to send soules again into the earth, but that it is his will so to do, or that it is necessary especially at these dayes, is not yet proued. Moses and Helias appeared not to al the Apostles but only to thre, neither did they speake to those thre, they brought no new Doctrine, they commanded them not to build Churches in their honor, or to do any such like thing, whether that their soules came alone, or their bodies: also sure it is, they were not sent to the Apostles, but to Christ onely.

It was very necessary, that they which should be Christs witnesses, shuld very wel understand, that both ꝧ Law and the Prophets, do beare record unto our Sauior Christ, that he shuld die for the world, and come again in the latter day, to raise up the dead bodies, to glorifie them, & to carry them with him, into eternal blisse. And for this cause, God would haue these two excellent Prophets sene of the Apostles.

Lazarus came againe on earth. *Iohn* 11.

Lazarus soule did not only appeare, but he came againe both in bodie & soule, as Iohn witnesseth in his 11. chap. he is as it were a sure token, of our true resurrection, which shall be in the last day, as also others, which our Sauiour Christ, the Apostles, and in auncient time, the Prophets haue raised from the dead. You shall neuer read that either Lazarus, or any other haue tolde where they were while they were dead, or what kind of being there is in the other world, for these things are not to be learned and knowne of the dead, but out of the word of God.

The like may be said to that which is in the 27. chap. of S. Matthew, that when Christ suffered on the Crosse, the graues were opened, & afterwards on the day of his resurrection, many dead bodies did arise, & appeared to many at *Hierusalem*. The soules of the dead did not only appeare, neither did they warne the liuing, or command them to do

Matth. 27. At the resurrectiō of christ many rose againe.

this

this or that for ŷ deads sake, to wit, either to pray for them, or to go on pilgrimage to saints, &c. But ŷ dead with their soules and bodies togither, came into the earth: for hereby God would shewe, that he by his death hath ouercome and destroyed death to the faithfull, and that at the last day their soules and bodies shall be knit togither, and liue with God for euer. Now what these holy men were that rose againe, and whether they remained any time in this present life, or died againe, or went with Christ into heauen, looke the iudgement of S. Augustine in his 99. Epist. to Euodius, and his 3. booke *De mirabilibus. cap.* 13. Augustine.

To these we may ioyne that which Ruffinus writeth in his ecclesiastical historie, 1. boke, 5. chap. and which Socrates repeateth in his first booke & 12. chap. touching Spiridion Bishop of *Cyprus*. He had a daughter called Irene, with whome a certaine friend of hers left gorgious apparrell, she being more wary than needed, hid it in the ground, and within a while died. Not long after commeth this man ŷ owed the apparel, & hearing say ŷ maiden was dead, goeth to her father whom somtimes he accuseth, & sometimes intreateth. The old father supposing this mans losse to be his owne calamitie, commeth to his daughters graue, & there calleth vpō god, beseeching him ŷ he wold shew him before ŷ time, the resurrection which is promised. And his hope was not in vaine, for the virgin being reuiued, apeared to her father, & shewed the place wher she had hid the apparel, & so departed again. Spiridion raised his daughter. Ruffinus.

I wil not deny this thing to be true. For the like historie hath Augustine in his 137. epist. A certain yong man which had an euill name accused Boniface, Augustines priest, ŷ he inticed him to filthinesse. Now whē ŷ matter could neither be proued, nor disproued by sufficient reasons: both of them were bid to go to the graue of one Felix a Martyr, that by a miracle the truth might be knowen. They had not bin sent, vnlesse before this time also some secrete matters had bene knowne by this meanes: it may be wel answered, that they were good, or rather euil angels which did appeare.

CHAP. XI.

Whether the holy Apostles thought they sawe a mans soule, when Christ sodeinly appeared vnto them after his Resurrection.

Luke 24. WE reade in the 24. Chapter of Saint Lukes Gospell, that two Disciples whiche returned from *Emaus* to *Hierusalem*, told the Apostles, that they had séene Christ aliue againe, and whiles they yet spake, the Lorde stood in the midst of them, and saide vnto them, Peace be vnto you: but they being amazed & afraid, thought they sawe a spirit. &c.

Christs Disciples supposed they sawe a ghost. Out of this some go about to proue, that the Apostles beléeued that spirits or soules did walke and appeare vnto men, and that they themselues did thinke they sawe the spirit of Christ (as certaine of the old Writers do expound it) or else some other mans spirit.

This argument may be answered two wayes. First if they thought they sawe a soule, they thought a misse. But they were no lesse deceiued with the common sorte now, than when they thought Christ would raise vp an outward and earthly kingdome, in which they should be chiefe.

Many kindes of spirites. Secondly, it may be, that they supposed they sawe an euill or good Angell, for there are more kindes of spirites than one. There is a spirit that created all things, to wit, God the Father, the Sonne, and the holy Ghost. Againe there be spirits that be created, as good and euil Angels, as also the soules of men, which either are in the bodie, or by death seuered from the bodie, and abide either in euerlasting life, or in eternall damnation. As touching the state of soules in Purgatorie, where they are prepared to the heauenly iourney, and of *Limbus puerorum*, there is nothing extant in holy scripture.

It is manifest in scripture, that God appeared vnto the holy Patriarches, to the Prophets, to Kings and others, in diuers visions and formes, and that he shewed himself vnto them and spake with them. Iacob sawe a ladder reache from the earth vp to heauen, and God leaning on it. Isaias sawe the Lord sitting vpon an high throne. Daniel sawe an olde man sitting, and his sonne comming vnto him and receiuing all power of him.

Tertullian and other holy Fathers do teach, that the son of God, which at the appointed time should take vpon him humaine flesh, did appear vnto the Patriarches in an angelicall shape.

When Iohn Baptist did baptise our Sauiour in *Iordan*, the holy Ghost was séene in the shape of a Doue. The holy scriptures in many places do testifie, that good Angels haue oftentimes appeared to Gods Ministers.

That euill spirits are often séene, and that at this day they shewe themselues in diuers formes, to Inchaunters and Coniurers, and to other men also, as wel godly as wicked, both histories and daily experience doth witnesse.

Truly we reade not, that soules haue appeared on this fashion. By these we may easily gather, that the Apostles, when they thought they sawe a spirit, did not beléeue they sawe a soule. Could they not thinke I pray you, they sawe an euill spirit? Or rather that they sawe a good spirit, or a good Angel? For it may be shewed by many examples, that euen the faithfull haue bene troubled, and feared at the appearing of good Angels.

In the eight and tenth Chapter of Daniel, we read that the Prophet fel into a sicknesse at the sight of Angels. The Virgin Mary her selfe was afraide when she sawe the Angell Gabriel. So was Zachary the Priest, & many others. *Dan.8.10.*

In the 12. of ẏ Acts, we reade, that Herode killed Iames the Apostle with the sworde, and when he sawe that it pleased the Iewes, hée caught Peter also, and when hée had *Acts 12.*

put him in prison, hée deliuered him to .16. Souldiours to be kepte, entending after the feast of Passeouer to kill him. But the Angell of the Lorde led S. Peter out of the prison by night through the Souldiours watch, and sette him in the right way to the house of Mary, the mother of Iohn, whose surname was Marke (where many were gathered togither and prayed.) And when he had knocked at ẏ entrie doore, a maid came forth to harken, named Rhode. But when she knew Peters voice, she opened not the entrie doore for gladnesse, but ran in and tolde howe Peter stood before the entrie, but they said vnto hir thou art mad: yet she affirmed constantly that it was so. Then said they it is his Angell, but Peter continued knocking, and when they had opened and saw him they were astonied. In like maner, now also when the Apostles saw Christ, peraduenture they thought they sawe a good Angel. For there are Angels giuen of God vnto men to kéepe them. Of this matter there is somwhat red in the. 18. of S. Matthew, & in

Mat.18. the 19. Psal. & we will note somwhat more of it hereafter.

Psal.19. The Gentiles also beléeued (as may bee gathered by their writings) that euery man had a good & an euil Angel, and that the good Angel did stir men vp to vertue, & defend them, but that the euil Angell did hurt men wheresoeuer he could, and did prouoke them to wickednesse.

If our Elders, when they haue séene or heard any thing of one that hath bene trauelling or dead, did say it is his spirit, it may be, they ment not his soule, but his Angel: for if when as spirits were séene now in this place, and by and by in an other place, they did thinke them to be soules (as in these latter times all men haue beléeued:) in this they were deceiued, as they haue bene in many other things also, for soules are by and by receiued, eyther into euerlasting ioy, or into eternall damnation.

If the Preachers and Teachers had done their duties, and had in this and other pointes of Christian Doctrine, rightly

CHAP. XII.

Concerning the holy Fathers, Councels, Bishops, and common people, which say that soules do visibly appeare.

The holy Fathers say that soules appear.

Ambrose.

Augustine.

Gregorie.

THe authoritie of the holie Fathers is obiected against vs, as that which Saint Ambrose writeth of Saint Agnes, and Saint Augustine of Saint Felix, of which we haue spoken before. And that which Abdias hath in the life of the Apostles, that Thomas appeared after his death and preached. Saint Gregorie in his Dialogues, doth write diuerse and wondrous things, among others he rehearseth many examples of the dead which appeared, and desired helpe of certaine Saintes, yea and of the Apostles themselues, whiche haue visited some vppon their death beddes, a little before they departed, and many other suche lyke matters, which they that list may read themselues. It is saide that Hierome appeared to Saint Augustine.

Many things fabulous in Gregories Dialogues.

I will not in this place accuse the holie Fathers of vanitie, yet this we must note, they say not they haue beleeued that they whiche appeared, were the soules of dead men, but they spake after the common manner. As touching S. Gregories Dialogues, I cannot hide, this (which many haue noted before mee) that many things are conteined in them that are nothing true, but altogither like old wiues tales. Not because the holie Father hath written these things of malice, but for that he being too too credulous, hath put many things into his bookes, rather vppon other mens report, than that he himselfe knew them certainly to be true.

At-

At this day also there are many honest and godlie men which haue this faulte, that they are too quicke of beléefe, and altogither ruled by others. They iudge other men by themselues, they would be ashamed to reporte any thing that were false, and thinke suche men in like manner to be affectioned, which doe abuse their simplicitie and goodnesse. Oftentimes these men, through their too muche lightnesse of beléefe, fall into great daungers.

Moreouer, in that age wherin Gregorie liued, men began to attribute much to those apparances and visions. And at that time the true and sincere Doctrine began greatly to decay. Truly the time in which a man happens to liue, is much to be regarded: he himselfe confessed that his times was the latter times. Therefore the Scriptures shoulde haue béene more diligently lent vnto, neither should any thing haue bene retained that was not agréeable vnto them. Some going about to excuse him, for that he hath stuffed his Dialogues ful of miracles and wonders, say he did it to mollifie by those examples, the peruerse and hard hearts of the Longobardes, to the end they might embrace the true Religion, which they had so gréeuously persecuted. But that it is in no wise profitable to make knowen the true faith, by these helpes which are nothing else but vaine tales, euen Viues himselfe, in his first booke *De tradendis disciplinis* doth acknowledge.

Counsells approue the appearing of Soules.

Some vrge vs with the authoritie of councels, which haue allowed certain apparances of soules, and haue suffered some bookes, whiche are extant of such apparitions, to be read for the edifying of the simple, and some againe togither with their visions, they haue cleane reiected.

It is reported that the Counsell of *Constance*, hath allowed this vision:

A certaine Deane when he had giuen ouer his Deanrie, went into the Wildernesse to doe penaunce: after his deathe he appeared to his Bishop, and tolde him that the

the same houre in which he departed this life, there died thirtie thousand men, among whome only his soule and S. Barnarde were made partakers of eternall saluation, and thrée went into Purgatorie, and all the rest into endlesse damnation. &c. They say that Councels & the churche cannot erre, because they are guided by the holy Ghost. Counsels may erre. Also in the 24. of Matthew, the Lord doth say in the later *Matth.* 24. dayes there shalbe signes and wonders, that the very elect if it were possible might be seduced, therefore they conclude those things which Councels do saye of such apparitions, are to be beléeued. Christs wordes are not so to be vnderstood that the chosen can neuer be broughte into errors (for the contrary may be shewed by many examples) but that they do not abide in erroure, albeit some do very hardly get out of the same againe. Tell me, I pray you, who they were that came togither in auncient Councels? were they not holy fathers? It is manifest that in many points they were at variaunce among themselues, and that they haue shewed by their contrary writings: yea and many times they are contrary to themselues, and therfore they haue not alwaies thought aright. Sometime they send vs to the word of God, as to the most certaine rule and leauell of faith. There are examples inough, by which it may be shewed, that the old Councelles haue erred in some of their determinations. The Councell of Ariminum hath allowed the Arrians doctrine. The second Ephesin councell did subscribe to Eutiches. The Councell holden at *Carthage*, which Ciprian gathered, pronounced flatly against the scriptures, &c. What shall we say was done in latter times? It is well inough knowen by histories who hath resisted Councels, and ruled them, and what hath bene chiefly handled in them for certaine hundred yeares: And what for the most parte hath by and by followed after them, euen cruel warres and bloudy slaughters. If nowe those auncient Councels coulde erre, who will marvaile that they which haue assembled since haue erred? But as touching the apparitions, that I may (all other things omitted) talke only of them, tell me I pray you who should certifie the Councels, whether this or that vision were true or false? Certainly no Councels can bring to passe that the lyes which haue bene scattered abroade, shall now begin to be true tales, although they of the Councel haue saide they are true.

Popes haue approued the appearing of soules.

It is euen as foolishe to say, the Pope (who wil be counted aboue all Councels) hath confirmed this or that miracle to be true, which they say was wrought in some one monasterie or other. How can the bishop of Rome being so far off, knowe any thing better than they which dwell in the same places? If the bishop hauing no other assuraunce than out of their words or writings, which perhaps go about to erecte newe pilgrimages, and newe deuises to get money, confirme once that this or that soule was seene, it must straight way without any gaynsaying be beleeued. But if any other men who haue with diligence sought out the truth of the matter, do testifie the contrary: al that they say must not be regarded. Consider (I beseeche you) of this matter. Before, all haue doubted whether the thing were so or no, but assoone as the Pope doth giue his verdicte, or some Church man do in his dreame see it to be so, it is a heynouse matter afterwards to doubt of it. O time! O manners!

Many affirme they haue seen soules.

As touching other common and lay men as they terme them, which say they haue seene one after his death, and haue heard and knowne him, and haue spoken with him: I easily graunt they haue seene and heard some thing, and haue thought verily they were soules, and that they did speake with them. But it followeth not therfore, that they were soules indeede, much lesse that any dead man hath appeared in bodie & soule vnto them. For at domes day only, the soules shall returne to their bodies againe. Soules are

spirits.

spirits, but spirits are inuisible, wherefore they cannot so be séene, vnlesse they take some outward shape vpon them. But it can neuer be proued by the testimony of holy scripture, that as good and euil Angels, so soules take som shapes vpon them. Besides this, it is most true that oftentimes the shapes and formes of them whose soules are not yet sundred from their bodies by death (as when one lieth vpon his death bed) are no lesse séene than theirs which are already dead. Therefore it is not necessary that we beléeue ẏ ghostes which are séene, to be soules. By these things you vnderstand what is to be thought of the tale of Platina, Nauclerus, and others, which write that a certaine Bishop sawe Pope Benedict the eight (lately dead) in a solitary place sitting on a blacke horse, and being demaunded why he was so carried about with the blacke horse, he warned the Bishop that he should distribute the money which was giuen to the vse of the poore (but now wickedly kept to other purposes) vnto those poore folkes to whom of right it belonged. Other tales of like stampe are rife euery where.

CHAP. XIII.

Whether soules do returne againe out of Purgatorie, and the place which they call *Limbus puerorum*.

THat soules, which are gone either to heauen or to hell, returne not thence, nor appeare againe before the latter day, perchaunce some men would easily graunt: but they imagine there is a third place, (which is Purgatorie) out of the which soules do returne vpon earth. For as yet the last sentence hath not passed on them, and therefore as yet they may be helped, and therfore also they do craue help, and shewe themselues vnto men. But we haue proued before at large, both out of the scriptures, and also out of ẏ writhings of the auncient Fathers, that the soules of the faithfull are saued, and that the soules of the vnbeléeuers are damned immediatly without delay, and therefore there is no Purgatorie. Against this, they alledge sundrie arguments, amongst the which this, albeit it be very common, yet is it the chéefest, when they say, that no man is saued except he bee purged from all his sinnes, and that sinne cleaueth vnto vs euen vnto the graue. If we say that puritie and cleannesse consisteth not in our workes, or in the paines which wee endure, but that God through faith in his sonne Iesus Christ (who is our onely redemption, iustification, satisfaction, and raunsome for our sinnes) doth iustifie vs: they straight aunswere, that our faith is vnperfect, and that the moste godly men complaine when they depart hence, of the weakenesse of their faith. And therefore that God doth not take vp suche kinde of men straightwayes into heauen, nor yet because they are not vtterly voyde of faith, thrust them presently downe into hell. And therefore, that there is a middle place betwéene both, which is called Purgatorie, in which the soules are purified from the imperfection whiche remained in them at the time of their death, and out of the which they are deliuered by the merits of the liuing, and by large pardons. Is not this as much as to attribute that vnto our owne paines and to externall fire, which ought only to be ascribed vnto the death of Christ? Doth not Christ teache vs, that if at any time we féele any weaknesse of faith, we shuld crie out with the Apostles, Lord increase our faith? Doth God disdaine to heare the prayers of his faithfull people in the extremitie of death? Christ saith, he that is washed hath no néede saue to washe his féete, but he is cleane euery whitte: Hée will saue vs, not for the worthinesse of our faith, but by his méere grace onely. He doth bestow these things amongst vs, as if some riche man did fréely giue meate and drinke vnto others, whereof some of them

recei-

receiueth it in wodden, some in earthen, and some in siluer or golden vessels: or as if a Prince did distribute vnto euery one a piece of golde, and some receiue it with a féeble hand, and some with a strong and lustie hand. He that hath the hand, receiueth money as well as he that hath the strong hande. Saint Paule exhorteth the Thessalonians in his first Epistle and fourth Chapter, that they mourne not for the dead as the Gentiles doo. If there had bene a fire of Purgatorie, as they haue falsely imagined, he could not haue bene angry with them, although they had taken their friendes departure somewhat impatiently, &c. Other arguments which are brought for the confirmation of purgatorie, are of late so confuted by many godly and learned men, that it is maruaile our aduersaries will so often repeate them. 1. Thess. 4.

But before I leaue this matter, I will here insert this historie following. A certaine Germain being accused by the Inquisitours of heresie (as they terme it) that amongest his companions he denied Purgatorie, contrarie to the common consent of the Catholike Churche, made his answeare thus: If our parish Priest (quoth he) whome I credite very much, preach vnto vs true doctrine in the Pulpet, either there is no Purgatorie at all, or else it is cleane emptie. For hée oftentimes saieth, that Turkes, Iewes, heretikes, and wicked men, goe not into Purgatorie, but straight into Hell fire, from whence they shall neuer bee deliuered: Then that by Pardons whiche are euery where solde for money, many soules are restored to their first perfection. And moreouer, that the Masse is of such force, that there is not one sung in all the world, by whiche one soule at the least is not deliuered out of the flames of Purgatorie. If these things (quoth he) be true, (for I will not go about to refell that which maister Parson hath saide) I will stande in this my opinion. For you doo all complaine, that the nomber of the Catholikes is verie small, the greater part of men being diuided into sundry sectes, and the multitude of Epicures daily increasing. Then are all mens purses many times drawne drie by pardoners, which for mony sell their indulgences, that by them the soules of men may bee deliuered out of the torments of Purgatorie. Furthermore, there is no village but there are a great many Masses sung in it, before any one husbandman dieth. What followeth then, but that there is either no Purgatorie, or one vtterly voyde and emptie? When the Inquisitors (who knew very well that their men commonly taught such doctrine) heard these things, they were amazed, and taking aduise togither, they all berated him for occupying his head about questions nothing appertaining vnto him, which they commaunded him to leaue vnto Diuines, and to follow his owne businesse.

Dilemma, is a kind of argument or reasoning, which euery way conuinceth him vnto whome it is spoken.

There was in our Countrey an honest and sober man, who before the light of the Gospell began to appeare, vsed this Dilemma: The Bishop of *Rome* either hath authoritie to bring soules out of the paines of Purgatorie, or else he hath no authoritie: If he haue that power, and will not vse it, except he receiue money, he cannot escape the fault of crueltie and couetousnesse: But if hee haue no such authoritie, surely it is great villainie to robbe so many widowes and fatherlesse children, and so arrogantly to boast himselfe of authoritie whiche hee hath not. And if there bee no Purgatorie (as by the holy Scriptures it plainly gathered there is not) surely then mennes soules can neyther returne from thence, nor offer themselues to be seene of men.

Limbus puerorum.

Nowe as touching the fourth place, namely Limbus puerorum, (in the which innocent children, as as they call them, are saide to be) Papistes themselues scant dare affirme, that they returne againe and appeare vnto men, and craue their helpe: for they teache, that if they depart without baptisme, they shall neuer enioy the sight of God, and

for

scriptures do not attribute so much unto external baptisme, which is by water. Was the condition of infants better in the olde Testament than in the new? You do not reade that the olde Fathers, supposed that infants which died before the eight day, and therfore were not circumcised, should be separated from the sight of God for euer. Dauid the king and prophet, said he should follow his sonne, whom God had called out of this life before he was circumcised. But it was not Dauids meaning that hee should goe into a place where he should bee depriued of the sight of God for euer. But it appertaineth not much unto our purpose to dispute any further hereof. Thus haue I now answered the cheefest arguments of our aduersaries, whereby they would proue the soules of good and euil men, to offer themselues to be seene sometimes of them that liue, after their departure by death from their bodies.

CHAP. XIIII.

What those things are which men see and heare: and first that good Angels do sometimes appeare.

BUt thou wilt say, I do not yet clearely and plainly understand what manner of things those are, whereof (as it is sayd before) Historiographers, holy Fathers, and others, make mention: as that holie Apostles, Bishoppes, Martyres, Confessours, Virgines, and manie other which dyed long agoe, appeared unto certaine men lying at the poynt of death, gaue them warnyng, aunswearedunto certaine questions, commaunded them to doe this or that thyng: and that some thing is seene and heard at certeine times, whiche not only affirmeth it selfe to be this or that soule, but also sheweth howe it may be succoured, and afterwardes returning againe, giueth great thankes vnto them of whome it hath receiued such a benefite: that the husband being dead, came in the nighte vnto his wife nowe a widowe, and that seldome times any notable thing hathe happened, whiche was not foreshewed vnto some man by certaine signes and tokens. You wil say, I heare and vnderstand very wel that these things are not mens soules, which continually remaine in their appointed places, I pray you then what are they? To conclude in fewe wordes, If it be not a vaine persuasion procéeding through weakenesse of the senses through feare, or some suche like cause, or if it be not deceit of men, or some naturall thing, wherof we haue spoken muche in the firste part, it is either a good or euill Angell, or some other forewarning sent by God, concerning the which we will

Angells appeare. speake more orderly and fully hereafter. Our sauioure witnesseth in the Gospell, that children haue their good An-

Matth.18. gells: and we reade in the 18. of Matthew, that the Lorde saide: Take héede ye contemne not one of these litle ones: for I saye vnto you, that their Angels in Heauen do alwayes behold the face of my father whiche is in Heauen. Which wordes are not so to be taken, as though they were neuer sent downe into the earth, but the Lord here speaketh after the manner of men. For as seruaunts stande before their maisters to fulfill their commaundement, euen so are the Angels prest and ready to serue God. E-

Esay.63. say the 63. The Angell of his face, that is, which standeth ready in his sight, preserued them. And further they which often stand in presence of their Lorde, are acceptable vnto them and priuy to their secrets. Out of this place of Math. Sainct Herome in his commentaries, and other fathers do conclude, that God doth assigne vnto euery soule assone as he createth him his peculiar Angell, which taketh care

of

of him. But whether that euerie one of the elect haue his proper Angell, or many Angels be appointed vnto him, it is not expreslly set forth, yet this is most sure and certaine, that God hath giuen his Angels in charge to haue regarde and care ouer vs. Daniel witnesseth in his tenth Chapter, that Angels haue also charge of kingdomes, by whom God keepeth and protecteth them, and hindreth the wicked counsels of the diuell. It may be proued by many places of scripture, that all Christian men haue not only one Angell, but also many, whome God imployeth to their seruice. In the 34. Psalme it is sayd, the Angell of the Lord pitcheth his tentes round about them which feare the Lord, and helpeth them: which ought not to bee doubted but that it is also at this day, albeit we see them not. We reade that they appearing in sundry shapes, haue admonished men, haue comforted them, defended them, deliuered them from daunger, and also punished the wicked. Touching this matter, there are plentifull examples, which are not needfull to be repeated in this place. Sometimes they haue either appeared in sleepe, or in maner of visions, and sometimes they haue performed their office, by some internall operations: as when a mans minde foresheweth him, that a thing shall so happen, and after it happeneth so indeed, which thing I suppose is done by God, through the ministrie of Angels. Angels for the most part take vpon them the shapes of men, wherein they appeare. And so it may be, that S. Felix, and Saint Agnes, and other which haue appeared vnto honest and godly men, were the Angels of God. Angels haue appeared not only one at a time, but also whole Armies and Hostes, of them, as vnto Iacob the patriarch, and Heliseus the Prophet. It is read in the Ecclesiasticall history written by Socrates and Sozomenus, that Archadius the Emperour receiued Gaina, with all his Armie of souldiers, into the Citie of *Constantinople*, to defend it, but this traitor went about to get the rule of the Citie into his owne hands, and therefore

Dani.10.

Psal.34.

Whole armies of Angels.

Cōstantinople preserued by the appearing of Angels.

fore he sent a band of men to fire the Emperours Pallace, which sodeinly espied a great hoste of Angels, of large stature, armed like unto souldiers, whereupon they gaue ouer their enterprise of fiering. Then sent he others who reported the very same: At the last he went himselfe, and sawe it to be so, and so left his purpose: and thus God by a miraculous meanes, preserued the Cittie and Church of *Constantinople* from the craftie subtiltie of the tyrant.

Augustine.

Whereas S. Augustine in his booke *De cura pro mortuis agenda*, Chapter 10. writeth, that dead men, haue appeared unto the liuing in dreames, or any other meanes whatsoeuer, shewing them where their bodies laie unburied, and requiring them to burie them. There he supposeth, that these are the workes of Angels by the dispensation of Gods prouidence, using unto good purpose, both good and euil Angels, according to the unsearchable depth of his iudgements. He saith not that such soules appeare in sleepe, but the similitude of soules. He addeth further, if the soules of the dead had any thing to do with matters of the liuing, and that we might talke with them as often as we list in our sleepe, his mother no night would leaue him, who to liue with him, followed him both by sea and by lande, suche loue bare she towards her sonne.

That

CHAP. XV.

That sometimes, yea and for the most part, euill Angels do appeare.

Contrariwise, euill angels are hurtfull and enemies vnto men, they followe them euery where, to the ende they may withdrawe them from true worshipping of God, and from faith in his onely sonne Iesu Christ, vnto sundry other things. These appeare in diuers shapes: for if the diuell (as Paule doth witnesse) transformeth himselfe into an Angell of light, no lesse may he take the shape of a Prophet, an Apostle, Euangelist, Bishop, and Martyr, and appeare in their likenesse: or to bewitch vs, that we verily suppose we heare or see them in very deede. He taketh on him to tell of things to come, whether hee hit them right or wrong. Hee affirmeth that hee is this or that soule, that he may bee deliuered by this or that meanes, that by these meanes he may purchase credite and authoritie, unto those things which haue no ground of scripture. Paule.

By meanes of false myracles, he decreeth new Hollydayes, Pilgrimages, Chappels, and Aultars: by Coniurations, blessings, enchauntments, he attempteth to cure the sicke, to make his doings haue authoritie.

You shall reade marueilous straunge things in Arnobius, Lactantius, and other holie Fathers, who wrote against the Gentiles and their superstition, after what sorte Diuels haue deluded the miserable Gentiles, and haue entrapped them in many errors. He ioyned and hid himselfe in their Idolles, he spake through them from one place to an other, he made them to moue, and did such straunge myracles, that verie lame men leauing their stilts whereon they leaned in the Temples of their Idols, returned home to their houses, without any helpe or stay of them, but especially in the temple of Æsculapius (who was counted the Patron of Phisicke) many of these kinde of miracles are reported to haue happened. Wherefore there is no cause, why the Papistes at this day, shoulde so insolently glorie of the like myracles, by the which they goe about to proue their intercession of Saints, and such lyke trumperie.

CHAP. XVI.

Of wondrous Monsters, and such like.

Nowe as concerning other straunge things, we must hereafter search what nature they are of: as when one dieth that there is somewhat séene, or some great noyse is sodeinly heard, but especially that many signes and wonders happen before the death of great Princes. It is well knowne by Histories, what signes went before the death of Iulius Cæsar, amongst the which, a great noyse was heard in the night time, in very many places farre and neare.

As concerning other Emperors, and Kings, and other great mens deathes, we reade that some certaine forewarnings were heard or séene, we must also consider what those straunge things are, which for the most part happen before the innouations of kingdomes, before battailes, seditions, and subuersions of Cities.

I say flatly, euen as I sayde before concerning spirits: if they be not vaine perswasions, or naturall things, then are they forewarnings of God, which are sent, eyther by good Angels, or by some other meanes vnknowne vnto vs, that we might vnderstand that all these things happen not by aduenture, without the wil and pleasure of God, but that life and deathe, peace and warre, the alteration of Religion, the exchaunge of Empires, and of other things, are in his power, that we might thereby learne to feare him, and to call vppon his name. In the meane season, Sathan also fayneth and worketh many things to terrifie men, and to plant superstition in their hearts. But that all things are done by Sathan, hereby we may vnderstand: It chaunceth that one is thrust throw and slaine by one with whome he neuer was at variance, but hath euer vsed him as his friende, some man is drowned, or falleth from some high place, or otherwise is miserably slaine, an euill spirit can haue no foreknowledge hereof (for there are no naturall signes, or coniectures going before them, as there are in diseases) yet notwithstanding, some signes and rare casualties fall out before. Hereof do I gather, that these things are wrought by God, who onely knoweth that they shall come to passe, and they are not onely admonishments vnto them, whom they especially concerne, but also vnto them which heare them, and are present at the doing of them.

There was a certaine Magistrate within the liberties of *Tigurine*, not long before I wrote this, whome certaine of his friendes tarried for to breake their fast with him before hée tooke his iourney, and thus waiting, they supposed they heard a knife falling from the vpper part, or floore of the stewe, wherein they were, yet sawe they nothing, and sodeinly as they communed togither of this straunge wonder, they thought they heard it againe. In the meane while commeth the Magistrate, vnto whome they declare what had happened, and as they had scant ended their talke, the knife fell againe the third time, in the hearing of the Magistrate, who before doubted very much of the matter. And therefore taking occasion hereby, he began to exhort them, that whereas within fewe dayes after, a great marriage should be kept in the same place, they should all endeuour to maintaine peace, and obserue sobrietie, least perchaunce through quarrelling and murther, it should bee a bloudie marriage. After he taking his iourney, and within a day or twaine dispatching his businesse, as he was returning towards his Castle, (his horse falling into a riuer, whiche was sodeinly encreased with raine) after he had long striued with the water, at the last died miserably.

And that the diuell doth delude men with straunge happes, hereof I gather, that if any be taken with greeuous sicknesse, so that not onely the Phisitian, but also the sicke themselues dispaire of their owne health, in the night time there is heard a noyse as if one were making a coffin or chest to laie one in, or were burying a dead bodie: that suppose I to be an illusion of the diuil, for he thinketh verily the diseased will die, whom God by meanes of godly and earnest praiers, doth restore againe to his former health.

Plinie. Whereas Plinie writeth that rauens are of such sharp senses, that they will flie three or foure dayes before, vnto the place where carryon will afterwardes be, it is altogither vaine and fabulous. If this were graunted, it were no absurditie to say, that the diuell hath a knowledge of things to come, yea euen where there are no naturall causes, &c. Moreouer he may by Gods permission, if warres and mutinies be towards, stirre the instruments of warre, and all other kinde of munition as it lyeth in the Armorie, he can make a noyse and reare a clamour and crie, as it were of a great Armie in the aire, and play as it were on a Drum, and do other such things, which all Histori ographers affirme with one voyce, haue oftentimes chaunced.

That

CHAP. XVII.

That it is no hard thing for the Diuell to appeare in diuers shapes, and to bring to passe straunge things.

BUt it is no difficult matter for the Diuel to appeare in diuers shapes, not only of those which are aliue, but also of dead men, (whereof I spake also before, when I entreated of Samuels appearing) yea, and (which is a lesse matter) in the fourme of beasts and birds, &c. as to appeare in the likenesse of a blacke Dog, a Horse, an Owle, and also to bring incredible things to passe, it is a thing most manifest: for hee may through long and great experience, vnderstand the effects and force of naturall things, as of hearbes, stones, &c. and by meanes hereof worke maruellous matters. And then he is a subtile and quicke spirite, which can readily take things in hand, which in each thing is of no small weight. By his quicknesse, and by his knowledge in naturall things, he may easily deceiue the eye sight, and other senses of man, and hide those things which are before our face, and conuey other things into their places. Whereof the holy scriptures, and histories, and continuall experience beareth record. How did the wicked spirit handle Iob? what did he not bring to passe in short space? What straunge workes of an euil spirit did Bileam bring to passe: did he not purchase a famous name by his Magicall Artes? what wonderfull great miracles did Pharaos Sorcerers? Did not Simon Magus so bewitch the *Samaritanes* with his vnlawfull Artes, that he would say he was the great vertue of God? Touching this Coniurer, the olde Fathers write many things, as Ireneus in his first booke and tenth Chapter, Eusebius in his second booke and thirteenth Chapter.

Egesippus

Egesippus writeth in his third booke and second Chapter, of the destruction of *Hierusalem*, that this Symon came to *Rome*, and there set himselfe against Peter, boasting that he could flie vp into heauen, and that he came at the day appointed vnto the Mount *Capitoline*, where leaping from the rocke, he flew a good while not without the great admiration of the people, who now began to credit his wordes, but sodeinly he fell downe and brake his leg, and after being carried vnto *Aritia*, there died.

Iohannes Tritenhemius, Abbot of *Spanheimium*, writeth in his Chronicles concerning the Monasterie of *Hirsgraue* of the order of S. Bennet, in the yeare of our Lorde 970, that Peter and Baianus, the two sonnes of one Simon a Monke, ruled ouer the *Bulgarians*, wherof the one, namely Baianus, was throughly séene in the Arte of Necromancie, and thereby wrought many myracles. He chaunged himselfe into a Wolfe so often as he list, or into the likenesse of an other beast, or in such sort as he could not be discerned of any man, and many other straunge things hée could doo, and did, whereby he brought men into great admiration.

And after in the yeare 876. he writeth, that there was a certaine Iewe named Sedechias, sometimes Philosopher and Phisitian vnto Lewes the Emperour, who being very cunning in sorcerie, did straunge miracles and wonderfull sleights before the Princes, and before all other men. For he brought it to passe by his cunning, that he séemed to deuoure an armed man with his horse, and all his harnesse, and also a carte loaden with hay, togither with the horse and carter. He cut off mens heads, their hands and féete, which he set in a basen before all the lookers on to behold, with the bloud running about the basen: which by and by he would put againe vppon the places whence they séemed to haue bene cut off, without any hurt to the parties. He was séene and hearde of all men to exercise hunting and running

running, and suche like things in the aire and cloudes, as men are accustomed to exercise vpon the earth. He practised so many and diuers deceites, that all men marueiled and were astonished out of measure.

In the yeare of our Lord. 1323. when Frederike Duke of *Austrich*, who was chosen Emperour against Lewes, as the same author witnesseth, was vanquished in a great battail betwene *Ottinga* and *Meldorfius*, and deliuered into the hands of Lewes, who sent him away into a strong castell to be safely kepte: It chaunced shortly after, that a coniurer going vnto his brother Lupoldus in *Austriche*, promised, that by the helpe of a spirit, he would within the compasse of an houre, deliuer Frederike safe and sounde out of captiuitie, if he would promise him and giue him a worthie reward for his paines. The Duke aunsweared him: if thou wilt (quoth he) do as thou makest promise, I wil worthily reward thee. So the Magitian with the Duke entring his circle of coniuration in an houre moste conuenient, calleth the Spirit whiche was accustomed to obey his commaundement. Whome, when he appeared in the likenesse of a man, he commaunded by the vertue of his coniurations, that he should spedily bring vnto him into *Austriche*, Duke Frederike, deliuered safely out of prison. Unto whome the spirit aunswering, said, If the captiue Duke will come with me, I will willingly obey thy commaundement. This saide, the spirite flieth awaye into *Bavarie*, and taking vppon him the forme of a Pilgrime, he entreth into the prison where the Duke was kepte prisoner: whome assone as he sawe, the Spirit whiche was sente as messenger vnto him, said: If thou wilt be deliuered out of captiuitie, mount thee vp vpon this horse, and I will bring thee safe and sounde without any hurte into *Austrich* vnto Duke Lupoldus thy brother. Unto whome the Duke saide: Who art thou? The Spirite aunswered: Aske not who I am, because it appertaineth nothing to the purpose, but get thée vp on the horse which I offer thée, and I will bring thée safe and sound, and fréely deliuered into *Austrich*. Which when the Duke heard, hée was taken with a certaine horror, and feare, being otherwise a hardy knight: and when he had blessed himself with the signe of the holy crosse, the spirite sodainly vanished away with the blacke horse, which he had proffered him, and returned emptie againe vnto him that sent him: of whom being rebuked because he had not brought the prisoner, he declared all the matter vnto him in order. Duke Frederick at the last being deliuered out of prison, confessed that it had so happened vnto him in his captiuitie the very same day they named. This historie is also to be séene in the Chronicles of the *Heluetians*.

There are also Coniurers found euen at this day, who bragge of themselues that they can so by inchauntments saddle an horse, that in a fewe houres they wil dispatch a very long iourney. God at the last wil chasten these men with deserued punishment. What straunge things are reported of one Faustus a Germane, which he did in these our dayes by inchauntments?

I will speake nothing at this time, of those old Sorcerers, Apollonius, and others, of whom the histories report straunge and incredible things. Hags, Witches, and Inchaunters, are said to hurt men and cattell, if they do but touch them or stroake them, they do horrible things wherof there are whole bookes extant. Juglers and Tumblers, by nimblenesse do many things, they will bid one eate meate, which when they spit out againe, they cast forth ordure and such like. Magitians, Juglers, Inchanters, and Necromanciers, are no other than seruants of the Diuel: do you not thinke their maister reserueth some cunning vnto him selfe?

Howbeit this is not to be dissembled, that the diuel doth glory of many things which indéede he cannot performe: as.

as that he saith, that he raised the dead out of their graues. &c. He may in very déede by Gods sufferaunce, shewe the shapes of them unto men, but he hath no such power ouer the dead bodies.

CHAP. XVIII.

Diuels doo sometimes bid men doo those things which are good, and auoide things that are euill: sometimes they tell truth, and for what cause.

If those spirites which séeke helpe at mens hands be not soules, but Diuels, many will say, why then do they perswade men unto good things, exhort them unto vertue, and call them from vice. For they say, Judge uprightly, take héede of theft and extortion, restore goods uniustly gotten unto their owners, beware of periurie, surfets, and drunkennesse, enuie and hatred, lying and deceit, pray earnestly, come to church often, &c.

The Diuell is not pleased when wée doo good, and auoide euill: nothing woulde gréeue him more, than that we should liue according to the prescript worde of God. Therefore they are not Diuels which bid us doo good, and eschue euil.

Moreouer, those Spirites speake truthe, but the Diuell is a lyer, and is called by Christe, the father of lyes. Therefore wée may not say that they are diuellish Spirits.

Unto this argument I aunswere thus: hée dooth this for his owne aduantage. If he should shewe himselfe so, as he is by nature, he should little profit. That whiche he doth, he doth it to this ende, that he may purchase credite unto his wordes, and that he might the better thrust other things upon men, and bring and driue them into sundry errours, whereby they forsaking the worde of God might giue eare vnto Spirites. Did not the seruaunts of vncleane Spirits, I meane false Prophets, come in times past vnder sheepes skinnes, and fayned themselues to tender the peoples commoditie, whereas in very deed in the meane space they sought after another thing, that is, that when they had obteined great authoritie, they might pill and poule other men, and fill their owne bags with golde and siluer? Do not all herretickes yet at this day say, they are sent from God, and that we must eschue wickednesse, and seeke after vertue. Didst thou neuer heare that theeues trauelling by the way with those on whose company they light, haue talked of liuing honestly, and of the punishment of wicked men, and the rewarde of good men, to the ende that after they might take ẏ aduantage of them vnawares? Whereas the Diuell hath fayned himselfe to bee otherwise than he is, it hath brought forth innumerable errors, superstitions, and false worshippings in the Churche of God. For Bishops in proces of time neglected the word of God, they would accept the Diuell and receiue him as an Angell of light, when he came not in a blacke and horrible, but a pleasaunt and acceptable forme. He speaketh some good things, that he may intermedle euil things therwith, he speaketh truth, that he may scatter abroade lyes, and roote them in mens hearts. So Simon in Virgil, mingled falshood with truth, that he might the better entrape the *Troians*.

Sathan doth imitate craftie gamesters, who suffer a plaine and simple yong man to winne a while of them, that afterwards being greedie to play, they may lurch him of all his golde and siluer. He followeth them which once or twise iustly repaie vnto their creditors such money as they haue borrowed, keeping their promise duly, that afterwards they may obtaine a great summe of them, and then deceiue them.

The

The diuel sometimes uttereth the truth, that his words may haue the more credit, and that he may the more easily beguile them. He that would utter euil wares, doth not only set them forth in words, but doth also so trim and decke them, that they seeme excellent good, whereby they are the more saleable: this Art also the diuel knoweth, for he painteth out his stuffe that he may obtrude it unto other men in the steede of good ware. S. Ambrose writeth in his Commentaries upon the first Epistle to the Thessalonians, and fift chapter, expounding these words: Quench not the spirit. Despise not prophecying. Examine all things, and keepe that which is good. Euill spirites are went to speake good things craftily, as it were by imitation, and amongst those they priuily insinuate wicked thinges, that by meanes of those things which are good, euil things may be admitted, and because they are supposed the words of one spirit, they may not be discerned asunder, but by that which is lawfull, an unlawfull thing may bee commended by authoritie of the name, and not by reason of vertue, &c. Ambrose.

Hereunto appertaine those words which we reade in S. Chrysostomes second sermon De Lazara. There he sheweth that many simple men haue bene in this erroure, that they haue thought the soules of those which were slaine by some violent death, did become Diuels. He saith further, that the Diuell hath perswaded many Witches, and such as serue him being in this erroure, that they should kill the tender bodies of many yong men, hoping they should become Diuels, and doo them seruice. And by and by he addeth; But these things are not true, no, I say, they are not. What is it then that Diuels say? I am the soule of such a Monke? Verily I beleeue it not, euen for this, that Diuels doo auouche it: for they deceiue their auditours. Wherefore Paule also commaundeth them to silence, albeit they speake truth, lest taking occasion by truth, they mingle lyes therewith, and so purchase themselues credit. Why the diuel doth somtimes tel truth

Acts 16. of the most high God, shewing vnto you the way of saluati-
on: The Apostle not content herewith, commaunded the prophecying spirite vnto silence, and to come foorth of the mayd. And yet what harme speake they? These men are the seruantes of the most high God. But because the most parte of simple men haue not vnderstanding alwayes to iudge of those things which are vttered by diuels, he at once
Marke.1. excludeth them from all credit. Thou art (saith he) of the
Luke.4. number of infamous spirites, it belongeth not to thee to speake freely, hold thy peace, keepe silence, it is not thy office to preach. This is the authoritie of the Apostles: why takest thou vppon thee that which appertaineth not vnto thee, hold thy peace, be thou infamous. So also did Christ sharply rebuke the diuels saying vnto him: We know thee who thou art, therein prescribing vnto vs a lawe, that we should in no wise trust the diuel, albeit he tell the truth.

Sith we know these things, let vs in no wise beleeue the diuel, nay rather if he say any thing that is truth, let vs flee from him and shunne him. For it is not lawfull exactly to learne sounde and wholesome doctrine of diuels, but out of the holy scriptures.

That you may therfore know that it can in no wise be, that a soule once departed out of the bodie can come vnder the tyrannie of the diuell, heare what S. Paule saith: For he that is dead is iustified from sinne, that is, he sinneth no more. For if the diuil can do no hurt vnto the soule while it is in the bodie, it is euident, he cannot hurt it when it is departed out of the bodie. &c. By all these things it is plaine, what manner of things those are which are heard and seene.

The

The third parte of this Booke, in which is shewed, why, or to what ende God suffereth Spirits to appeare, and other straunge thinges to happen: as also howe men ought to behaue themselues when they meete with any suche things.

CHAP. I.

God by the appearing of Spirits doth exercise the faithfull, and punish the vnbeleeuers.

IT foloweth now hereafter to be intreated of, why God suffreth spirits, ghosts, and horrible sightes to appeare, &c. And also why he doth permit other straunge and miraculous things to happen: And furthermore, how men ought to behaue themselues when they see anye suche things.

God doth suffer spirits to appeare vnto his elect, vnto a good ende, but vnto the reprobate they appeare as a punishment. And as all other things turne to the best vnto ẏ faithfull, euen so doo these also: for if they be good spirits, which appeare vnto men, warning, and defending them, therby do they gather the care, prouidence, and fatherly affection of God towardes them. But in case they bee euill spirites, (as

Causes why God suffereth spirites to appeare.

(as for the most part they are) the faithfull are moued by occasion of them unto true repentance. They looke diligently unto themselues so long as they liue, least the enimie of mankinde, who is readie at all assaies, and lieth allwaies in waight, should bring them into mischiefe, and take further vauntage to vexe and hurt them. God also by these meanes doeth exercise and trie their faith and pacience, to the end they continue in his word, and receiue nothing contrary to the same, haue it neuer so faire a shewe, nor do any manner of thing against his worde, although those spirites do not straightwayes ceasse to vexe them.
God doth also suffer them to be exercised with haunting of spirites, for this cause, that they should be the more humble and lowely. For in the second Epistle to the Corinth. and. xii. chap. Paul saith: And least I should be exalted out of mesure, through the excellencie of reuelations, ther was giuen unto me unquietnesse through the flesh, euen the messenger of Sathan to buffet me, because I should not be exalted out of measure. For this thing besought I the Lord thrice, that it mighte depart from me. And he said unto me: My grace is sufficient for thée, for my strength is made perfect through weakenesse. Except God did shut up the way before us with certaine stops and lets, we should not know our selues, we shoulde not understande whereof we stand in néed, we should not so earnestly pray unto God, to deliuer us from euill, to strengthen our faith, and to giue us patience, and other necessarie things. Neither should we be touched with compassion of other mennes miserie which are vexed with spirits: but we woulde rather say, that they cannot tell what they speake, and that they imagine many vaine feares. Moreouer, if other understande that godly men are for their exercise vexed by spirits, they become more patient whensoeuer they are sicke, or otherwise troubled, acknowledging their owne harmes to be but small in comparison of other mens. For nothing is more

more gréeuous, than when a man is tormented by the Diuel.

Now as touching infidells, they are constrained, will they, or nill they, to confesse, that there are diuels, for there are many which would neuer be persuaded, there are good or euill Angels or spirits, except sometimes they had experience thereof indeede. God suffereth these things to chasten them. For so muche as they will giue no place vnto truth, but are wilfully deceiued, it is good reason they be taught by diuellish illusions what they must doo, or leaue vndone, and that they be illuded by euil spirits, after some other meanes. Seeing of spirites to the wicked is a punishment.

Thus we reade in the 13. chapter of Deuteronomie: if there arise among you a prophet or a dreamer of dreames, and giue thée a signe and wonder, and that signe or wonder that he hath saide come to passe, and then say, let vs goe after straunge Gods, which thou hast not knowne, and let vs serue them: hearkē not thou vnto the words of that prophet, or dreamer of dreames. For the Lorde thy God prooueth you, to wit, whether ye loue the Lord your God with all your soule. Ye shall walke after the Lorde your God and feare him, kéepe his commandements, and hearken vnto his voice, serue him and cleaue vnto him. And he addeth further, that the same prophet or dreamer shall die the death. *Deut. 13.*

By these words we do not only sée that God doth suffer suche lewde fellowes to worke maruellous thinges, but also to what ende and purpose he permitteth it, that is, to trie his faithfull, how constant they be, and how faithfully they would beléeue in him, if at any time spirits do come and foretell things to happen hereafter. Our Sauiour Christ saith in the third Chapter of Saint Iohn: This is the condemnation, that light is come into the world, and men loued darknesse more than light, because their déedes were euill: for euery one that doth euill, hateth the light, *Iohn 3.*

neither commeth he to the light, least his deedes should be reproued,&c. By the which wordes our Sauiour sheweth the cause why the worlde is condemned, which is, because they receiue not the light of the word of God, or Christe himselfe, who is the light of the worlde, set forth vnto vs in his word: but rather shut their eyes against the cleare light, preferring darkenesse, that is, errors, superstition, and wickednesse, before the word of God. If God then condemne and reiect the vnthankfull world, what maruell is it, if hee vexe them with spirites and vaine apparitions?
John 5. Christ saieth in the fifth of Iohn, I come in my Fathers name, and you receiue mee not: If an other come in his owne name, you receiue him.

Christe laboured for their health and saluation: this they would not acknowledge, but refused him: therefore was it the iust iudgement of God, that they shuld receiue others, that hunted after their owne commoditie and profit: suche as were Theudas, Iudas of *Galilee*, and many other false doctors, and seditious seducers. Wherefore if any refuse to giue eare to Christ and his Ministers, it is by the iust iudgement of God, that they hearken vnto spirites, and suche lyke things. Sainte Paule in the seconde to the
2. Thessa. 2. Thessalonians and second Chapter, writeth of Antichrist, that he shoulde exercise great tyrannie in the Churche of God, and shewes against whome, and for what cause God will suffer him so to doo, saying: Among them that perish: because they receiued not the loue of the truth that they might be saued. And therefore God shall send them strong delusions, that they shoulde beleeue lyes, that all they might be damned, whiche beleeue not the truth, but had pleasure in vnrighteousnesse. And in the fourth Chap-
2. Timo. 4. ter of his seconde Epistle to Timothie, he earnestly beseecheth his scholler to be diligent in preaching daily. He giueth this reason: for the time will come, when they shall not suffer wholesome doctrine: but after their owne lustes

shall.

shall they (whose eares itche,) get them an heape of teachers, and shall withdrawe their eares from the truth, and shalbe turned unto fables. Now we see the cause why god dothe suffer seducers, false teachers, and wicked spirites, to deceiue men in the place of true doctours: which is, for that eyther they utterly despise his worde or little esteeme it, and cannot abide godly and constant preachers.

Touching whiche matter, wee will alleage a fewe examples. Pharao contemned God and his seruants, Moyses and Aaron, wherefore God blinded his eyes, that he gaue himselfe to be ruled by his Magi or wise men, and at the last perished miserably in the red Sea.

Examples of the Wicked punished by delusions of spirits pharao. Exodus. Samuel.

Saule would not giue eare unto Samuell, who bare a right hart and good affection towardes his king: he loued him not (as by reason he shoulde haue done) but hated him, and all other that loued him right well, for he contemned the worde of God. Wherefore it came to passe, that being in extreme daunger, he sought helpe of a witch to reare Samuel from the dead, ỳ he might now use his aduise, whō he dispised beeing aliue, and disdained to heare him. This woman reareth one, who is no otherwise called Samuell, than when false gods, are called gods, when in very deede they are not gods, but wood and stones, or rather (as Paul saith). 1. Corin. 10. very diuels. This counterfait Samuel giueth him neither comfort nor Counsell; but driueth him to utter desperation. The same hapned unto Saule which chaunceth unto those stubborne children, whiche despise their parents, contemne their counsel, & would gladly wish their death, and at the last grow unto ỳ point, ỳ they would willingly take in hand a great iorney on condition it might be graunted them to heare them giue their last counsell. 1. Cor. 10.

An other example hereof. Acab king of Israel, & Iezabel his wife had many godly prophets, amongst whō Elias was a man indued with the gifte of shewing and working miracles. But they did not only contēne these prophets, but also Achab.

cruelly murthered so many of them as they coulde catche. Yet amongst the rest, they especially laboured to intrape Elias, who was excéeding zealous. The Baalamites were in greate fauoure with the King: but especially with the Quéene, as her chief dearlings. And when the time approched, that Achab should suffer due and worthie punishment for his Idolatrie and wickednesse, wherein he had long time liued, he entred councell with his kinsman Iosaphat, that they ioyning their powers togither might recouer againe the Citie of *Ramoth Gilead*, which the Assirians had taken from him. Iosaphat allowed well this deuise, notwithstanding hée woulde in any wise aske counsaile hérein of God. Achab, therefore gathereth togither a Councell of 400. priests of Baall, who all with one voyce, exhorted him to goe on with his enterprise, assuring him of most certaine victorie. One of them named Sedechias, was so vainly bold, that putting hornes of yron on his head, he saide: With these hornes shalt thou pushe the Assirians. But Iosaphat suspecting the matter, asked if there were any one Prophet of God to be found, of whome they might séeke counsell. Achab answered: There is (quoth he) yet a certaine man by whom we might enquire of the Lorde, but I hate him, for he doth not prophecie góod vnto me, but euill; his name is Micheas. Iosaphat thought góod in any wise to heare him. Wherfore the king presently sent for him by one of his Chamberlaines. And thus the messenger spake vnto him. All the Prophets with one voice, prophecie góod lucke vnto the king, I pray thée therefore, that thou speake nothing to the contrary. When he was nowe brought before the two kings sitting in their thrones, clad with sumptuous apparell, and before the other Prophets, which stood in their presence, king Achab asked him, whether they should make warres against *Ramoth Gilead*, or no? Unto whom he scoffingly answered: go (saith he) thou shalt haue prosperous successe. The king

3. *Reg.* 22.

who

let euery one returne home to his owne house in safetie. Then saide Achab, Did I not tell thee, that this fellow doth prophecie me no good? The Prophet went on, saying: Heare the word of God: I sawe the Lord sitting in his seate of maiestie, and all the hoste of heauen stande about him on his right hande, and on his lefte hande. And the Lorde saide, Who shall entice Achab that he may go and fall at *Ramoth Gilead*. And one saide on this manner, and an other saide on that manner. Then there came forth a spirit, and stoode before the Lorde and saide, I will entice him. And the Lorde saide vnto him, wherewith? And he saide, I will goe out and be a false spirite in the mouth of all his Prophets. Then he saide, thou shalt entice him, and shalt also preuaile: go forth and do so. Now therefore beholde, the Lord hath put a lying spirite in the mouth of all these thy Prophets, and the Lorde hath appointed euill against thee. Then Sedechias came neare and smote Micheas on the cheeke, and saide: when went the spirit of the Lord from me, to speake vnto thee? And Micheas prophecied what should happen also vnto him. So the king commaunded him to be cast into prison, and to be fed with bread and water vntil he returned from the wars. Then saide Micheas, If thou returne in peace, the Lorde hath not spoken by me: and therewith he willed all all the people to hearken what he spake. Notwithstanding the kings went foreward with their enterprise, and prepared themselues, and led forth their armies against their enemies. Achab was slaine in the battaile: Iosaphat because he ioyned himselfe with the wicked, was in very great daunger, &c.

I haue handled this historie somewhat at large, that we might vnderstand, how God by his iust iudgement sendeth spirites vnto those which despise his word, whereby they may be beguiled and deceiued.

The very same happened vnto the Christians after the Apostles time. For when the word of God began to be lesse esteemed than it should haue bene, and men preferred their owne affections before the hearing thereof: and when as they would incurre no maner of daunger, for the defence of their faith, and of the truth, but accounted of all religions alike, God so punished them, that now they began to giue eare vnto false teachers, which framed themselues vnto their vaine affections, they learned of images, whom they called Lay-mens bookes, they kissed these mens bones, and shrined them in golde (if happily they were their boanes) whose doctrine before they disdained to receiue: they gaue credit vnto false apparitions and diuellish visions: and so suffered they worthie punishment for their great ingratitude. Euen as yong men, which will not be ruled by their maisters, are after compelled to obey other men with great shame: so also happened it vnto those men: for they fel daily more and more from the word of God, in so much that when they had once lost the truthe, some ranne one way, and some an other, to finde a meanes for the remission of their sinnes: and one man beleeued this spirite, an other that, which no man can deny.

The like chaunced vnto the Gentiles in times past, as it appeareth by the first chap. to the Romanes, and also by their owne writings. They worshipped many gods, many miracles were shewed amongst them: they had many visions of gods, and many oracles: which when the Apostles began to preach, all ceased. S. Athanasius in his booke De humanitate verbi. Fol. 55. and 64. writeth, that in auncient time there were oracles at *Delphos* in *Bœotia*, *Lycia*, and other places which hee nameth: but nowe since Christ is

Rom. 1.

Athanasius.

preached euery where vnto all men, this madnesse hath ceased, &c. In the like maner writeth Lactantius and others. But in these our dayes, since we haue refused mens traditions, and willingly imbraced the doctrine of the Gospell, all appearings of soules and spirits haue quite vanished away.

Who (I pray you) heareth now of any soule or spirit, which doth wander, and as they call it, craue mens deuotions? Those rumblings of spirits in the night, are now muche more seldome heard than they haue bene in times past.

CHAP. II.

What the cause is that in these our dayes so fewe spirites are seene or heard.

THe cleare light of Gods word driueth away all such spirits, which vse to worke their feates in the darke. The cleare light approaching, the shadow & darkenesse vanisheth. The prince of darknesse shunneth light, and hath nothing to do where men worship God the Father, only through Iesu Christ, beleeuing only on him, and committing themselues wholy vnto his protection. If men esteem the word of God, and haue it in price, he will in no wise suffer them to be so ouerseene and deceiued, as they are which do all things without the warrant of his word.

Here I cannot ouerpasse with silence a certaine merry iest: when once there chaunced to be talke in a certaine place of visions and spirites, a certaine professour of the Gospell saide vnto a Papist in this maner: You ought (quoth he) euen by this to gather, that our religion is true, and youres false, for that since the Gospell was preached vnto vs, very fewe spirits haue bin seene of any man.

To

To whome the other made aunswere by way of reasoning called Violentum: Nay (saith hee) hereby ye may gather, that your religion is naught, and oures good: for the diuell assaulteth those, whome he feareth will shortly reuolte from him.

A storie of S. Benedict, seing many diuels in a monastery and fewe in the market.

It is not much vnlike whiche Æneas Siluius (who was afterwardes made Pope, called Pius. 2.) reciteth in his Historie of the Councell of *Basill*, out of the life of holy Benedict, father of the Monkes called after his name. Hee sometimes visiting a certaine Monasterie of holy men, espyed an infinite route of diuels, who as it were fighting with the holy fathers, laboured to disturbe the good workes which they went about. And he forthwith going to a faire full of marchandise and buying and selling, sawe there but one diuell, and he also idle and sad, sitting vppon a watchtoure, wherat saint Benedict maruelling, that he saw the place which was holy and dedicate to praier, full of diuels, and that he founde the prophane place which was occupied with periurie and other offences, guarded but with one Diuell: coniures the same Diuell to declare and shewe vnto him the true cause thereof: who straight answered him, that it was needfull the holy place shoulde be assaulted by many diuels, but those which sinned of their voluntarie accorde, had no neede to bee deceiued by the Diuell.

But I aske thee this question O thou Papist, mighte not the Gentils in ancient time haue obiected the same to the Christians, when they demaunded of them why their Oracles ceassed? and why there were so fewe Visions? If those Spirites or bugges be Diuels, why doe you then saye and beleeue that they are the soules of deade menne, whiche desire helpe of you? I will shewe you the verye true cause why those visions are nowe so seldome times seene: forsothe because the Diuell perceiueth, that wee vnderstande his subtilties and craft, therefore hee

hunteth

of his deede, if thou perceiue he bee acquainted with thy sleight, by and by thou leauest him, and goest vnto an other which is fast a sleep, and cannot perceiue the deceit.

There be other causes also why these things happen now more seldome. If any man deceiue thee once, twice, or thrice, afterwards thou openest thy eyes, and espiest what he doth and what he goeth about: so when we haue bene often beguiled with false apparitions, we will not easily be persuaded, if any man tell vs that a soule or spirite hath appeared (as the prouerbe saith,) Burnt childe, dreads fire. Moreouer, whereas now adayes fewe stand in feare of spirits, many might be easily found, who would seeke them, feele them, yea and also handle them. This is well knowne, and therefore no man will gladly put on a visor, or otherwise counterfeit himselfe to be a ghost. A man may soone persuade a childe that there is a black man, a tall woman, which will put children that cry in their budget, &c. but after they are come to maturitie of yeares, they will no more bee feared with visours and such like persuasions: they will laugh at thy follie, if afterwards thou goe about to make them so afraide. Euen so when we were children in the scriptures, that is, when we vnderstood them not, we might be easily seduced to beleeue many things: But now that we reade them in all manner of tongues, and do daily profit in them, we do not suffer our selues to be so mocked, neither doo we beleeue euery vaine apparition. How many sights of spirits did the knauerie of the Monkes of *Berna* driue away, after it was once detected? Things are set vp in the fields to feare away the birdes, which at the last also they perceiue to be but trifles, and are not driuen away any longer with suche toyes. What maruel is it then, if after so great a shipwracke

A burnt child dreads fire.

of godlinesse and truth, men albeit they are simple, doo at the last open their eyes.

CHAP. III.

Why God doth suffer straunge noyses, or extraordinarie rumblings to bee heard before some notable alterations or otherwise.

IN that there happeneth certaine straunge things before the death of men, and also before notable alterations, and destructions of countries, as maruellous crackes, and terrible roaring, surely it turneth to good vnto the iust, and to further damnation to the wicked. For by these means God sheweth that nothing commeth to passe by chance, or by aduenture, but that the life and death, the prosperous or vnfortunate estate of al men, is in the power and hand of God. It is nothing so as the Epicures affirme, that God hath no regard whether any man liue, or be borne, or do well or euill, or otherwise, or whether commõ wealths do florish, or be made waste. Christ himself teacheth vs, that not so much as a sparrow falleth vnto the grounde without the will of God. Salomon and Daniel say, that the hearts of kings are in Gods hands, and that he appointeth or deposeth kings at his pleasure. Wherfore if we happily do heare any noises or such like, they ought rather to put vs in good comfort, thã to make vs afraide. And againe, God hereby admonisheth vs, that we be not idle and secure, for he hath in all ages stirred vp his seruants, not only with word, but also with rare and straunge apparitions. The very Gentiles accounted these miraculous things, as the admonitions and warnings of their gods, as it may be seen euery where, in their histories. And albeit it be very likely, that most of these things happen by the diuels procurement, yet neuerthelesse, we herein perceiue Almightie God his fatherly care, loue, and preseruatiõ of vs against ŷ deuises of the diuel. For albeit the diuel take no rest, but is alwayes in readinesse to destroy

vs,

vs, yet can he not hurt vs, so long as God kéepeth watche and defendeth vs. The wicked who despise the preaching of Gods word, are sore terrified with these things, in so much that they not knowing whither to turne themselues, are constrained to confesse, that God doth gouerne all mens actions, and that there are good and euil spirits. Otherwise they coulde in no case be repressed, but that they would doo greater mischiefe vnto the faithfull, except God by these meanes did cast feare vppon them, and as it were with a snaffle or bridle, did hale and drawe them backe.

CHAP. IIII.

After what sort they should behaue themselues, whiche see good or euil spirits, or meete with other straunge aduentures: and first how Iewes and Gentiles behaued themselues in the like cases.

That we may rightly vnderstand how we ought to behaue our selues, if any thing either good or euill, appeare vnto vs, we wil first declare how the Gentiles and Iewes vsed themselues in like cases. Amongst the Gentiles, not only those wandring spirits beare men in hand that they were mens soules, but also shewed what were good and expedient for them to doo for their sake, to wit, that they should do sacrifices for their soules, obserue their obsequies, burie their bodies, erect Temples, make holy dayes, and such like stuffe. Suetonius writeth, that the Emperor Caligule his bodie was priuily conueyed into the gardeins called *Lamiam*, and there with a hastie fire being but halfe consumed, was cast into a pit, and couered with a litle earth. But afterwards, whē his sisters returned from exile, it was taken vp, and thorowly burnt, and afterward solemnly buried. But before they had so done, the gardē kéepers were very much troubled with appearing of spirites. And moreouer, no man could passe any night in the same house where he was slaine, without some great feare, vntil such time as the house was vtterly destroyed with fire.

What the Gentiles did when they sawe spirits.

Suetonius.

We read also in other writers, that the ghostes of them which were not orderly buried, or whose accustomed rites and ceremonies in the time of warres were omitted, did appeare either to their friendes or unto others, complayning and intreating that their funerals, and all other ceremonies might be obserued for their sake: whereof came the hearses, weekeminds, monthminds, and anniuersaries, whereof we reade many things in the Ethnike writers, and many things are recited out of the olde Poets, and in Lilius Giraldus, in his booke *De sepultura*, and also in Polid. Virgilius *De Inuentione rerum.lib.6.cap.*10. We haue shewed before in the second part and first Chapter, that some haue desired others, that they might bee buried after that they were dead. Cicero writeth in his 1. booke *De legibus*, that Romulus the first founder of *Rome*, walking after his death not farre from Atticus house, appeared unto Iulius Proculus, and told him that he was now a god, and that his name was *Q*uirinus, and therwith commanded that there should be a Temple erected and dedicated unto him in the same place.

Septimæ Tricesimæ Anniuersaria.

Lilius Giraldus.

Cicero.

Ouid.

Ouid writeth *Lib.4.Fastorum*, that Remus appeared in the night time unto Fastulus, and to his wife Accia Laurentia, sometime his Nurse, complaining unto them of his miserable death, and desiring them to make laboure, that the same day wherein he was slaine, might bee accounted amongst their holy dayes. The people of *Rome* (as Ouid witnesseth, *Lib.2.Fastorum*) kept a feast in the moneth of Frebruarie called *Feralia*, in the which they did sacrifice unto the infernall goddes, and those whose duties it was to celebrate the funeralls of their Auncesters, carried dishes of meat to their sepulchers. Whereof Fastus and Varro called the same feast by the name of *Feralia*. These dishes of meate were set upon a stone, at the time of these sacrifices: for the which cause, as *S*eruius saith, they were called *Silicernium*, by the which word some will haue a

Feralia.

certaine

certaine feast signified, which is bestowed uppon old men. Donatus sayth, that *Silicernium* is a supper, which is made to the infernall Gods, because *Eam silentes cernant*, that is, the deade soules do receiue it, or because those that doe serue it, do onely *cernere*, see it, and not taste thereof, &c. There were also certaine holie feastes called *Parentalia*, in the which meate was carried to the Sepulchers, for the soules of Parents and Auncestours before deceased. And albeit they suppose, that soules were pleased with small giftes, as of milke, wine, and such like, whereof mention is made in Ouid, yet notwithstanding they also killed sacrifices, whereof some suppose that *Feralia* tooke their name, *à feriendis pecudibus*, of killing sheepe. Unto their sacrifices they also added praiers, and kindled lightes. When in times past the Romanes being troubled with warres, had let passe the feast of *Parentalia*, they therefore supposed (that the infernall Goddes being for the same cause angrie) there arose stormes and pestilence, and that soules rising out of their graues, did wander with pittifull complaintes about the graues, and by the highway sides, and in the fieldes. This feaste endured by the space of fifteene dayes, in the whiche married women lay not with their husbandes, neither those whiche were marriageable did marrie, and the Images of their Goddes were couered. The soules of them that were dead, when they came to the meate, they wandred about the graues, and were fed (as they thought) with the banquet. Parentalia.

In the moneth of May, there was holden a feast in the night time, which at the beginning they called *Remuria*, and afterwardes *Lemuria*. This did not differ much from the feaste called *Feralia*, whiche was instituted to pacifie soules. Touching the originall of them, and the rytes belonging therto, looke Ouid in his *Lib. 5. Fastorum*. One who tooke on him to pacifie the soules, arose in the night verie late, he went barefooted, and washed himselfe euer with Lemuria. Ouid.

fresh springing water, and then taking beanes whiche he had rolled in his mouth, he threw them behinde his backe, and said, that with them he did redeeme himselfe, and after beating on a peece of brasse, he prayed the soules to depart from thence: which thing if they had done nine times, they thought they had ended their holy seruice. These were celebrated by the space of three dayes. The sacrifices which are done for the infernall gods, are called *Inferiæ*.

We reade in Lucan, of the soules of Sylla and Marius, which were purged by sacrifice. We shewed before how Athanagoras commanded the bones which were digged vp in the entrie of his house at *Athens*, to bee orderly buried againe. &c.

Touching the Iewes behauiour.

The auncient Iewes had an expresse commandement of God, not to bee any thing moued with the miracles of false Prophets, and God in plaine words forbad them, not to seeke counsel of dead bodies. Saule in the beginning of his raigne, while he yet gaue himselfe vnto godlinesse, vtterly destroyed all Coniurers and Witches. I doo not remember that I haue euer heard or read, how the Iewes behaued themselues when any spirits appeared vnto them: yet I doubt not but that they are superstitious as well in these things, as in all others.

CHAP. V.

How Christian men ought to behaue themselues when they see Spirites, and first that they ought to haue a good courage, and to be stedfast in faith.

How Christian menne oughte to behaue themselues in this behalfe, it is fully and amply declared in the holie Scriptures, in like manner as all other things are, whiche appertaine vnto our saluation. To wit, that first we ought to be of good courage

courage without feare, being assured and constante in true faith.

For if they be good Angels which shew themselues vnto vs, then are they sent vnto vs from God, to a good ende and purpose. But if they be wicked and euill, they can do vs no harme be they neuer so desirous, excepte God giue them leaue thereto. If it be nothing but a vaine imagination that we haue, or an idle sight obiected vnto our eies, surely it is great follie to be any thing afraid. In déed it is naturall vnto vs, to be amazed with feare when we sée suche things: for very godly menne, as we read both in the olde and newe Testament, were stricken with excéeding feare when they sawe good Angels, but yet a man must pull vp his heart againe. When Christes Disciples sawe their Maister walking vpon the water, and approching neare the shippe, they thought they sawe a spirite, and they were astonished, and cried out through feare. But the Lorde saide vnto them, be of good comforte, it is I, be not afraide.

The like is reade in the foure and twentie Chapter of Saint Luke, when he appeared vnto them after his resurrection, and sawe that they were maruellously afraid. Matthew the 10. Feare not saithe Christ, those whiche slay the bodie, but cannot kill the soule, but rather stande in awe of him, who can cast both bodie and soule into hell fire. The Diuell would like it well, if we would alwaies stand in feare of him.

Luke.24.

Math.10.

Be not dismaide, although thou heare some spirit stir and make a noise, for in case hée rumble onely to make thée afraide, care not for him, but lette him rumble so long as he will, for if he sée thée without feare, hée will soone depart from thée. And if thou thinke good, thou maiest boldly say vnto him, get thée hence with a mischiefe thou wicked Diuell, thou hast nothing to do with me, who haue sette my onely beléefe in Christ Iesu my Sauiour.

I am

I am owner of this house,and not thou, vnto whome there is an other place appointed.&c. If he perceiue ẏ there is no feare or dreade of him, and that his bustling is not estéemed, he will not continue long time. I will make this matter manifest with a similitude, which is well knowne. There be certaine men, which if they thinke other men stande in feare of them, they make wise to drawe their sworde, and sometimes two they draw it, and strike the stones therewith,chafing and swearing lustily: But if they knowe their aduersaries haue a good courage, and that (if néede require) they will fight it out stoutly,they will quickly put vp their sworde into their scabberde. In like manner, if the Diuill sée thou art of a good stomacke, and well armed with Gods worde, he will soone séeke after others whome he may mocke with feare.

But if it please God to exercise thée by the Deuill for a certaine time,as he did sometime Iob, thou must patiently suffer all things which he laieth vppon thée, and that willingly for Gods commaundement sake. And knowe thou well, that he cannot thus much hurt,neither thy goods, nor bodie,nor soule,without the permissiō and sufferance of Almightie God: if God giue him leaue to plague thy bodie, thinke with thy selfe howe so euer it be done,that God hath so done for thy profitte and commoditie, who also sendeth gréeuous sicknesses vppon other men,by other meanes & instruments, or else doth exercise them with other kindes of calamities. Be therefore strong and constant in faith, yet lette euery one beware of boldnesse, temeritie, and headdie rashnesse.

Christ hath conquered the diuel. *Luke* 11. *Iohn*.12.16.

Let it comforte thée,that thou knowest Christe hath conquired the Deuill, as he himselfe teacheth in the eleuenth chapter of Luke,by the example of a strong man at armes. In the 12.&.16.of John he saith: the Prince of this worlde shalbe cast out of the dores, that is to say, out of the hearts of them which cleaue to the worde of God, and are not in loue

loue with the world, whereof he is prince and ruler. For he hath power ouer such, which do greedily loue the world.

In the first of Iohn the third chapter, it is saide: The sonne of man appeared, that is, came into the world for that cause, that he might destroy the workes of the diuel. There are many miracles in the Gospell which shewe that Christ cast out diuels. Albeit God for a time do suffer the diuel in many things, yet hath he appointed him his bounds, which he may not passe. And he doth not suffer the faithfull to be tempted any more of him than they are able to endure. He giueth his grace plentuously vnto them, vpon whome he laieth great afflictions. 1. Iohn. 3.

We ought not to maruel if spirits sometimes be seen or heard. For as Saint Peter saith: Sathan raungeth euery where, in houses, fieldes, water and fire: and yet he is not alwayes espied of men, neither can he so bee, except God giue him leaue to shewe himselfe. In that that we doe alwayes see him (for he being of an inuisible nature, taketh on him diuers shapes) or heare him, we haue to thanke the goodnesse of almightie God: for otherwise we should not be in rest one moment of time. But if sometime wicked spirits meete with vs in a visible forme by the will of God, or do otherwise trouble and disquiet our houses, we must not think therfore that they were neuer in house before. The diuel is conuersant among men.

CHAP. VI.

It behoueth them which are vexed with spirites, to pray especially, and to giue themselues to fasting, sobrietie, watching, and vpright and godly liuing.

NOw because good Angelles appeare vnto vs more seldome in this oure time (for there is a verie greate difference of men liuing vnder the newe Testament, from them that liue vnder the olde, vnto whom God many and oftentimes sent his Angels) and that euill angels very often appeare, we ought the rather to commit our selues more diligently to the tuition of almightie God, both when we go to bed, and also when we arise againe.

Our Sauiour amongst all other things, taught vs to pray to this purpose: Deliuer vs from euill. And moreouer he saith in the 17. Chapter of Matthew, that some kinde of diuels are not driuen away by any other kinde of meanes than fasting and praying. As touching those which suppose that diuels ought to be cast out with coniurations, and execrable cursings, I will entreat in the end of this my booke. Watch and pray, least ye fall into temptation. Matthew 26. And in the 22. of Luke, Christ saith vnto Peter, Sathan hath desired to sift you euen as corne, but I haue praied that thy faith faile not. And euen at this present also he maketh intercession for vs sitting at the right hand of his heauenly father.

The auncient Fathers in olde time, call vppon God in all their daungers and troubles, whereof it were a needlesse matter to auouch many examples. It is also very profitable and good to craue the prayers of the whole congregation, when soeuer we are vexed with euill spirites and vaine fantasies. For we know right well that the prayers of the Church haue bene very profitable and effectuall vnto others, and that the godly in their distresses haue euermore desired them.

It is Gods pleasure, that the faithfull should succour one an other with their good prayers. Howbeit that the Saintes after their departure from hence, should pray for vs, that we should in any wise desire their prayers, surely there is no commandement of God, or any example thereof in the holy scriptures.

Moreouer, the Apostles teach vs to withstand the craft and subtiltie of the diuell by this meanes. Saint Paule to the Ephesians the 6. Chapter, and Peter in his first Epistle

and

and fifth Chapter saith: Be ye sober and watche, for your aduersary the diuel, as a roaring lyon walketh about, seeking whom he may deuoure: whom resist stedfast in faith, &c. *Ephe.6.* *1 Pet.5.*

When men are secure and negligent, wholly giuen unto pleasures, and as it were drowned in surfetting, couetousnesse, adulterie, and such other wickednesse, then hath the diuel place to shewe himselfe. Wherefore we ought to giue our selues to watching, praying, fasting, and godly liuing: we must heare the word of God often and gladly, we must desire to reade and talke of him continually, that we may thereby put from us those diuellishe illusions and sightes. We must fight against the diuel with good life.

If thou haue any publike office or charge, do it faithfully: restore thy goods euil gotten, either unto their true owners, or else imploy them to some good and godly ende. If men care neither for God, nor his word, it is no maruell if vaine sightes appeare unto them. For God suffereth such things to happen unto them, to humble them and to make them know themselues.

It is an horrible thing, that there are some which giue ouer themselues to the diuel, because he should not torment them: they ought rather to weigh with themselues, that if they so do, they shall be perpetually tormented of euil spirits, except they truly repent and turne againe to God.

CHAP. VII.

That spirits which vse to appeare, ought to be iustly suspected: and that we may not talke with them, nor enquire any thing of them.

WE ought not without great cause to suspecte all Spirites, and other apparitions. For albeit God doth vse the helpe and seruice of good Angels, for the preseruation of his elect, yet notwithstanding in these our dayes they appeare vnto vs very seldome. For things are nowe farre otherwise since Christes comming into the worlde, than they were before in auncient time. Although perchaunce thou thinke thou haste seene a good Angell, yet doo not easily and vnaduisedly giue him credite. If the euent of the matter declare afterward, that it was a good Angell, which gaue thee notable warning of some matter, or deliuered thee out of some great dangers: giue God thankes that he hath dealt so fatherly and mercifully with thee, and hath suche care ouer thee, and endeuour to frame thy selfe to his wil and pleasure. But if thou see an Angell whiche flattereth and speaketh thee faire, suche a one as those are whiche craue thy helpe, (as thou hast heard before) in no wise credite their wordes. Men which blaunche and flatter with vs, are alwayes suspitious, why then should not such spirites be suspected? Enter into no communication with such spirites, neither aske them what thou must giue, or what thou must doo, or what shall happen hereafter. Aske them not who they are, or why they haue presented themselues to bee seene or heard. For if they be good, they will like it well, that thou wilt heare nothing but the word of God: but if they be wicked, they will endeuour to deceiue thee with lying. When the Angell in the first Chapter of Matthew, instructed Ioseph in a dreame, he by and by alleaged testimony out of the prophet. If it be so, that we must not beleeue an Angell comming from heauen, who can iustly blame vs, if we giue no credite to spirits and suspitious dreames? Although Christ and his Apostles had the full power to shew miracles, yet did they establish and confirme their doctrine by the holie scriptures.

Matth.1.

When Almightie God himselfe had enquired of Adam in Paradice, touching the breaking of his Commaundement, and that he had layde the fault vpon his wife Eua,

and

and she had put it ouer to the Serpent, which caused her to eate of the forbidden frute, God woulde not demaund of the Serpent, that is, of the Diuell, (whiche had vsed him as an instrument) why he had so done, for he knewe right well that he was a lyer. Except Eue had talked with the Serpent, she had neuer transgressed Gods Commandement.

If Spirites of their owne accorde woulde gladly tell vs many thinges: yet wée must not giue eare vnto them, much lesse ought we to coniure them to tell vs the truthe. God commaunded in his lawe, (as wée haue oftentimes said before) that no man should enquire any thing of the dead.

God himselfe sent his faithfull seruants, the Prophets, Apostles, Euangelists, and especially his onely begotten sonne Christ Iesu our Lord and Sauiour into the worlde, by whoms he truly and plentifully taught his faithfull seruants what they ought to beléeue, to do, to leaue vndon, and what kinde of worshipping did best please him, with many other such things. By them he enformed vs concerning great and waightie affaires, which should happen in his Churche, and in kingdomes, euen vnto that blessed day wherein Christ shall iudge the world, and shall call togither his generall Councell, and shall pronounce finall sentence vppon them who haue done well or ill, and wherein he shall make a diuision and separation betwéene the good and euil.

God hath alwayes giuen vs teachers.

Christ himselfe after his Resurrection did not immediately ascend into heauen, but aboade a while in earth, appearing vnto his Disciples and others, least we should at any time say: Who euer came again to tell vs what estate is to be looked for in the other world?

Moreouer, God among suche great and long persecutions, wherein many profitable bookes haue perished, hath miraculously preserued the holy Scriptures for our profit,

God hath preserued the scriptures.

lite, euen vnto this day, and hereafter will preserue them in despite of all impious and wicked men.

God hath instituted the holy ministerie. He hath also ordeyned the ministerie of the worde, that vnto the ende of the worlde, there shoulde be some men, whiche bothe by liuely voyce, and also by their writings, shoulde interprete his worde, and enfourme others of his will and pleasure. His word is a shining

Psalme.119. John.8. lanterne, which shineth in this darke worlde, which is full of errours, as we reade Psalm. 119. And our sauiour saith in the eight chapter of Saint Iohn, that he is the light of the worlo, whome if any man follow, he walketh not in darkenesse.

This standeth as a sure grounde: wherefore no other reuelations are to be looked for, neither by myracles from Heauen, nor by wandring spirites or soules, as the common people misterme them. But lette vs imagine, that they are the wandring spirites of deade bodies, then is it necessarie, that they be the soules, either of faithfull men, or of infidels. If they be the soules of the faithfull, they wil say with God the father concerning his sonne Christe Jesus, *Heare him*. But if they be the soules of Infidels and of wicked men, who I pray you, will vouchsafe to heare them, or beléeue any thing they say? Morcouer those things whiche these counterfeite soules doo speake, eyther agrée with the holy Scriptures, or else are contrary vnto them. If they are agréable, then are they to be receiued, not because spirits speake them, but because they are comprysed in the word of God. But in case they are repugnant to the worde of God, they ought in no wise to be receiued, albeit an Angell from Heauen vtter them. Thou wilt not beléeue a man of thy familiar acquaintaunce, otherwise worthy of credite, who sounde of bodie and soule, nowe liueth togither with thée, if hée affirme any thing which thou knowest to be contrary to the holy Scriptures; why then wouldest thou beléeue a spirite which thou

doest

doest not knowe? In ciuill causes the euidence or witnesse of dead men is reiected, why then in causes of religion shuld we giue eare to the testimonie of runagate and wandring spirites.

It is no harde or difficulte matter for the Lorde oure God to sende his Angels unto vs, whome otherwise hee vseth for our profite, and by them to instructe vs in the Faith: but it hath pleased him to appoint the matter otherwise.

Wee reade in the tenth chapter of the Actes, that by an Angell he commaunded Cornelius to sende for Peter, that he might instruct him in the faith. He mighte haue commaunded the Angell to teache Cornelius, but he followed an orderly meanes. It shalbe best for vs therfore to stand to the holy Scriptures simply, and that all appearing of spirites, as also all dreames and reuelations be tried by the holy Scriptures, as vpon a touchstone, and so to admit nothing but that which is set forth in the holy Scriptures: for except we go thus warely to worke, there is greate danger least wee bee deceiued. If the auncient Fathers had so done, they had not estrayed so farre from the Apostles simplicitie. *Acts.10.*

S. Augustine in his third booke and 6. chapter, writing against the letters of Petilianus saieth thus: If concerning Christe, or any other thing, whiche appartayneth to faith and euerlasting life, (I will not say, we: for comparing with him that said: Albeit that wee) but simply, whereas he going on, sayd: If an Angell from Heauen shall teache you any thing besides that whiche you haue receiued in Scriptures conteining the law and the Gospel, bee he accursed. S. Augustines counsell. Scripture to be only beleued.

S. Chrisostom vnto the Epistle to the Galathians the firste chapter: Abraham (saith he) when he was desired to send Lazarus, said: They haue Moises and the prophets, if they will not heare them, they will not giue eare vnto them Chrisostomes aduise.

them which rise up from the dead. And when he bring in Christ uttering these wordes, he sheweth howe he woulde haue the holy scriptures more worthy of credite than any raised from the dead. S. Paule (when I name Paule, I name likewise Christ, for he stirred up his mind) preferreth the Scriptures before Angels descending from Heauen, and that for very iust cause. For albeit Angels are great, yet are they seruants and ministers. For all holy scriptures were not commaunded to be written and sent unto us by seruants, but by almightie God ye Lord of all things. Thus write these two holy fathers.

All things necessarie to saluation are conteined in the scriptures.

What things soeuer are necessarie for us to know, are conteined in the holy scriptures: those things which are not expressed in them, we must not curiously enquire of, as things profitable for our saluation. Who will therefore say against the commaundement of God, that these things are to be sought and learned of dead men, and by diuellish visions? These things which are secret and hidden, we shall throughly see when we come to eternall life. May not God, if we be not content with his holy word, say that unto us, which sometimes he spake by the mouth of Helias unto the messengers of king Ochosias. Is there no God in *Israell*, that you now go to Accaron to aske counsell of Belzebub? Yea Thomas Aquinas denieth that diuels are to be heard, whiche deceiue simple menne, feyning themselues to be the soules of dead men: and by that coloure especially terrifie menne, whiche sometimes also happened unto the Gentiles.

If it were certaine and sure that the Diuell coulde not appeare and deceiue menne, and also shewe greate and straunge miracles, then perchaunce some men would thinke that we shoulde giue eare unto such Spirites: but nowe we see the contrary happen. An euill spirite cloaketh his erroures under the colour of diuine seruice, and under the pretence of religiō, he endeuoureth to ouerthrow religion.

religion. For as S. Hierome saith, the diuell sheweth not himselfe with all his deceits, that he may be knowne what he is. And therefore it behoueth vs to be very circumspect and warie. Hierom.

Moreouer, miracles are onely testimonies and seales of the word, neither may any thing be approued by them, which is repugnant to the word of God. All miracles which lead vs away from our Creator vnto creatures, and do attribute that vnto our workes, which is onely due vnto the merites of Christ: and to be short, all those which induce vs any wayes into errour, are to be eschued. If we must néeds beléeue these appearing soules, no man could be assured of his estate: for new things should be continually deuised, as we sée plainly it happened in the olde time. Therefore we must let passe all maner of spirits, and embrace true religion, and therein constantly abide. Miracles are seales of the word.

CHAP. VIII.

Testimonies out of holie Scripture, and one example whereby it is prooued, that such kinde of apparitions are not to be credited, and that we ought to bee verie circumspect in them.

That wee ought not by and by to beléeue all thinges which we heare, not onely experience and many common Prouerbes, but also the holy Scriptures teach vs, especially in cases concerning our saluation, touching the which thing, we will alledge only a fewe places and examples.

When Christ first sent abroad his Disciples to preach the Gospell, he said vnto them, Matthew 10. Be yée wise as Serpents, and simple as Doues, beware of men: howe much more than ought we to take héede of diuels? Christ prophecieth in the 24. of Matthew, that many false teachers Mat. 10. Mat. 24.

 shall

shall come in the latter daies, and shall shewe straunge myracles to confirme their erroures, and therefore hée commaundeth the faithfull, to be héedefull and circumspect, and not without cause hée addeth: Beholde I haue tolde you before. Sainte Paule to the Galathians the firste Chapter, saith in greate earnest vnto them, that if an Angell come from Heauen, and preache vnto them any other Gospell, hée shoulde be accursed. Euen so, if at this time spirites appeare, and doe vtter any thinge repugnant to the Doctrine of the Apostles and Prophets, they are to be reiected. The Apostle in his firste Epistle and fourth Chapter to Timothie, dothe prophecie of false tea-

1. *Tim.* 4. chers whiche shoulde come, and saithe, the spirit speaketh euidently, that in the latter times some shall departe from the faithe, and shall giue héede vnto spirits of errour and doctrines of Deuils, whiche speake lies through hipocrisie, and haue their consciences burned with an hote yron, forbidding to marrie, and commaunding to absteyne from meates which God hath created to be receiued with gyuing thankes of them whiche beléeue, and knowe the truth. &c. By the worde (spirite) are vnderstoode false teachers, whiche vaunt themselues of the spirite of God: But what cause is there, why it may not be vnderstoode of suche wandring spirites, which haue induced men to take in hande many things? In the seconde Epistle to the

2. *Thess.* 2. Thessalonians, and the seconde Chapter, when certaine affirmed the latter daye to be presente at hande, Paule foretelleth them, that there shall be a defection, and that Antichrist shall first come, saying: Nowe we beséech you brethren by the comming of our Lorde Iesus Christe, by our assembling vnto him, that yée be not sodenly moued from your intent, nor troubled, neither by spirits, nor by word, nor by letter, as it were from vs, as though the day of Christ were at hande. Let no man deceiue you by any meanes. &c. Whiche wordes truly in my iudgement may

also

also be verie aptly vnderstood of those wandering spirites. Saint Iohn saith in his first Epistle and fourth Chapter: *1.Iohn.4.* Dearly beloued, beleeue not euery spirit, but trie the spirits whether they are of God: for many false prophettes are gone out into the world. Hereby shall ye knowe the spirit of God. Euery spirit that confesseth that Iesus Christ is come in the flesh, is of God, and euery spirite whiche confesseth not, that Iesus Christ is come in the flesh, is not of God. &c. Here he speaketh not of spirites which falsly affirme themselues to be mens soules, but of those teachers whiche boaste of themselues that they haue the spirite of God. But in case we must not beleeue them being aliue, much lesse ought we to credite them when they are dead. And albeit that neyther Christe nor his Apostles, had so diligently giuen vs warning, not to suffer our selues to be seduced with myracles, and with the talke of spirits, yet notwithstanding, daily experience teacheth vs to bee circumspect and warie in these cases. For assoone as false teachers see that they haue no testimonie of Scripture to defende themselues withall, by and by they turne themselues to spirites and visions, whereby they may confirme their doctrine, which thing hath opened a large windowe to many errors. To what inconuenience ambition, couetousnesse and enuie, hath brought many of the Clergie, it is both well knowne by many examples, and it hath also as it were by the way bene before declared. Haue not the orders of Monkes striued amongest themselues for the preheminence? haue not they inuented newe miracles? haue they not counterfeited gods, pilgrimages, saintes and spirits? The holy Virgin is a famous and notable example, that we should not rashly beleeue euery spirit. For at what time ÿ Angell Gabriel appeared vnto her in a visible shape, and saluted her, shewing her before of ÿ incarnatiō of the sonne of God, she thought with her selfe, what maner of saluation that should be, how this thing could come to passe,

The holy virgin did not by & by beleeue the appearing of the Angell.

 seeing

of God.

CHAP. IX.

After what sort the faithful in the primitive Church, vsed themselues when they met with spirits.

I Haue declared out of the word of God, how good and godly men ought to behaue themselues, when soeuer any spirites appeare vnto them. And truly the auncient Christians behaued themselues after this sort. For they were couragious and without feare, they gaue themselues to godlinesse, and all good workes, they diligently auoyded all things which were displeasing vnto God: and they were also very circumspect, not to attribute to much vnto spirits and visions.

The signe of the Crosse. Tertullian.

It was a common custom amongst them, to blesse themselues with the signe of the Crosse, when they mette with these things, which many also vse at this day. Tertullian writeth in his booke *De corona militis*, that the auncient Christians did many times marke their foreheades with the signe of the Crosse. S. Hierom exhorteth Demetriades, that he often crosse his foreheade, least that the destroyer of *Egipt* finde any place therein. Origen also, Epiphanius, Chrisostome, and Augustine, write many thinges of the vertue of the holie Crosse. S. Athanasius writeth in his booke *De Humanitate verbi, eiusque corporali aduentu. Fol. 67.* In times past (saith he) the diuels by vaine shewes, and mockerie, ensnared men, abiding somtimes in wels, sometime in riuers, in stones, and woods, and so by craftie deceytes, brought vnwise men into sottishnesse. But nowe since.

Hierome.

Origen. &c.

Athanasius.

since Gods word hath appeared vnto vs, suche sightes and vaine fantasies haue surceased. Fol. 56. and 72. and in other places also he handleth the same matter.

Lactantius writeth of the same in his fourth booke *Diuinarum Institutionum* 26. Chapter, and also throughout the 27. Chapter. He saith that the diuel can haue no accesse vnto those, nor any wayes hurt them, which signe their foreheads with the Crosse. He addeth moreouer, that the Christians vsed this ceremonie in old time, in casting out diuels and healing diseases.

Not for that they ascribed such efficacie and force to the externall signe of the Crosse, (for that were superstitious) but vnto the Crosse, that is, to the merites of Christe, whose worthinesse and excellencie, they called withall to their remembrance. Touching the holy Apostles, or Apostolike Churches, we reade not, that they euer vsed the signe of the Crosse, in expelling diuels, in curing diseases, or in any other thing. God spared the Iewes in *Egipt*, whiche marked the doore postes with the bloude of the Lambe: not that Lambes bloude is able to deliuer men from death, but it was a figure of the bloud and passion of Christ Iesus. And the Iewes sprinkled not bloud of their owne good deuotion, as they terme it, but by the commandement of God. The holy Fathers by the ceremonie that they signed themselues with the Crosse, ment to testifie their confidence in the crosse, that is, in the death of Christ Iesus, which abandoneth all euill and mischiefe. The Diuell neuer a whit feareth the Crosse, wherewith we signe our selues, nor yet those pieces and fragments of Christes Crosse, which are shewed for reliques, but he trembleth at the power and force of Christs death, by the which he was conquered and ouerthrowne. If any man attribute too much vnto ceremonies, he cannot be excused from superstition, which worthily deserueth blame.

Whether the bare signe of the Crosse haue anie force.

We read more in the auncient writers, that they vsed

Coniurations agaiust diuels

exorcismes, or coniurations in the primatiue Churche against diuels.

Tertullian.

You may read in Tertullian in his booke *De anima*, that uncleane spirits haue oftentimes deceiued men, haue taken on them the persons of others, and haue fained themselues to be the soules of dead men, that men should not beléeue that all soules descended into Hell (what is to be understood by the word Hell, I haue shewed before) and so to bring the beléefe of the latter iudgement of the resurrection of the dead, into doubt and question.

Moreouer, we reade that the olde Fathers haue cast diuels out of men, and out of such places wherein by their rumbling, they haue put many in horrible feare. Such an historie of Saint Iohn in Abdias Babylonius, for the holy Apostles, and many godly men after them, were endued with this grace from God, that they could cast out unclean spirits: which gift continued a long season in the Church, to the great profit of the faithfull, but afterwards it ceased as other miracles did also. It maketh unto this purpose, that Tertullian writeth in his Apologetico, Fol. 858. and 159.

Thus we haue sufficiently séene after what sort the holy Fathers and auncient christians behaued themselues when any spirits appeared unto them.

CHAP. X.

That sundrie kindes of superstition haue crept in, whereby men haue attempted to driue away spirits.

2. *Thess*. 2.

In proces of time, superstitions encreased more & more. Paule complaineth, that in his time Antichrist beganne to practise his misterie of iniquitie, and that many opinions and sects beganne to spring up. Saint Iohn writeth,

1. *Iohn*. 4.

that in his time, there were many Antichristes. What maruell

Sainte Augustine in his 22. booke *De ciuitate Dei*, Augustine.
and eighte Chapter, after that hee hadde recited certaine miracles, whiche were therefore shewed that men might beleeue in Christ, he setteth forthe this historie Hesperius a man of good worshippe and calling amongest vs, hath a piece of land in the territorie of *Fussalum* called *Cubedi*, in the which, perceiuing by the languishing of his cattell and seruauntes, that his house was infected with the force and rage of euill spirites, he desired our fellow Priestes, (I being then absent,) that some one of them would take the paines to go thither, that the spirit by his good praiers might giue place: one of them went thither, and there offred the sacrifice of the bodie of Christ, praying very earnestly, that the same disquieting of spirites might cease, and by and by God had compassion, and it ceased. He had giuen him of a friend of his, some parte of holy lande brought from Hierusalem, where Christ being buried, rose againe the third day: that earth he hung vp in his chamber, least any euill might happē vnto him. But when his house was deliuered frō that trouble, he deuiseth with himselfe what he might do with the saide earth, which for reuerence sake, he would not keepe any longer in his chamber. &c. Hereby it is manifest, that superstition began immediatly, and (as it hapneth alwaies) grewe bigger with great increase, as if one shoulde roll forthe snowe clodded togither, or as when huge lumpes of snowe begin to fall down from the *Alpes*, all things on euery side are filled with snowe. Shortly after menne began to praye, and offer sacrifice for dead mennes soules, yea and that with a good intention, as it may euidently appeare in many of the auncient fathers.

After-that which S. Paule saith to the Romanes the tenth. (For I wil let passe at this time all other arguments,) how shall they call vpon him in whom they haue not beleeued? The Papists themselues cannot deny, but that we must beleeue onely in God, and therefore he onely is to be worshipped through his sonne.

The Aue Marie is no praier.

Some write that it is a soueraign remedie to driue away diuels, if we pray *Aue Maria*. Where by the way is to bee noted, that the same salutation of the Angell is no prayer, but onely a greeting, and historicall narration, to witte, howe the Archangell Gabriell tolde the Virgin Mary before of the Incarnation of Christ. But I pray thee weigh the sense of the wordes, and whether thou wilt or no, thou must needes say that these wordes conteine in them neither asking, nor thankesgiuing, which are the parts of prayer. When the Angell came vnto her, he saluted her, saying: χαῖρε *i. salue*, that is, God speede, or reioyce (for as Festus saith, the Greeke and the Latin word haue one signification.) Then he addeth further, full of grace, which is to be vnderstood passiuely, as they terme it in the schooles) for because God bestowed his grace vpon her: for so the Angell himselfe expoundeth it, when he saith afterwardes, that she had founde grace, that is, that God is mercifull and louing towardes her. Those wordes may not be so vnderstoode, as if she were the fountaine of grace (as some haue expounded it) and that she hath grace of her selfe, and bestoweth it vpon such as call vppon her, or speake vnto her with the salutation of the Angell. For neyther the Greeke worde, nor any other places of the Scriptures admit this sense. The Apostle saieth to the Ephe-

Ephesians the first Chapter, that God hath made vs his faithfull seruants, deare by his grace through his beloued, that is, through Jesus Christ. In the which saying, the same word is put, which the Angell vsed in saluting the holy Virgine. It is written in the first Chapter of saint Iohns Gospell in plaine wordes, that Iohn Baptist bare witnesse of Christ with a loude voyce, and saide, that we all haue receiued of his fulnesse, grace for grace. For the lawe was giuen by Moses, but grace and truth sprang vp by Christ. Many other suche places I omit for breuities sake. The Virgin Mary her selfe saith, the Lord hath done maruellous things vnto me. She setteth forth the grace of God, giuen vnto her from God, without any of her deserts. For he neuer bestowed greater grace on any woman. And there is a very great difference betweene him that conferreth grace, and them which receiue or obtaine grace. Grace is only to be sought at his hands, who giueth grace, and not of them which themselues receiue grace. A fewe yeares past, all men besought the Virgin for helpe, hoping for more grace and succour of her than of Christ himselfe. The Angell addeth further: Blessed art thou amongst women, that is, God hath conferred more grace vnto thee, than vnto any other woman. The wordes which are ioyned herevnto, Blessed is the frute of thy wombe, are not the wordes of the Angell, but of her cousin Elizabeth, who also saluted her. Vnto these wordes some religious men added, Jesus Christ, Amen. Therefore the Angell vttered not all those wordes of the Aue Marie (as it may manifestly be gathered out of the very text of Saint Luke, Chapter 1.) not because we deny these wordes to be good and holy, for the text saith of Elizabeth, that she was full of the holy ghost: but that which the Angell spake not, is not to be attributed vnto her. You shall not finde in any allowed Authors, that in the time of the Apostles and many dayes after, this greeting was accounted as a prayer, or that any godly men did

Ephe.1.

Iohn.2.

salute, and call vpon the holy Virgin. Which thing I write not, because I would bereaue the holy Virgin of hir honor, but least that against hir will, we giue hir that honour which is only due to God the Father, and to his sonne Iesu Christ. For he is our onely mediatour and redéemer. 1. Timoth. 2. Otherwise the Aue Marie, and other such places of holy Scripture full of consolation and comfort, touching the humanitie of Christ, his punishment, death, and merites, are to be often read, and diligentely considered: neither are the Scriptures to be pulled out of the handes of the lay people, in whiche they may sée all these things with their owne eyes. Indéede I denie not but Spirites haue many times vanished away vpon the saying of Aue Marie, but it was so done, that men might therby be confirmed in their superstition.

1. Timo. 2.

Holy Water.

But these men procéeding further, did coniure or consecrate water with certain peculiar ceremonies, and kept it in vessels in their churches, houses and else where: amongest many other vertues, ascribing this force vnto it, that it chaseth away spirites, and vaine sights. They also consecrated saulte, and taught, that whether socuer it were cast, it draue away spirites, and all deceites of the diuil, yea and the diuel himselfe also. Moreouer, they coniured with certain cerimonies and wordes, candles, palme, herbes, and other creatures, to driue away fantasies (as they terme them.) They laide these and such like things, as also the relikes of Saintes, in those places wheras Spirits had bin séene or heard. They also bare men in hande, that greate belles and sancebelles by their noise fraied spirites out of the ayre. All these things are founde more at large in the Papists bookes whiche are written of the consecration of suche things, and are publikely extant. If belles be rong on S. Iohns day, or S. Agathes day, they say it is a most excellét remedie against spirits. Some vsed to burne a bundell of consecrated herbes, that with the smoke therof they

might

might chase away diuels. Many haue their peculiar and straunge blessings against spirites. There haue bene also many holy rites instituted by the commaundement of wandring soules, as Masses for the dead, vigils, prayers, and twelue months minds: as though the soules of godly men, being deliuered from all trouble, were not immediately translated into eternall rest. And it is also plaine by reading the Poets and Historiographers, that the Gentiles had their sacrifices for the dead, as their rites called Nouendialia, which were obserued the ninth day, and their yearely feastes, &c. Howbeit those counterfait ghostes craued nothing so earnestly, as that many Masses might be sung for their sakes, for they bare men in hand, that those had great and marueilous force to redeeme them out of Purgatorie.

Iohn Tritenhemius writeth in his Cronicles of the Monasterie of Hirsgauium, about the yeare of our Lorde 1098. Henricus the fourth then being Emperour, that at such time as the order of the Cistercians first began, there appeared many dayes and nights, not far from the citie of *Wormes*, great troupes of horsmen and footmen, as if they were now going forth to battail, running now here & now there in troupes, and that about .ix. of the clock at night they returned again to the hill nere at hand, out of ye which they vsed to come forth. At last a certaine Monke of the Abbey of *Limpurge*, which stood not far from ye hil whence they issued, associating certain other vnto him, came on a certain night to ye place of the hil, & blessing himselfe with ye signe of ye holy Crosse, adiured them in the name of the holy and vnseparable Trinitie, as they came out of the hil, to declare vnto him who they were: vnto whom one of the company made answer: we are (quoth he) no vain things, neither yet liuing souldiers, but ye soules of earthly men, seruing in this world vnder our prince, who not lōg since was slain in this place. The armour, furniture, & horses, which were vnto vs instruments of sinne while we liued, are euen now after our The order of Cistercians.

death, certaine signes and tokens of tormentes. Whatsoeuer ye sée about vs, is all firie vnto vs, although you nothing discerne our fire. When the Monkes enquired whether they might be holpen by men, the spirit answered: we may (saith he) be holpen by fasting and praiers: but chiefly by the oblation of the bodie and blood of Christ, which thing we beséech you do for vs. Assoone as he had so saide, all the whole rout of spirits cried thrée times with one voyce: pray for vs, pray for vs, pray for vs. And sodeinly withal, they séemed to be all resolued into fire, yea and the hill it self, as if it had bin on fire, cast forth as it were a great crashing and rushing of trées. They had in Churches a peculiar order of them whom they called Exorcists, or Coniurers, whose dutie was to coniure and driue away diuels, but they were not so endued with that gifte, as the auncient Christians were, and therfore they did but vaunt & boast of themselues.

Exorcists.

Afterwards certaine Monkes and Priests well séen in Magicall sciences (for they were neuer without such trimmen) tooke vpon them to coniure and driue away euill spirits out of houses into woods & desart places. They wroght marueilous and straunge things, and they said that a spirit in the name of Saints, and by the vertue of their coniuring and charecters, was constrained to giue place whether he would or not. Indéede the diuel giueth place, but he doth it as enemies doo, which by flying chuse a more fit place to fight in, or more apte to embushe themselues. That which Sathan doth, he doth it willingly and of his owne accorde, that he might withdrawe men from trusting in God onely, and driue them headlong into Idolatrie. Christ and his Disciples cast out diuels, but they were loth and vnwilling to depart. Moreouer they vsed to hang Saint Johns Gospell about their neckes, and carried about with them hallowed ware inclosed in a purse, which they call an *Agnus Dei*. There are certaine bookes abroade, especially one written by Iacobus de Clusa, a Carthusian, concerning

them, in departing from them, in the place where they ap-
peare, and what questions are to be proposed vnto them: touching which things I spake before, in the second part of this Booke and second Chapter, where if you list you may finde them.

I haue heard men which haue confessed themselues to haue bene so superstitious, that when the priest lifted vp the host (as they call it) in saying masse, they woulde presently wipe their face with their hands, because they were perswaded, that it was good to stop all spirits from meeting with them in a visible forme.

But tell mee I pray thee whosoeuer thou art whiche doest so, by what places of Scripture canst thou confirme those ceremonies? Where doth Christ and his Disciples teach vs to expell the diuell (which is a spirit, and therefore without any bodie) by bodily things? Shew we but one example, that they haue cast forth the diuel by this way or means. If you bring out of the bookes of Tobie, that the heart and liuer of the fish being laide on the coales, drone away the diuel with the smell, we say that the same booke is not accounted amongst the Canonicall scriptures: and moreouer that the same diuel was rather vanquished by the praiers of Tobias and his wife, than by any fumigation. Did Christ ordaine the holy Supper to this ende, that thereby diuels should be cast out? Albeit that an euil spirit do faine to giue place, because of these things, yet he bringeth to passe in the meane season, that superstition is more deeply rooted in the hearts of men.

CHAP. XI.

That spirites are not to bee driuen away by cursing and banning.

HEre I cannot ouerpasse, that certaine do vainly persuade themselues, that spirites may easily be driuen away with cursing and banning, for that (as they say) spirits approach neare vnto such as pray, and do more egerly disturbe and vex them. Our Lord Jesus Christ who can best tell how we should fight against the craft and subtiltie of the diuel, teacheth vs in many places to pray continually, he biddeth vs to pray in ẏ Lords praier, that we may be deliuered from euil, calling Sathan by the figure κατ' ἐξοχὴν, Euil it selfe, because he exceileth therein. Nothing can be more acceptable and pleasing to the diuel, than when any man vseth cursing and banning. He feineth that he is hereby driuen away, but in the meane season he creepeth inuisibly into their bosomes. If you list ye may driue away the diuel, in saying that he hath no place with you, but his place is in Hell, and that he hath nothing to do with those which put their only trust and confidence in Christ Jesus. For in the eight Chapter to the Romanes in the beginning, it is

Rom.8. said: Now there is no condemnation vnto them, that are grafted in Christ Jesu, who walke not according to the flesh, but according to the spirit. A man may commaund the diuel to depart from him without any cursing or banning. And that is also to be blamed, that certaine wicked and rash men talke very beastly, and filthily with spirits, if they appeare at any time vnto them.

Some others, when spirits appeare vnto them, will by and by set on them, and driue thē away with naked swords: and sometimes throw them out of the windowes, not considering with themselues, that spirites are nothing hurt with weapons. In the Grecian histories we reade, that a certaine

certaine *Lacedemonian* passing by a sepulchre in the night season, when a spirit seemed to appeare vnto him, ranne towards it thinking to run it through with his speare: saying: Whither fliest thou, O thou soule which shalt twice die? Surely it is praise worthie when a man meeting with a spirit is not afraid, but yet boldnesse and rashnesse cannot be commended. If thy enemy, albeit he be very weake be not to be despised, much lesse ought an enemy so mightie and so craftie, to be neglected. There haue bene some who when they would haue striken a spirit with their sworde, haue thought they haue striken the featherbed, the diuel so mocked them. Others supposing they had throwne a spirit out of the window, by and by thought they heard shingles falling and ratling amongst the trees.

It is reported that there haue bin some, who supposing with their weapons to hurt spirits, haue wounded themselues, for their armes and other members of their bodie haue neuer serued them after. We must not vse a materiall sword against spirits and vaine shewes (for it profiteth nothing) but we must vse the sword of the spirit. They which will strike spirits and ghosts with a sword, indeed σκιαμαχοῦσι, that is, fight with their owne shadow. In the booke of Iobe the diuel is signified by Leuiathan, which careth not for the speare, for he appeareth in diuers shapes, and cannot be put to flight with pikes. The diuel is a spirit, he hath not bones and flesh, but he only taketh on him a shape for a time. But in case spirits which haue bodies do wander (that is, coniurers, priests, whores, & whoremongers, which faine themselues to be spirites) there can be no better coniuration inuented, than to bang them well with a cudgell. For thou shalt not so much preuaile with these kindes of diuels with words as with stripes.

Hitherto I haue shewed howe they ought to behaue themselues which meete with spirits. As touching them which neuer heard or sawe any thing (for there bee many

which

which neuer chaunced on such things) let them be thankful vnto God for so great a benefit, let them not be rashe and bolde, nor desirous to see such things, but rather let them pray vnto God for them which are vexed with such euils. Let them not do, as they many times vse which were neuer greatly sicke: for they feele not other mens griefes, and therefore they thinke they are litle sicke, or that they counterfeit their sicknesse, vntill such time as they themselues fall into some great and daungerous disease: euen so God can cause them to see spirites, which neuer sawe any before, that afterwards they may be the more touched with other mens griefes, and diligently pray for them.

CHAP. XII.

After what sort we ought to behaue our selues, when we heare straunge crackes, or when other forewarnings happen.

BUt nowe as concerning other matters, as in case any straunge crackes and noyses be heard, or any rare and marueilous things happen before the alteration of kingdomes (which we speake of before) what shall we then do? Surely we must not attribute to much vnto such things, for they sometimes, yea and most commonly chaunce by the deceit of the diuell, who hath a great pleasure to haue men muse night and day on such matters, and to imagine before their eyes and mindes many horrible things, that thereby they may fall into some greeuous sicknesse, and neuer be at rest. When such things happen in deed, they ought to put vs in minde, that we casting from vs all these things which displease God, should wholly consecrate our selues vnto God, and so frame our selues, that at what houre soeuer he come, and please to call vs out of this life, we should be readie for him euen as he himselfe teacheth

teacheth vs, and also endure patiently all vnfortunate chances, how many soeuer happen vnto vs, knowing that they come not by chance, but by the prouidence of God.

Plutarch, albeit he be an Heathen writer, is of a sounde iudgement (as me seemeth) concerning Monsters and wonders. For writing of Alexander the great, in his booke *De vitis*, he saith; that there happened certaine prognosticatiions before his death, which sometimes Alexander cared not for, but contemned them, and contrariwise, sometimes he toke smal and trifling things, as signes of euil lucke. Plutarches Christian opinion.

He addeth further, how dangerous a thing it is, to despise tokens and signes sent from God vnto men, and on the other side, how pernitious and hurtfull it is to be afraid of euery trifle, for as in all other things, so is there a measure to be obserued herein. The same opinion is he of, touching other wonders and miracles. For ye may reade in the life of Camillus, that when he being Captain, had taken and destroyed the *Veians*, he made a solemne vow, to translate the Image of Iuno vnto *Rome*. And therefore he commaunded certain men to take vp the Image: he offered sacrifice vnto the Goddesse, and besought her that she would vouchsafe to follow him, and to be fauourable vnto the Romanes, as other Goddes were which now dwelt at *Rome*. The Image made him answere that she would goe with him. He also writeth, that those men which noted and recorded these things, report other such straunge matters, as that Images did sweate, that they gaue great grones, that they turned away their faces, or hanged down their heads: he saieth, that men whiche liued before his time, gathered many suche examples togither, and that he himselfe hath heard many maruellous things of men liuing in his time, which were not by and by to be neglected and contemned: and yet mans infirmitie is such, that it cannot attribute either too much or too little, vnto those things without great daunger, for men obserue no measure, but are either too superstitious and attribute ouer much to such matters, or else do vtterly reiect and contemne them. And therefore the safest way is, to be aduised, and to kéepe a meane in suche affaires. Valerius Maximus confesseth in his first booke, that the very Gentils themselues had many miracles and wonders happening among them in great suspition, and that not without iust cause. True wonders ought to stir vs vp from sléepe. A couragious horse goeth well inough of his owne accorde, and yet if you do but make signe vnto him with a wande, or put spurre vnto him, he will be more readier and quicker. Euen so must we go in the way that leadeth vnto heauen so long as we liue, but in case we sée any foretokens, or some great alteration séeme to hang ouer vs, we ought to bee the more stirred vp, to giue our selues to praier, and to exercise godlinesse. The Gentiles if at any time such forewarnings were shewed vnto them from heauen, did institute certaine solemne praiers and processions to pacifie their Gods: how much rather ought all Christian Princes and Magistrates, Doctors and Preachers of our time, to bend themselues wholly herein, when so euer plagues hang ouer our heads, that all men generally and particularly shewe forth true repentance?

Valerius Maximus.

Hitherto (I trust) we haue sufficiently shewed what we may thinke, concerning visions and appearing of spirites, and other straunge things which haue great affinitie and likenesse vnto them. And that in times past, Doctors wrote and taught farre otherwise concerning them, than the very truth it selfe was, we haue also shewed the causes thereof. It might be also declared in many wordes, that the like hath happened in other pointes of Christian doctrine, yea and many excellent learned and godly men, haue at large opened the same in their bookes which are now extant concerning such matters.

The conclusion.

And that I may conclude this my booke, I shall beséech all those, for the glorie of God, that shall happen to reade it,

that

ther giue God thankes for that great and unspeakable benefit, whereby he doth daily deliuer them out of great errors and feares, and doth continually more and more bring his truth to light: let them not so lose the raignes to their affections, that they reiect the truth which they haue once acknowledged.

The Senat and people of *Rome* as stories witnesse, granted libertie to the people of *Cappadocia*, when the stocke and issue of their kings was utterly extinct, to be free, and Lords of themselues for euer after. But the Nobilitie consulting on the matter, refusing libertie whiche they coulde in no wise disgest, desired to haue a King. The Romaines wondring heereat, gaue them leaue to choose whome they would to be their King. Let not us bee such fooles, but rather let us imbrace the libertie of our soules, whiche God doth daily offer unto us by his word.

Many Noble nations fighting couragiously, haue put themselues in present daunger of life, to obtaine and keepe this sweete externall libertie. How muche more ought we Christians to fight against the subtiltie and deceit of the Deuill, least the libertie of our soules, whiche is much more precious than the other, shoulde be oppressed by diuers errours and superstitions.

Men sitting in darkenesse, desire the light very earnestly. Let not us therefore cast away light freely offered unto us by God in his Scriptures. We haue nothing here in earth more deare unto us, than the libertie of our soules and consciences. Let us not then (as Paule saith,) withhold truth in unrighteousnesse, let euery man of what age soeuer he be, weigh with himselfe how fraile and brittle

this

this life is which God hath giuen vnto vs, and that wee must depart from hence, sooner then we thinke for, and render an account to the iust Iudge, of our faith, wordes, and deeds.

Glorie and praise be vnto Almightie God for euer and euer, and I beseech him to vouchsafe to stretch forth his hande, to deliuer all suche as are still entangled in superstition and errours, and to graunt those whome he hath deliuered his heauenly grace, that they be allwaies thankfull for so great a benefit, least they be wrapped againe in the same mischiefe.

FINIS.

LONDON
Printed by Thomas
Creede. 1596.

www.ingramcontent.com/pod-product-compliance
Lightning Source LLC
Chambersburg PA
CBHW030405270326
41926CB00009B/1283
9783744670876